Fascism, Totalitarianism and Political Religion

09/11 and its aftermath has demonstrated the urgent need for political scientists and historians to unravel the tangled conceptual and causal links that characterise the relationship of secular ideologies and organised religions to political fanaticism in the age of high modernity

Fascism, Totalitarianism and Political Religion uses a series of case studies by world experts in their topic to further our understanding of these complex issues. They examine the nexus between fascism, political religion and totalitarianism by exploring two inter-war fascist regimes, two abortive European movements, and two post-war American extreme right-wing movements with contrasting religious components.

The corner-stone of the collection is a major article by Emilio Gentile, recently awarded an international prize for his contributions to our appreciation of the central role played by political religion in the modern age. It is preceded by an editorial essay by Roger Griffin, one of fascist studies' most original theoreticians, on the value of the conceptual 'cluster' to investigating the dynamics of fascism

This book marks a profound step not only towards locating fascism within broader historical processes, but towards recognising and understanding the modern manifestations of totalitarianism both as movement and regime

This book was previously published as a special issue of the journal *Totalitarian Movements and Political Religions* entitled *Fascism as a Political Religion*

Roger Griffin is Professor of History at Oxford Brookes University. He has published widely on the subject of Fascism.

Totalitarian Movements and Political Religions
Series Editors: **Michael Burleigh,** Washington and Lee University, Virginia and
Robert Mallett, University of Birmingham

This innovative new book series will scrutinise all attempts to totally refashion mankind and society, whether these hailed from the Left or the Right, which, unusually, will receive equal consideration. Although its primary focus will be on the authoritarian and totalitarian politics of the twentieth century, the series will also provide a forum for the wider discussion of the politics of faith and salvation in general, together with an examination of their inexorably catastrophic consequences. There are no chronological or geographical limitations to the books that may be included and the series will include reprints of classic works and translations, as well as monographs and collections of essays

International Fascism, 1919–45
Edited by Gert Sorensen University of Copenhagen and
Robert Mallett University of Birmingham

Totalitarian Democracy and After
International colloquium in memory of Jacob Talmon
Edited by Yehoshua Arieli and Nathan Rotenstreich

Faith, Politics and Nazism
Selected essays
Uriel Tal with a Foreword by Saul Friedlander

The Seizure of Power
Fascism in Italy 1919–1929
Adrian Lyttleton

The French and Italian Communist Parties
Comrades and culture
Cyrille Guiat, Herriott-Watt University, Edinburgh
Foreword by David Bell

The Lesser Evil
Moral approaches to genocide practices
Edited by Helmut Dubiel and Gabriel Motzkin

Fascism as a Totalitarian Movement
Roger Griffin

The Italian Road to Totalitarianism
Emilio Gentile
Translated by Robert Mallett

Religion, Politics and Ideology in the Third Reich
Selected essays
Uriel Tal
In memoriam Saul Friedländer

Totalitarianism and Political Religions
Volume I: concepts for the comparison of dictatorships
Edited by Hans Maier
Translated by Jodi Bruhn

Stalinism at the Turn of the Millennium
Russian and western views
John Keep and Alter Litvin

Fascism, Totalitarianism and Political Religion

Blackburn
College

Edit

Rog

R
Taylor & Francis Group

LONDON AND NEW YORK

First published 2005 by Routledge
2 Park Square, Milton Park, Abingdon, Oxon, OX14 4RN

Simultaneously published in the USA and Canada by Routledge
270 Madison Ave, New York, NY 10016

Routledge is an imprint of the Taylor & Francis Group

© 2005 Roger Griffin

Typeset in Classical Garamond BT by
Genesis Typesetting Ltd, Rochester, Kent
Printed and bound in Great Britain by
Antony Rowe Ltd, Chippenham, Wilts

British Library Cataloguing in Publication Data
A catalogue record for this book is available from the British Library

Library of Congress Cataloging in Publication Data
A catalog record for this book has been requested

ISBN 0–415–34793–9 (hardback)
ISBN 0–415–37550–9 (paperback)

CONTENTS

Acknowledgements

Roger Griffin would like to pay tribute to the extensive work which Matthew Feldman devoted to getting several of the articles which comprise this special issue into a fit state for copy-editing, and to Paul Jackson, Valentin Sandalescu, and Marius Turdu for help in filling the gaps in the bibliographical information provided in two of them. He would also like to thank TMPR's general editor Robert Mallet and the Journals Editor at Taylor and Francis, Glyn Lavers, for their patience and support at times when it looked as if the project would never 'come together' in time.

About the Contributors

Chip Berlet has been writing about right-wing social and political movements in the United States for over 25 years. A journalist by craft, he has also written for academic and peer review journals and scholarly collections, most recently a chapter in Abby Ferber (ed.), *Home-Grown Hate: Gender and Organized Racism* (2004). He is co-author (with Matthew N. Lyons) of *Right-Wing Populism in America: Too Close for Comfort* (2000) and *Eyes Right! Challenging the Right Wing Backlash* (1995) – both of which received the Gustavus Myers Center Award for outstanding scholarship on the subject of human rights and bigotry in North America. His byline has appeared in publications ranging from the *New York Times* and *Boston Globe* to the *Progressive* and *Amnesty Now*. He is senior analyst at Political Research Associates, a progressive think tank in the Boston area.

Martin Blinkhorn is Professor of Modern European History at Lancaster University and a member of the editorial board of *Totalitarian Movements and Political Religions*. As a researcher, writer and teacher he has worked on the twentieth-century Spanish and wider European Right throughout his academic life. Among those of his publications most relevant to this special issue of *Totalitarian Movements and Political Religions* are the edited collection *Fascists and Conservatives* (1990) and his *Fascism and the Right in Europe, 1919–1945* (2000).

Martin Durham is Senior Lecturer in Politics at the University of Wolverhampton. He is the author of *Women and Fascism* (1998) and *The Christian Right, the Far Right and the Boundaries of American Conservatism* (2000) He is presently working on a study of the American extreme Right.

Emilio Gentile is Professor of Contemporary History at the University of Rome 'La Sapienza'. Among his recent books are: *The Sacralization of Politics in Fascist Italy* (1996; Italian edn. 1993), *La via italiana al totalitarismo: Il partito e lo Stato nel regime fascista* (1995; English edn. forthcoming), *La Grande Italia: Ascesa e declino del mito della nazione nel ventesimo secolo* (1997; English edn. forthcoming), *Fascismo e antifascismo: I partiti italiani fra le due guerre* (2000), *Le religioni della politica: Fra democrazie e totalitarismi* (2001; English edn. forthcoming), *Fascismo: Storia e interpretazione* (2002), *Il* *totalitarismo alla conquista della Camera Alta* (2002), *Renzo De Felice: Lo storico e il personaggio* (2003), *The Struggle for Modernity: Nationalism, Futurism and Fascism in 20th Century Italy* (2003).

Roger Griffin is Professor in the History of Ideas at Oxford Brookes University, and the author of *The Nature of Fascism* (1991), and numerous articles and chapters on fascism, as well as three readers, *Fascism* (OUP, 1995), *International Fascism: Theories, Causes and the New Consensus* (Arnold, 1998) and *Fascism* in Routledge's Critical Concepts in Social Science series (2003). He is currently working on a monograph on the relationship between fascism and modernism.

Radu Ioanid studied at the University of Bucharest, the University of Cluj, where he received a PhD, and the Ecole des Hautes Études en Sciences Sociales in Paris, where he received a doctorate in history. He is the author of *The Sword of the Archangel: Fascist Ideology in Romania*, *The Holocaust in Romania*, *The Destruction of Jews and Gypsies Under the Antonescu Regime, 1940–1944* and of numerous articles and contributions to collections of essays. He is currently the director of the International Archival Programs Division of the United States Holocaust Memorial Museum, located in Washington, DC.

Thomas Linehan is currently a Lecturer in History at Brunel University. He is the author of *British Fascism, 1918–1939: Parties, Ideology and Culture* (2000), and *East London for Mosley: The British Union of Fascists in East London and South-West Essex 1933–1940* (1996). He has also co-edited a collection of essays on the British Far Right and culture with Julie Gottlieb, entitled *The Culture of Fascism: Visions of the Far Right in Britain* (2004). He is currently working on a study of the Communist Party of Great Britain during the inter-war years.

Richard Steigmann-Gall has been an Assistant Professor of History at Kent State University since 2000. He received his BA and MA at the University of Michigan, then obtained his PhD in history at the University of Toronto in 1999, specialising in Nazi Germany. He has published articles on various aspects of the relationship between Christianity and Nazism in the journals *German History*, *Kirchliche Zeitgeschichte*, *Social History* and *Central European History*. His book, *The Holy Reich: Nazi Conceptions of Christianity, 1919–1945*, was published last year.

Preface

The debate on fascism and totalitarianism is now one of the longest ongoing scholarly discussions in the fields of modern history and political studies. In its main phase, nearly half a century old, it is fueled by a large and steady volume of new monographic research which shows little sign of abating. During the past decade the debate has been further broadened by Emilio Gentile and Hans Maier, who have drawn more attention than ever before to the religious and cultic aspects of fascism and other revolutionary movements and regimes, fostering a new discussion of political religion.

The present volume has been very carefully designed to broaden and illuminate this debate through an extended discussion of some of the key aspects of fascism and political religion on the theoretical and comparative level, and presents an illuminating series of studies of individual movements from this analytic perspective. It is an unusual volume in achieving a clearer conceptual focus than is common in collective enterprises and provides the fullest collaborative discussion ever to have appeared in English. On the one hand, it contributes further to the analysis of generic fascism and, yet more significantly, offers the reader the most up-to-date comparative and theoretical treatment of political religion.

These studies were first published as a special issue of the new journal *Totalitarian Movements and Political Religions*, founded by Robert Mallett in 2000. In its five years of existence, *TMPR* has become much more than another of the endless number of "niche" journals which frequently spring up. It has established itself as an important cross-over journal for history, the humanities and the social sciences in probing a wide range of topics in modern revolutionary movements and regimes, and in the analysis of fascism, communism, totalitarianism, political religion, and many other related subjects.

The two theoretical studies by Roger Griffin and Emilio Gentile, which begin the book, will be extremely useful to scholars because they provide highly polished, state-of-the-art discussions of major aspects of the debate on generic fascism and, much more extensively, on the theory and analysis of political religion, and on the relationship between the two. Nowhere else can a comparative analysis of this caliber be found. Roger Griffin expertly brings these different foci together in the introductory study, while on several major points

Gentile carries his examination of political religion even beyond his earlier publications. He clarifies complex issues, responds to critics and makes clearer than ever before what is and is not claimed by his theoretical approach, so that this lengthy study will become a key reference point in future discussions of political religion.

Richard Steigmann-Gall has become a controversial scholar at an early age. His contribution gives him an opportunity to comment on how he views the conclusions of his book *The Holy Reich* with respect to the question of political religion. Thomas Linehan takes what might have seemed an unlikely candidate – the British Union of Fascists – and probes its relationship to the general problem. Radu Ioanid then examines in some detail the Iron Guard, arguably the most religious form of fascism, and the one that students in this field have found the most strange and exotic. Since the key study of this movement is in German, Ioanid makes a notable contribution to the scanty literature in English by clarifying in some detail its relationship to and exploitation of Romanian Orthodoxy.

The last two monographic chapters extend the study of political religion to different forms of exotica—the extremist movements in the United States related to neofascism. Martin Durham explains the "cosmotheism" of William Pierce's National Alliance, in some ways the most influential movement of the American extreme right in the late twentieth century, while Chip Berlet probes the doctrines of the Christian Identity group, a movement which originated in England in the late nineteenth century but assumed a new extremist form a century later in the United States. Both these studies reveal the usefulness of applying the concept of political religion to some of the key recent fringe phenomena.

The accomplishment of this volume is to raise the comparative study of fascism and political religion to a higher level by offering fresh perspectives and new case studies. It marks an important step in the clarification and application of the seminal theory of Emilio Gentile and, with the addition of new empirical dimensions, helps to place the broader problems of fascism and totalitarianism in a different, more original, context

Stanley G Payne
University of Wisconsin-Madison

Introduction: God's Counterfeiters? Investigating the Triad of Fascism, Totalitarianism and (Political) Religion

ROGER GRIFFIN

Even when he turns for religion, man remains subject to it; deplet-
ing himself to create false gods, he then feverishly adopts them: his
need for fiction, for mythology triumphs over evidence and absur-
dity alike ... We kill only in the name of a god or of his counter-
feits: the excesses provoked by the goddess. Reason, by the
concept of nation, class, or race, are akin to those of the Inquisi-
tion or the Reformation

Emile Cioran, 'Genealogy of Fanaticism' *A Short History of*
Decay (1949)

Ideological Storm-fronts

When the first issue of *Totalitarian Movements and Political Religions*
appeared in the summer of 2000 it was not building on an existing
specialism so much as identifying the site where the edifice of a new
one might arise at the conjuncture between several specialisms. It was

an act of the social scientific and historical imagination, or perhaps of the archetypal human faculty that Ernst Bloch calls the 'not-yet-conscious'. 'Totalitarianism' and 'political religion' have their own convoluted histories as analytical terms, both so contested and value-laden that the proliferating connotations they have acquired seriously compromise their heuristic value for investigating concrete historical realities. A journal whose title linked them, conjoining 'totalitarian' with 'movement' rather than 'regime', opened up new cognitive spaces. It provided a forum for academics keen to explore the nexus between two seemingly unrelated class of phenomena: ideologically motivated onslaughts against the civic institutions and plural forms of social existence fostered by liberal humanism, and the capacity of politics in the age of the accelerating 'disenchantment of the world' to reassert the primacy of a religious tradition or to turn the secular world itself into a new source of faith and the re-enchantment of reality.

In 2001 the attacks on the World Trade Center had placed the need to understand the relationship between political violence, religion and sacralized modes of secular politics at the top of the agenda of the international social science community. It involved a reordering of research priorities comparable to the rapid promotion of 'nationalism' to pole position once the unexpectedly sudden collapse of the Soviet Empire had not only created new nation-states, but unleashed a spate of hitherto repressed xenophobias and ethnic conflicts. After the Islamic Revolution of 1979 had so unexpectedly established a theocracy in Iran, Middle East watchers in the Pentagon were said by one political satirist to be 'speed-reading the Koran' for clues to what had happened. Events since 9/11 have made it clear that mapping the rapidly shifting contours of the emerging ideological world order involved a process more reminiscent of what Walter Benjamin called the 'storm of progress' than the gradualistic scenario of an ever-advancing warm front of neo-liberalism implied by George Bush Senior or Francis Fukuyama. It is a turn of events that makes particular demands on contemporary historians and social scientists in the West, requiring them not only to be receptive to the experiences and constructions of reality born of other cultures, but also to be prepared to re-read some recent chapters in our own history more slowly.

This painstaking, sometimes painful, process of revision and professional soul-searching is one that, among other things, means re-opening the investigation into episodes of right-wing extremism in modern political history that may until recently have seemed dead and buried as academic issues, but with hindsight can be seen to offer important case studies in the complex relationship between political violence, ideological fanaticism, religious politics and totalitarianism. In particular, it means revisiting the two fascist regimes of inter-war Europe, for decades routinely treated as the products of capitalism in crisis, idiosyncratic national histories, dysfunctional political cultures or personal megalomania. It is now becoming increasingly apparent that they are also to be interpreted as fruits of an inherently unstable and destabilizing. Western modernity (a term embracing capitalism) which after the First World War gave rise to various types of authoritarian regime and *totalitarian movement* bent on overthrowing parliamentary democracy in the name either of restoring stability or of creating a new order.

The group of essays that follows has been specially 'commissioned' (in the non-mercenary sense that still (against all odds) prevails among academics) to contribute to the emergence of greater conceptual lucidity and methodological sensitivity in the way the nexus of generic concepts bound up with fascism is approached by historians and political scientists. The original intention was admittedly more utopian. A number of leading specialists on different manifestations of fascism would be asked to analyse 'their' variant of it as a 'totalitarian movement', paying particular attention to its relationship to religion, both traditional and 'political'. They would be encouraged to carry out their analysis within a common conceptual framework informed by two articles previously published in *TMPR*, namely Emilio Gentile's 'The Sacralisation of Politics: Definitions, Interpretations and Reflections on the Question of Secular Religion and Totalitarianism',[1] and Michael Burleigh's 'National Socialism as a Political Religion',[2] as well as an article on 'the new consensus' in fascist studies (of which more later) which first appeared in *The Journal of Contemporary History*.[3] I thus approached the task of editing the project with the naivety of a student teacher who plans a seminar on the assumption that all students will turn up having immersed themselves in the prescribed preparatory reading, and proceed to engage in a passionate discussion of the topic without what Germans call 'talking past each other'. The synergy thus generated would unearth subterranean linkages between the apparently disparate phenomena of totalitarianism and political religion on the basis of specialist empirical knowledge of particular specimens of fascism, both past and contemporary. Naturally, the special issue of *TMPR* that resulted would have profound implications for both political scientists and modern historians studying the various assaults of the 'extreme right' against liberal democracy, Enlightenment humanism or socialist concepts of progress.

Inevitably the shadow between idea and reality, the conception and the creation about which T. S. Eliot wrote about so memorably in *The Hollow Men*, fell on this enterprise too. Perhaps inevitably, there remain significant differences between the contributions in the degree of conceptualization that their authors brought to their case study and in how far they addressed the notion of 'totalitarian movement' and its relationship to 'political religion' using a common vocabulary. As a result many feel these essays do more to document current academic confusions and conflicts over key definitional questions in this field of enquiry than to elucidate them. Nevertheless, at the very least they should help establish the pitfalls and merits of the multiple-perspective that results when 'clusters' of key terms are applied to conceptualizing modern forms of the extreme right in a comparative context instead of the single-point perspective imposed when only one key concept is applied.[4] After the six specialist analyses Martin Blinkhorn offers a provisional evaluation of the success of this exercise in fulfilling this more modest and realistic ambition. He does so in his capacity as a professional historian who has written extensively on aspects of generic fascism and expressed considerable scepticism about the value of protracted navel searching over its definition.[5]

Much Light, Deep Shadows[6]

To place this exercise in applying a 'multiple-point perspective' to the study of the modern extreme right in context it may be helpful to be reminded of the tangle of definitional and taxonomic confusions that have grown up around each of the three key terms of the 'cluster' within the human sciences.

Totalitarianism

'Totalitarianism', a term apparently making a comeback after being left out in the cold for a time, now carries with it such cumbersome semantic baggage that several books and doctorates have appeared which might be classified 'tertiary literature', devoted mainly to taking stock of the conflicting connotations it has acquired within secondary literature.[7] A recent doctorate treats the superabundance of secondary literature surrounding the topic under four main headings: utopianism, modernity, political religion, and post-modernism, each of which subsumes a plethora of conflicting conceptual approaches and definitional border disputes.[8] What emerges from such surveys are deep historical conflicts and intellectual divisions over how far totalitarianism should be seen 'functionally', and hence also phenomenologically, focusing on the type of radically authoritarian state it produces and the marks of coercion it inscribes on the minds and flesh of those it attempts to bend or subjugate to its purpose, or 'intentionally' in terms of the goals that an autocratic regime sets out to achieve through its efforts to exercise total authority over the state and civic society. In the second case deeply divergent interpretations result from assuming that the intention is reducible to the destructive and ultimately nihilistic one of gaining power as an end in itself, as opposed to the utopian one of using the power accumulated to realize an ideal new order.

How treacherous this terrain can be conceptually is illustrated by considering the way one academic, Leonard Schapiro, summarizes a crucial passage in a canonical text in the (Anglophone) history of the concept, Carl Friedrich and Zbigniew Brzezinski's *Totalitarian Dictatorship and Autocracy*, first published in 1956. This book is famous for defining totalitarianism in terms of a 'five-points' syndrome (increased to six in the 1965 edition), the first of which Schapiro summarizes as 'an official ideology, to which everyone is supposed to adhere, focused on a "perfect final state of mankind"'.[9] The purely coercive connotations of this criterion for Schapiro are reinforced in his conclusion which presents totalitarianism as being characterized 'by the predominance of the Leader of the victorious movement, who, with the aid of his subordinated elite and manipulated ideology, aims at total control over state, society, and the individual', an approach firmly rooted in the 'functionalist' mindset.[10]

Yet in the original this ideology is explicitly described in intentionalist terms as being 'characteristically focused and projected towards a perfect final state of mankind — that is to say, it contains a chiliastic claim, based upon a radical rejection of the existing society with conquest of the world for the new one [sic]'.[11] Earlier Friedrich and Brezezinski have cited with approval another expert's judgement that totalitarian dictatorship is a 'novel type of autocracy' established 'for realizing totalist intentions under modern political and technical conditions', the primary goal of which is the creation of a 'new man'.[12]

That the authors do not see this 'functionally' as a pseudo-revolutionary façade designed simply to indoctrinate and manipulate the masses is clear from their own exposition of 'point one' a few pages later. This not only states that 'totalitarian ideology involves a high degree of convinctional certainty', but that the 'Utopian, chiliastic outlook of totalitarian ideologies gives them a pseudo-religious quality' which elicits 'in their less critical followers a depth of conviction and a fervour of devotion usually found only among persons inspired by a transcendent faith'. In a phrase that has a direct bearing on the raison d'être of the present group of essays, they add 'whether these aspects of totalitarian ideologies bear some sort of relationship to the religions they seek to replace is arguable'. They then express their own sympathy for seeing totalitarian ideologies in terms of ersatz religion, highlighting the way they pervert conventional political programmes by substituting 'faith for reason, magic exhortation for knowledge and criticism', so that Marx's phrase 'the opium of the people' applies to them just as much as it does to organized religion.[13]

Given the book's influence on generations of students and scholars, the history of the term 'totalitarianism' would probably have taken a different course altogether had Friedrich and Brzezinski devoted an entire section of their work to elaborating on the relationship, only alluded to in its pages, between totalitarian ideology, transcendent faith, pseudo-religion and the creation of a 'new man'. Indeed, if they had then applied their embryonic 'cluster-analysis' to an extensive comparison of the 'chiliastic' projects of Stalinism and Nazism with the manifestations of totalitarianism that subliminally form the central focus of their analysis, this special issue of *TMPR* might have been redundant. As it is, the impact of the Cold War on the mood of the times ensured that the main theme of the book — as far as its 'reception' within the human sciences is concerned — was the nexus between a regime's totalizing ideology, its monopoly of state, cultural and military power, and the resulting destruction of liberty, a perspective which implicitly endorsed the claims of the 'Free World' to represent good in the Manichean struggle, against the evils of state communism.

Another major authority in this area, who might have helped save later generations of scholars much agonizing over taxonomic categories, is Juan Linz However, his seminal essay on authoritarianism and totalitarianism written three decades ago, while stressing that the radicalism of the latter stems from a vision of revolutionary transformation that cannot be countenanced by conservatives, still refers to 'fascist-mobilizational authoritarian regimes'.[14] To compound the confusions, his equally important essay on comparative fascism of the same period talks about fascism's 'totalitarian goals', which are directly linked in the text to 'new organizational conceptions of mobilization and participation' and a 'new synthesis' of political and social components.[15] Not only is there slippage between 'totalitarian' and 'authoritarian' in Linz's taxonomic scheme, but he does not develop the fleeting reference to fascism in his synthetic definition as 'anti-clerical, or at least non-clerical', so that the embryonic nexus of generic concepts remains no more than implicit.

Clearly Linz recognizes how germane the issue of religion is to the understanding of totalitarian regimes and fascism, and his essay contains a section entitled 'secularization, religion and fascism' on the structural role played by Catholicism in limiting the political space for fascism's success.[16] His more recent work on 'fascism, authoritarianism and totalitarianism' includes only a short passage on the transition 'from ideology to political religion'. It contains the tantalizing assertion that by the twentieth century secularization had created a spiritual void within the intelligentsia and educated classes that could be filled by 'total ideological dedication'. He continues; 'Once simplified and reduced to slogans by a political movement, such ideas became the powerful basis for a pseudo-religious political cause that justified totalitarianism and made it possible'.[17] Such passages provide the reader with no more than glimpses of a sophisticated conceptual framework that would identify the nexus between conservative authoritarianism, (anti-conservative) totalitarian movements and regimes, revolutionary nationalism, traditional and political (pseudo-) religion, and modernity that, with his encyclopediac knowledge of the twentieth-century extreme right, Linz has been ideally placed to construct, but clearly not felt drawn to as a central focus on his research.

A scholar of the younger generation who has made a concerted effort at 'tidying up' the definitional mess that has grown up around totalitarianism is Simon Tormey. One of his key contributions is to distinguish between the 'strong' theory of totalitarianism which assumes that a regime's systematic use of social engineering can be largely successful in its bid to destroy the inner freedom of its citizens, in contrast to the 'weak' theory which sees the external conformism thus imposed as largely perfunctory, destined to evaporate the moment the outer constraints are removed. This would enable the term to be applied even to regimes accommodating considerable pockets of personal freedom and cultural pluralism, such as Fascist Italy, which signally failed (and was genuinely reluctant) to impose the high level of regimentation and uniformity consistent with the Friedrich and Brzezinski model.

More important in the present context is Tormey's recognition that 'most theorists of totalitarianism agree that what distinguishes totalitarian rule from other forms of dictatorship is the commitment of a ruling elite to fashioning an entirely new form of society'. Thus 'totalitarianism is born above all of radicalism, a discontent with the present that is translated into a longing for the new',[18] which leads a regime to seek to implement a 'vision whose realisation would consist in a complete transformation of the very character of human existence'.[19] Yet the limitations of the single-point perspective are once again exemplified in Tormey's approach when he compares the applicability of his own model of Nazism and Stalinism. He has clearly not engaged with the works of G. L. Mosse or Stanley Payne, both of whom stress the centrality to fascism in general and Nazism in particular of the myth of new elites and the new man.[20] Thus he repeats the error committed by many in an earlier generation of academics that, in contrast to Marxism-Leninism, Nazism is at bottom a 'hotchpotch of prejudices and partialities', and that, whereas Marx's *The German Ideology* offered 'a vision of phoenix-like rebirth of humanity from the drudgeries of everyday life', *Mein Kampf* presents only a bleak picture of 'competition and struggle between races'.[21] The possibility of integrating totalitarianism into a nexus of generic concepts is precluded by this tunnel vision of one of the most important case studies of the phenomenon.

Fascism

One reason why Tormey may have been put off the serious engagement with fascist studies that would have corroborated his thesis in respect of Nazi Germany as well as Fascist Italy is perhaps that for several decades 'fascism' was an even more contested term than totalitarianism. It was thus difficult for a guest from another discipline to hear the voices of resident scholars who stressed the revolutionary thrust of fascism's ideology (e.g. Juan Linz, Eugen Weber, Zeev Sternhell, G. L. Mosse and Stanley Payne) above the babble of those stressing its nihilism, reactionariness, pathology or lack of a cohesive ideology, let alone of those who denied the very existence of a generic fascism. It was actually the same year in which Tormey published *Making Sense of Totalitarianism* that saw the appearance of the most authoritative work of comparative fascist studies to date, Stanley Payne's *A History of Fascism: 1914–1945*,[22] a milestone in the emergence of the partial consensus about the nature of fascism which forms part of the conceptual premise that underlies this special issue.

The suggestion that fascist studies has entered a period of fruitful convergence and synergy within fascist studies after years of fragmentation and polarization (code-named for the shake of brevity the 'new consensus' — an idea I first mooted in 1998)[23] has sometimes been misunderstood as the claim that unanimity now exists between theorists of fascism, which is patently absurd I should thus restate what is actually being claimed, namely that since the early 1990s there has been a significant degree of compatibility in the conceptual frameworks operated, consciously or not, in three types of contribution to comparative fascist studies: a) theories of generic fascism; b) comparative histories of fascism as an international phenomenon; c) monographic or comparative studies of specific political, social or cultural phenomena associated with fascist or putative fascist movements or regimes. The core component of this conceptual framework can be summarized as the premise that fascism is an ideologically driven attempt by a movement or regime to create a new type of post-liberal national community which will be the vehicle for the comprehensive transformation of society and culture, with the effect of creating an alternative modernity. Inevitably, since academia — though extensively influenced by cultural climates, social norms and prevalent 'schools of thought' (fashions?) — does not operate under the diktats and psychological constraints of totalitarian regime, each expert gives a particular nuance to this broad characterization and highlights certain features of the definitional core or lays particular emphasis on some of the organizational forms and techniques of establishing political and ideological power that are involved in realizing the transformation. As those familiar with the debate are all too well aware, my approach highlights the central role played in generic fascism by 'palingenetic ultra-nationalism',[24] namely the myth that the organically conceived nation is to be cleansed of decadence and renewed.[25]

I offered empirical evidence for the growth of consensus or convergence on this premise within Anglophone academia in an article published in 2001.[26] Since then there has been a steady trickle of publications which confirm the tendency, such as Sven Reichardt's *Faschis-*

tische Kampfbünde,[27] Philip Morgan's *Fascism in Europe, 1919–1945*[28] or Angelo Ventrone's *La seduzione totalitaria guerra, modernità, violenza politica,*[29] all of which associate the aspect of fascism under discussion specifically with the myth of national regeneration and the forces of palingenesis, even when, as in the case of Enzo Traverso's *The Origins of Nazi Violence*[30] and Jay Gonen's *The Roots of Nazi Psychology,*[31] the author seems oblivious of the wider debate over the definition of fascism. Another interesting symptom of the diffusion of the 'new consensus' are works by authors who specifically dissociate themselves from its claims, as if it were a club or sect, membership of which is the kiss of death of their intellectual autonomy, and may even go to the trouble of attacking the concept of palingenetic myth as a crucial component of fascism, yet proceed to offer characterizations of fascism that are entirely consistent with it. In the past this was true of Alexander de Grand,[32] A. J. Gregor[33] and Martin Blinkhorn.[34] More recently the list of experts operating a curious form of doublethink in the way they distance themselves from the new consensus but apply theories patently consistent with, and even indebted to, it must be extended to include Kevin Passmore's *Fascism: A Very Short Introduction,*[35] Marco Tarchi's *Fascismo Teorie, interpretazioni e modelli,*[36] Robert Paxton's *The Anatomy of Fascism*[37] and Michael Mann's *Fascists.*[38] It is when totalitarianism and political religion are applied to fascism, conceived in a way broadly consistent with the concise definition offered here (the 'new consensus'), that the possibility of a powerful conceptual cluster emerges. At least that is what this group of essays is intended to establish, and hopefully succeeds in doing so — even if not everyone involved chose to do the homework I had set, and the diversity of approaches of those who did counteracts any attempt on my part to 'impose' total harmony on the conceptual framework applied (in any case, a perverse impulse in an academic context!)

Political Religion

Of the three concepts whose relationship is being explored in this special issue, it is 'political religion' that poses the most intractable problems of definition and semantic demarcation from adjacent terms, and demands the most attention in the present context. Anyone acculturated to the (post-) Christian West tends to instinctively refer to 'God' in the context of political extremism as a rhetorical device to evoke the absolutist claims they make on an individual's faith and capacity for self-sacrifice, producing such titles as *The God that Failed*[39] and *The Psychopathic God: Adolf Hitler.*[40] It is thus not surprising if the fanatical convictions and liturgical rites generated by some modern regimes have often reminded outsiders of organized religions. In 1928 the American social scientist Herbert Schneider, having witnessed Mussolini's fledgling regime at first hand, referred to Fascism as 'a new religion'. However, he immediately qualified this observation by stressing that he did not mean that Fascism had developed 'its own theology', but that 'it has given to thousands of Italian youths an ideal for which they are ready to sacrifice all'.[41] On returning from his visit to Russia only three years after the Revolution, Bertrand Russell described Bolshevism as satisfying the generalized longing for a 'new religion' created by the mood of despair generated by the First World War, and as providing 'the only force capable of giving men the energy to live vigorously'.[42] Bolshevism was subsequently described metaphorically as a religion in a very different context by one of the foremost representatives of an ideology determined to wipe it out from the face of the earth. In his lecture on 'The Nature and Tasks of the SS and Police' given in 1937, Himmler stated unequivocally:

> Bolshevism is an organization of sub-humans, it is the absolute foundation of Jewish rule, it is the exact opposite of all that the Aryan people loves, cherishes and values. It is a diabolic outlook, because it appeals to the lowest and meanest instincts of humanity and turns those instincts into a religion. One should not be deluded: Bolshevism with its Lenin buried in the Kremlin will need only several more decades to plant its diabolic religion of destruction in Asia, this religion that is aimed at the destruction of the whole world.[43]

It is when attempts are made to turn such vivid impressions into the basis of a useful social scientific term that problems arise. First, there are problems of terminology, with political religion, secular religion and religious politics all vying for the same semantic space, and sometimes jostling for position with other closely related terms such as millenarianism (apocalypticism, chiliasm) or civil (civic) religion. Second, the concept of a political religion has had far longer to acquire conflicting historical connotations than either 'fascism' or 'totalitarianism', and a dense thicket of secondary literature has grown up around it.[44] Once it embraces aspects of 'civil religion' its history can at least be given a precise origin in the theory that was to have such a profound impact on the ideologues of the French Revolution, namely Section 8 in Book IV of Jean-Jacques Rousseau's *The Social Contract*. After considering the various relationships between traditional religions and the State demonstrated by history, all of which are found wanting as the basis of a tolerant and enlightened society, he postulates the need for a 'civil religion' whose dogmas should be:

> few, simple, and exactly worded, without explanation or commentary. The existence of a mighty, intelligent and beneficent Divinity, possessed of foresight and providence, the life to come, the happiness of the just, the punishment of the wicked, the sanctity of the social contract and the laws: these are its positive dogmas. Its negative dogmas I confine to one, intolerance, which is a part of the cults we have rejected[45]

Yet Rousseau's theory of a civic creed has its own venerable history and can be seen as an Enlightenment version of Plato's idea of a 'royal lie' or 'needful falsehood' which, once accepted unquestioningly by the citizens of the Republic, guarantees that they will 'care more for the city and for one another' and be prepared to sacrifice themselves for the community. There is a remarkable adumbration of both 'bourgeois capitalist' and Nazi uses of ideology when Plato's Socrates explains that the myth to be believed by both rulers and subjects is that God has created three different castes of citizen, corresponding to gold, silver and an alloy of brass and iron, and that 'there is nothing which they should so anxiously guard, or of which they are to be such good guardians, as the purity of the race'.[46]

The main problem posed by the idea of 'political religion' is not its antiquity, however, but rather distinguishing between its metaphorical power and its heuristic value as a conceptual tool and explanatory device. A comparison of Russell's observation on Bolshevism with the theory of Rousseau brings out two of several contrasting ways that the term religion can be approached in a secular ideological context. Russell implies that the Bolsheviks' passionately held political beliefs in a revolutionary new order constitute a new religion, which may be the substitute for a 'true' (revealed/scriptural/metaphysical/traditional) religion, but is based on genuine faith and deep-seated psychological need.[47] Rousseau contemplates the necessity of the state to contrive a form of supra-denominational, non-scriptural deistic religion which the State is somehow meant to inculcate in its citizens as the orthodoxy despite its obvious points of conflict with the Church, an attitude that comes close to Plato's idea of persuading citizens to believe in an outlandish mythic cosmology designed to promote civic virtues. The first approach leads to an emphasis on the 'phenomenology' of the 'subject's' experience of a political faith which has the normative, motivating and existentially 'grounding' force of belonging to a religious community and thus can be seen to all intents and purposes as a 'genuine' religion, even if it is clearly a travesty of traditional Christianity. The second stresses the instrumental aspect of an 'evangelistic' political ideology from the regime's point of view as a means of social control, and hence the way it acts as a modern equivalent for organized religion's legitimizing role in traditional societies; it is thus, functionally speaking, an 'authentic' religion, even if it is a manufactured one. It is a shift of perspective related to the distinction drawn by Hannah Arendt between 'the historical approach' and the 'social sciences' approach.[48] But such dichotomies are clearly simplistic, and a major expert in the field, Jean-Pierre Sironneau, identifies not two, but four approaches: the typological, the genetic and historical, the functional and the comparative.[49]

The Historical Versus the Archetypal View of Political Religion

Even with such fine distinctions, the stubborn fact is that few major theories in the debate fit neatly into any category. Arendt herself has reservations about the historical as well as social science approaches she identifies. Moreover, her own theory combines elements of both, for though she investigates in depth the almost literally soul-destroying function of totalitarianism in practice, she also argues that it can be seen 'as a new — and perverted — religion, a substitute for the lost creed of traditional beliefs' and the product of the human 'need for a religion'.[50] These statements were made in her rebuttal of the theory of Eric Voegelin's internationally famous but deeply idiosyncratic meta-theory of political religion, which identifies residues of what he (unhistorically) terms 'gnosticism' in all secular political ideologies. By this he refers to a travestied, 'immanentist' and heretical version of 'true' Christianity which is transcendental and metaphysically real, and whose telltale sign is the location of a suprahistorical paradise within a historically conceived, this-worldly future state of society, humanity or the nation. The elaborate philosophy of history Voegelin erects on this fragile premise leads to the thesis that nearly all modern ideologies, including positivism and liberalism — and not just the

creeds of totalitarianism — are not substitute religions, but modern-
ized, historicized versions of the 'immanentist' travesties of genuine
religion found in medieval Christian movements. They are thus not
just one, but two stages removed from 'the real thing'.[51]

No matter how abstruse such taxonomic and explanatory disputes
may seem, their relevance to the interpretation of concrete historical
phenomena is underlined by Barbara Spackman's criticism of what
she takes to be Emilio Gentile's concept of political religion. She
insists that when Giovanni Gentile declared in the 'Manifesto of
Fascist Intellectuals' that Fascism was a religion he was employing a
metaphor, 'just as "Achilles is a lion" is a metaphor', so that Emilio
Gentile displays considerable methodological naivety in not recogniz-
ing that the tope 'religion', used in the context of Fascism, is a
rhetorical strategy known as 'catachresis'.[52] What makes Spackman's
remedial lesson in rhetoric superfluous is that Emilio Gentile has
never claimed that Fascism is a religion, but that it can be seen as a
'political religion'. As such it was distinct from an established theology, in this case institutionalized Christianity, while making total
claims on an individual's capacity for faith and need for a 'higher'
reality in a way that led to a philosophical idealist such as Giovanni
Gentile to deliberately call Fascism a religion, meaning a total ethical
system. It is perfectly reasonable to argue that human beings have an
archetypal propensity to sacralize secular realities without making
them the object of transcendental religions based on a suprahistorical
notion of the divine Thus Emilio Gentile was being no more lexico-
graphically challenged when he explored the sacralization of the Italian state under Fascism then G. L. Mosse was when he traced the
history of the sacralization of the nation in nineteenth-century
Germany.[53]

Whether the term 'religion' should be used for this-worldy political
phenomena, shorn of their exclusive connotations of traditional religion, and suitably qualified by some such term as 'civic', 'political', or
'secular', is ultimately a matter of academic judgement in the creation
of a heuristically useful conceptual framework. But anyone who maintains that the application of the term 'sacred' should be limited exclusively to the sphere of transcendental, other-worldly realities revealed
by Christian scripture, ecclesiastical teaching and mystic texts could do
with a crash course in comparative religion and cultural anthropology.
This would highlight the existence of numerous 'monistic' or 'immanentist' belief systems such as Buddhism, Shinto and animistic 'nature

religions' which reject the metaphysical dualism of Christianity and make the drawing of clear distinctions between secular and religious deeply problematic. Even in the history of Judaism and Christianity the relationship between heaven and history, the sacred and the profane, religion and politics is far from clear-cut. One implication of this global 'anthropological' perspective is to be wary of any impulse to trace modern utopias of a new era or new order to Renaissance millenarianism in general or to Joachim de Fiore in particular. The works of Mircea Eliade and Joseph Campbell on comparative mythology and cosmology suggest that the myth of rebirth (palingenetic myth) is an archetype of human mythopoeia which can express itself in both secular and religious forms without being 'derived' from any particular source or tradition (an approach congruent with the theory of the 'not-yet-conscious', postulated by Hermann Broch in *The Principle of Hope*).

It follows from this line of reasoning that attempts to reconstruct the genealogy of a modern political ideology as a continuous lineage back to forms of traditional religion, whether genuine or heretical, are simplistic fictions.[54] A cogent case can be made instead for seeing the rebirth myths of modern political religions as an expression of something more universal than the Christian belief in resurrection and the rich symbolic world it generated in the West. Thus the millenarianism of such movements as the sixteenth-century Anabaptists is to be regarded as one expression of palingenetic myth which a deeply Christianized culture produced in the stressed social conditions of early modern Europe. Four hundred years later the no less stressed historical conditions of early twentieth-century Europe produced another, genetically distinct, expression of it in a variety of political movements promising a new secular order, many of which readily expressed themselves in the language of religion, and in some cases (e.g. the Romanian Iron Guard) made themselves out to be the true defenders and revitalizers of religious orthodoxy.[55] It is a perspective that suggests that the sacralization of the State, far from being a 'metaphorical' process, the profane simulacrum of a 'true' religion (spackman), a cynical 'aestheticization of politics' (Walter Benjamin) or the modern survival of medieval heresies concerning a kingdom on earth (Voegelin), is instead to be treated as the product of the archetypal human faculty for imbuing the home, the community, and hence the new home and the new community, with suprahuman, ritual significance, producing in the European context a symbology and liturgy certainly shaped by and articulated through the legacy of Christian discourse, but not descended from it 'genealogically'.

The Need for Joined-up Thinking

Clearly the ongoing academic debates being spawned by each of the three key terms under examination in this issue preclude the possibility that an aesthetically satisfying sense of closure could ever be derived from setting out to extract a definitive way of conceptualizing them. Indeed the very notion of definition is problematic in a humanities pervaded by the spirit of post-structuralist discourse analysis and postmodern relativism. However, as indicated earlier, the strategy being applied here is another, namely to pose the question whether, by consciously approaching the terms as components of a cluster that offer a multi-point perspective on a phenomenon, they acquire enhanced heuristic value as part of a conceptual framework.

As the earlier quotation from Arendt makes clear, there is certainly nothing new in linking the term 'totalitarian' to regimes driven by a powerful sense of ideological mission. The first of Burleigh's Cardinal Basil Hume Memorial Lectures 'Religion and the Totalitarian Challenge' documents how frequently contemporary observers of Nazism and Fascism associated its totalitarian destruction of freedom with a secular form of religion.[56] Karl Popper's *The Open Society and its Enemies*, first published in 1945, though part of the literature popularizing the idea of totalitarianism as a 'closed society', also recognized that its fascist variants blended elements of biology with Hegelian metaphysics to produce a 'materialistic and at the same time mystical religion'.[57] Three decades on, J-Lucien Radel distinguished between 'ordinary' (i.e. what Linz calls 'authoritarian') dictatorships that 'lack the *mass enthusiasm* in support of a leader and are not identified with a *programmatic ideology*', in stark contrast to totalitarian ones that are driven by 'a *charismatic ideology* with a suitable leader strongly contaminating people's emotions'.[58] Placed in this context we should not be surprised if Burleigh finds that 'theories of totalitarianism have rarely been incompatible with theories of political religions, and such leading exponents of the former as Raymond Aron,[59] Karl-Dietrich Bracher, Carl Friedrich and Zbigniew Brzezinski have employed these terms almost interchangeably'.[60] He rightly highlights the contribution of Jacob Talmon to this school of thought with his pioneering studies of the link between 'totalitarian democracy' and the messianic mentality of the revolutionaries who established it. The many articles and reviews that have appeared in the pages of this journal in its brief history underline how strong the nexus is in the political science imagination.

When it comes to fascism's relationship to political religion, the link is far less well established. Emilio Gentile and George Mosse both treat the sacralization of politics as a major aspect of generic fascism. Stanley Payne, on the other hand, ignores the concept in his own interpretation,[61] and does not even refer to it in his survey of approaches of fascism,[62] though in this review of Gentile's *Le religioni politiche* he extends a cautious welcome to seeing political religion as central to totalitarianism, a term which embraces fascism.[63] Walter Laqueur bases his prognosis of fascism's vigorous future on his use of the 'clerical fascism' to include radical Islamic politics, an idiosyncratic usage that blurs the distinction between what Gentile calls 'political religion' (i e. a sacralized form of politics) and 'politicized religions'.[64] Roger Eatwell's reflections on the subject emphasize the need to see fascism as a 'political *ideology*' rather than a 'political religion', insisting that the core of (the Christian) religion is a leap of faith in the Resurrection, something 'inherently absurd', whereas fascism's 'quest to forge a holistic nation and create a radical syncretic Third Way state' has 'nothing absurd' about it.[65]

Eatwell correctly points out that in *The Nature of Fascism* I had expressed considerable scepticism about the value of the term 'political religion' in the context of fascism, and have now become a 'convert to the cause'.[66] The reason for this is that, like Eatwell in his article, I was keen to dissociate fascism from being treated as a modern, secularized form of millenarianism or Gnosticism, while at the same time emphasizing the gulf that at least in theological theory (though tragically not in practice) should have separated fascism from all forms of established Christianity. However, after my original, somewhat dogmatic, pronouncements, correspondence with Emilio Gentile and Walter Adamson made me more sympathetic to the heuristic value of theories that distinguish clearly between established religion and political religion, using the latter to refer to the full gamut of rhetorical, organizational and ritualistic techniques used by a totalitarian movement or regime to engineer a cult of the reborn state, race or nation, while making the leader the focal point for charismatic sociopolitical energies. Since then, without becoming a zealot, I am one of its more active proponents, as this article shows. What Eatwell seems not to appreciate, like Spackman before him, is that in Gentile's terminology a political religion is *always* a secular ideology and an ersatz religion when contrasted with the world view based on an established ecclesiastical or scriptural tradition, because it seeks to mobilize the population to the point where the new political order is sacralized rather than any suprahistorical holy entity (even if this distinction is blurred in the minds of 'clerical fascists'). This usage of the term fully applies to a movement aspiring to create (in Eatwell's words) a 'holistic nation and Third Way state', no matter how much secular science, technology and appeal to rational choice is subsumed in the fascist synthesis of ideological components. In short, there is considerable uncertainty among political scientists over fascism's relationship to the term political religion, while the emergent consensus on fascism — whose stress on total national rebirth would bring it naturally into the orbit of both totalitarianism and political religion — remains contested

It is thus hardly surprising if several major historians, who are professionally concerned primarily with the 'idiographic' task of exploring the uniqueness of phenomena and not the way they fit into general patterns and generic concepts 'nomothetically', have yet to join up the thinking on the three terms in their interpretation of Nazism. This is only partially true of Michael Burleigh, whose recent publications show that he needs no convincing of the deep structural relationship between totalitarianism and political religion,[67] and that he finds the term 'political religion' a valuable heuristic device for exploring the messianic dimension of Nazism.[68] As a result he makes both terms the conceptual key to his history of the Third Reich,[69] observing that since the early 1990s it has 'once again become fashionable' to apply them to Nazism individually.[70] However, a political scientist would soon notice that at no point does he define them, spell out the connection between them, or make it clear how, once used in tandem, they provide potent heuristic devices for explaining Nazi policies for the transformation of Germany and what actually happened when they were implemented. More strikingly, given the abundant references to the centrality of the myth of rebirth and the new man to Bolshevism, Fascism and Nazism in his lectures and articles on political religion, and despite referring readers (in footnote 19) to G. L. Mosse's 'important essay' 'Towards a General Theory of Fascism',[71] he makes no allusion to the new consensus on generic fascism. As a result he fails to establish the obvious connections between totalitarianism, political religion and those theories of fascism (notably the one contained in the very essay by Mosse that he recommends) that precisely stress this 'palingenetic' aspect of fascism once it is combined with extreme nationalism to become a key definitional component.

Richard Evans's latest work on Nazism is revealing in another way. The last chapter of *The Coming of the Third Reich* is entitled 'Hitler's Cultural Revolution', announcing an interpretation of Hitler's political mission fully consistent with the new consensus of fascism, even if the correlation remains unacknowledged in a text that makes not a single reference to generic fascism. The next volume of the forthcoming trilogy immediately takes up this theme of cultural revolution. It opens with the passage from a speech delivered by Goebbels on 15 November 1993 in which he declared that 'The revolution we have carried out is a total one. It has taken over all spheres of public life and transformed them from bottom up. It has completely changed and remoulded the relationships that human beings have to each other, to the state, and to the questions of existence'. Like all revolutions it was not just affecting politics but 'economics and culture, science and art'. 'On 30 January the age of individualism finally died ... The single individual is henceforth replaced by the community of the Volk'. Yet despite the obvious relevance of 'totalitarianism' and 'fascism' in some of the usages encountered earlier to the interpretation of such a speech, they are both conspicuous by their absence from the conceptual framework that Evans deploys in the book. As for 'political religion', this is his response when I tried to make the case for its relevance to Nazism's 'mission' to build a new Germany:

> I don't think the concept of a political religion is very helpful. It is after all merely descriptive, and Hitler was at great pains to insist that Nazism was not a religion at all, poured scorn on Himmler and Rosenberg's paganism, banned the *Thingspiel*, and so on. Of course there were stylistic elements borrowed from religious ritual, just as there had been in the SPD culture, but religion by definition involves the primacy of the supernatural, and Hitler always insisted that Nazism was fundamentally about this world, not the next.[72]

Once again the qualifying, transformative force of the adjective 'political' when conjoined with 'religion' in the hands of most political scientists has been ignored

Perhaps the most significant case of a historian deeply unconvinced of the insights into Nazism offered by the group of terms under consideration is Ian Kershaw. Certainly he is not reluctant to deploy generic concepts per se, since it is Max Weber's concept of charisma that informs the organization of his magnificent two-volume biography of Hitler. He is also fully aware of the potential relevance of two of them, having devoted a chapter to comparing the heuristic value of both 'fascism' and 'totalitarianism' in *The Nazi Dictatorship*. Yet he applies neither of them himself in his voluminous writings on Nazism.

The recent article on 'Hitler and the Uniqueness of Nazism' has thrown some light on this anomaly. Here he states categorically that 'as long as we are looking for common features, not identity' he has 'no difficulty in describing German National Socialism both as a specific form of fascism and as a particular expression of totalitarianism'.[73] Moreover, when he identifies the key to the dynamism of Nazism and to its uniqueness in the 'explosive mixture of the "charismatic" politics of national salvation and the apparatus of a highly modern state', he makes a fleeting link between this dynamic and the 'quest for national rebirth' that he (now) acknowledges 'lay, of course, at the heart of all fascist movements'. However, since his concern is with Nazism's uniqueness and not its 'common features' he immediately qualifies this concession with his assertion that 'only in Germany did the striving for national renewal adopt such strongly pseudo-religious tones'[74] (a remark suggesting unfamiliarity with the intense pseudo-religiosity that also characterized the Romanian Iron Guard). While Kershaw finds only qualified value in applying 'totalitarianism' and 'fascism' to Nazism, he is utterly dismissive of 'political religion', describing it as 'a currently voguish revamping of an age-old notion, though no less [sic] convincing for being repeated so persistently'.[75]

Differentiation and the Transcendence of Indifference

It is against this background of continuing conflict among political scientists over several key generic terms and an understandable wariness of using those terms on the part of some major historians, all in principle engaged with studying aspects of the 'same' modern revolutionary right, that the following essays seek to leave their mark. Of course they can be consulted in isolation solely for the empirical information they offer about a particular movement, and in the case of the essays on phenomena relatively neglected in Anglophone research, namely the Iron Guard in Romania, and the National Alliance and 'religious right' in the US, that would certainly make sense. But their full value emerges when they are read as case studies in the application of the terms fascism, totalitarianism/totalitarian movement, and political religion/religion conceived not as alternative concepts, but as forming a cluster or constellation of overlapping and complementary heuristic devices.

The organizing principle that has determined the choice of subjects is that the first pair deal with the relationship to religion, political and traditional, of (what the new consensus considers the only) two fascist regimes; the second pair focuses on 'abortive' fascist movements from inter-war Europe with very different relationships to religion; and the last two discuss post-war extreme-right phenomena in the US which exemplify contrasting connotations that 'political religion' can acquire in the context of contemporary 'totalitarian movements' of the right. A provisional evaluation of the heuristic value of this group of essays to historians of the twentieth century closes the parabola opened by this introduction. For such diverse essays to 'hang together' at all it is important to start with Gentile's essay in which he has taken the opportunity to restate his theory of political religion and to address some of the criticisms and misunderstandings to which it has given rise. The first section of this essay proposes a theory of political religion, totalitarianism and generic fascism of rare precision and concision. The second offers students still tempted to read academic articles uncritically as unimpeachable 'truths' a rare insight into the continuous process of formulation and contestation, of thesis and counterthesis, of convergence and divergence, of verbal cut and thrust, that is the life-blood of the humanities, and conveys some sense of the subjective passions that drive the search for objective truths.

However, the main value of Gentile's essay for this special issue is that the terms 'political religion' and 'totalitarianism' are presented specifically as constitutive elements of fascism, whether in the form of movement or regime, which, as a result, becomes overtly identified with other key phenomena, notably the sacralization of the State, palingenetic myth, anthropological revolution and violence as a means to achieve the transformation of society. In this way connections that in the secondary literature surveyed above were at best only implicit become explicit, and none of the constituent terms can any longer be used in isolation. It then becomes impossible to confuse 'political religion' with a traditional 'suprahistorical' religion, or to see totalitarianism as the attempt to monopolize power for its own sake, or approach fascism as the externalization of national, class or personal pathologies.

The focus of Gentile's article for the construction and contestation of his model of political religion is Fascist Italy. The next piece was intended at the planning stage to dove-tail neatly by demonstrating the value of applying it to the Third Reich and the value of seeing Nazism as a totalitarian movement/political religion. However, the task of contributing to this special issue was taken on by Richard Steigmann-Gall, author of a major work arguing that there is persuasive empirical evidence to show that the Nazis' claim to represent a 'positive Christianity' was far less spurious than has been assumed by historians hitherto. In doing so he has unearthed a wealth of data that emphasizes just how permeable the membrane can be, both institutionally and ideologically, between organized religion and secular political movements. Far from corroborating or engaging with Gentile's conceptual model or Burleigh's interpretation in the pages of this journal of Nazism as a political religion, Steigmann-Gall chooses to side-step them. Instead, he offers his own sustained critique of the concept 'political religion' when applied to Nazism in a reductionist way that concentrates on its secular, anti-Christian, or neo-pagan strands to the exclusion of those which he believes constitute a genuine synthesis between Christianity and Nazism. This hybrid he sees not as marginal to Nazism but as its prevalent orthodoxy, to the point where he suggests that it is to be approached as a form of 'religious politics' (or what in Gentile's taxonomy is termed a 'politicized religion') rather than a 'political religion'. Were scholars to accept this interpretation[76] it would represent a major correction to received views on the essential character of Nazism as a political movement and social force. At the very least the article underlines how far scholars are still divided about fundamental issues relating to the religious content of Nazism and how best to conceptualize it. (I might also suggest that it indirectly emphasizes the shortcoming of applying a single-point perspective to Nazism, in this case based on the concept 'religion', without taking into account other terms in the cluster, totalitarianism and fascism, and the adjacent concepts found in Gentile's articles, such as revolution, palingenetic myth and modernity.)

With Linehan's study of the British Union of Fascists (BUF) as totalitarian movement and political religion the reader may be reassured finally to encounter an article that marshals considerable scholarship to fulfil the original brief of this special issue to the letter. In doing so he demonstrates the cogency of the concepts when applied in tandem to understanding the BUF's fascist dynamics (and at least Mosley did historians the favour of avoiding much future wrangling over taxonomy by specifically calling his movement 'fascist'). What also emerges is how in this case there is little danger of confusing the spiritual dimension of the BUF's 'political religion' with 'genuine' Christianity, though the presence of 'clerical fascists' within the BUF shows how far these categories could become confused and fused in the minds of some believers. This pocket of clarity seems to disappear immediately with the next article, for not only has Ioanid Radu chosen to discuss the Iron Guard without reference to the analyses of political religion carried out by Gentile or Burleigh in their *TMPR* articles, but in the Romanian case ideology is deeply enmeshed with traditional religion, in this case Orthodox Christianity. In fact the synergy of religion with fascism is so strong in the case of the Legion of the Archangel Michael that several scholars have suggested that it represents a hybrid of religion with politics, and thus is not a full member of the family of fascism (as long as this is conceived as secular revolutionary ideology), no matter how much it cloaks its racist utopia in the theological discourse of sacrifice, redemption and resurrection.[77] However, what does emerge clearly — thanks to Radu's profound familiarity with the primary sources relating to the subject in their original Romanian — is that, to cite the abstract, 'Despite its pronounced orthodox character, legionary mysticism did not signify the total assimilation of orthodox theology by a fascist political movement, but on the contrary an attempt at subordinating and transforming that theology into a political instrument'.[78] In a stroke this brings Romanian fascism into line with the way Michael Burleigh and Ian Kershaw (but not Steigmann-Gall) instinctively approach the 'theology' of Nazism.

Once we cross the divide between inter-war and post-war fascism and move to the other side of the Atlantic we enter what can be disorienting terrain for historians of the extreme right in inter-war Europe. Nevertheless, Martin Durham's essay on the National Alliance soon restores a sense of familiarity with its account of how a fascist movement has adapted neo-Nazism to an American and post-war context that turns the discourse of German nationalism into a pan-Aryan creed. In the absence of the conditions to generate a mass base, the NA has had to radically overhaul the inter-war concept of a fascist movement, the armed party and the charismatic leader. Durham suggests that it has also introduced a significant new element to the religious dimension of original Nazism by postulating the need to transcend the existing secular world order, a project that calls into question the adequacy of seeing political religion simply in terms of 'sacralizing the state'. The final essay by Chip Berlet on Christian Identity raises even more fundamental question about the adequacy of Gentile's taxonomy by considering specimens of political energy where the distinction between sacralized politics and politicized religion becomes highly elusive. He shows that the academic need for precise definitions is further thwarted by intractable issues of how to distinguish orthodox from heterodox modes of religion. Moreover, while the possibility that certain political cultures and social milieux, especially those saturated with non-conformist religions and with New Age cults, can generate hybrids of the secular and the religious which are neither fish nor fowl opens up another can of worms.

As for Martin Blinkhorn's afterthoughts, I will be as intrigued as many readers to learn what a historian of inter-war. European fascism not known for being particularly enamoured of taxonomic soul-searching makes of it all. Certainly, the articles justify a healthy scepticism about quests for 'nomothetic' clarity by documenting the extraordinarily diverse nature of the phenomena subsumed under the terms 'fascism' and 'extreme right', as well as the conspicuous differences in basic approach and conceptual framework that can still exist even among academics prepared to contribute to the same journal issue. However, they may hopefully also convince a sceptic that *Totalitarian Movements and Political Religions* would do well to adopt the policy of pursuing ever more deliberately and self-consciously the goal implicit in the act of its creation. This was surely to establish a new inter-disciplinary specialism based on maximizing the synergy, not only between political science and history, but between the concepts of totalitarianism and political religion, thereby reinforcing the ties of kinship and mutual support within the large extended family of terms, or conceptual constellations, to which they belong.

Whatever the practical outcome of this particular journey into collaborative scholarship and converging concepts, I would like to thank Robert Mallet (the series editor) and Glyn Lavers (the in-house editor at Taylor & Francis) for encouraging me as a reluctant captain to steer this special issue on such oceanic topics to a safe harbour, and express my appreciation to all the contributors for ensuring it did not arrive with its cargo bays empty. Whether it has reached its destination clarifying more than it obfuscates, and hence succeeds in moving the debate on rather than bogging it down even further in the terminological disputes that so alienate historians, I must leave it for readers to judge. Nevertheless, no matter how far this particular special issue may fall short of its original (necessarily utopian) objectives in the minds of some readers, it is worth emphasizing that debating the nexus between religion, politics and ideological assaults against civil society should never degenerate into the scholastic game or wrestling match of intellectual egos it may sometimes appear to outsiders. Nor is it simply a matter of satisfying the compulsive need of academic specialists to compare, contrast, discriminate and differentiate in their attempt to achieve some sort of conceptual grip on politics in the age of high modernity. An age in which Marx's prophetic phrase 'all that is solid melts into thin air' increasingly applies not just to external reality but to the terminology we create to capture them.

The prophylactic recommended by Cioran for the innate human drive to idolatry and fanaticism, the need to venerate even graven images representing secular authority, was to nurture 'the faculty of indifference', to become 'sceptics (or idlers or aesthetes) because they *propose* nothing, because they — humanity's true benefactors — undermine fanaticism's purposes, analysing its frenzy'. He also warns that 'in every man sleeps a prophet, and when he wakes there is a little more evil in the world'.[79] Undaunted, I will close in the guise of preacher rather than teacher by suggesting that the serious study of the nexus between politics and religion opens up — to use a trope employed by fascists, Dark Greens and first generation Blairites alike — a 'Third Way' of which Cioran is oblivious. It is one where academics engage with the historical fruits of fanaticism and analyse the political frenzies of modernity not with cold detachment but with a passionate humanist, or perhaps just human, commitment to establishing academically cogent interpretations, educating students and, if the chance arises, informing public opinion and the media that shape it, and enlightening government advisers and politicians, lest civil religion crosses once more the thin line that separates it from a religious one in times of crisis. We have a professional duty to take advantage of our privileged vantage point in society to avoid allowing the dissection of concepts to become desiccation, and to proactively disseminate the tolerance that is born of a sense of complexity and inflected by compassion. We have an obligation to combat any tendency for 'the goddess Reason' to degenerate into a modern Moloch or a Juggernaut. We have a mission to scrutinize and challenge the dangerous simplifications of fundamentalisms,[80] whether religious or secular, and do what we can to keep the minds and doors of our society open. It is a task that perhaps requires a benevolent fanaticism of its own, an academic equivalent of the passionate commitment to this-worldly life evoked on Sting's album *Sacred Love*: 'There's no religion but the joys of rhythm ..., There's no religion that's right or winning, There's no religion in the paths of hatred, Ain't no prayer but the one I'm singing'.[81]

NOTES

1. Emilio Gentile, 'The Sacralisation of Politics: Definitions, Interpretations and Reflections on the Question of Secular Religion and Totalitarianism', trans. Robert Mallet, *Totalitarian Movements and Political Religions*, 1/1 (2000), pp. 18–55.
2. Michael Burleigh, 'National Socialism as a Political Religion', *Totalitarian Movements and Political Religions*, 1/2 (2000), pp. 1–26.
3. Roger Griffin, 'The Primacy of Culture: The Current Growth (or Manufacture) of Consensus within Fascist Studies', *The Journal of Contemporary History*, 37/1 (2002), pp. 21–43.
4. I will be expanding on this concept of the cluster or 'constellar', concept in a forthcoming article in *Totalitarian Movements and Political Religions*, publishing the papers presented at a symposium on political religion. It was held by Bern University in conjunction with the award of the 2003 Hans Sigrist Prize to Professor Emilio Gentile for his services to the understanding of political religion.
5. For example, Martin Blinkhorn, *Fascism and the Right in Europe 1919–1945* (London: Longman, 2000), pp. 3–7. In his own reply to Tony Abse's review of this book published in 'Reviews in History' (24 September 2001), Martin Blinkhorn admits to being 'increasingly "impatient" (though this is less evident in the book than perhaps it should be) with the whole "generic fascism" grail quest'.
6. Johann Wolfgang von Goethe, 'Wo viel Licht ist, ist starker Schatten' (*Götz von Berlichingen*, Act 1).
7. For example, Simon Tormey, *Making Sense of Tyranny* (Manchester: Manchester University Press, 1995). Ian Kershaw offers a useful summary of the literature on Nazism as a form of totalitarianism in the chapter 'The essence of Nazism: form of fascism, brand of totalitarianism, or unique phenomenon', *The Nazi Dictatorship* (London: Arnold, 4th edn, 2000).
8. Richard Shorten, 'The Impact of Totalitarianism in Twentieth-Century Political Thought: From Hannah Arendt to Jürgen Habermas' (unpublished PhD thesis, University of Birmingham, 2004).
9. Leonard Schapiro, *Totalitarianism* (London: Pall Mall, 1972), p. 18.
10. Ibid., p. 119.
11. Juan Linz, *Totalitarian Dictatorship and Autocracy* (New York, Washington and London: Praeger, 1965), p. 21.
12. Ibid., p. 17, citing W. W. Rostow, *The Stages of Economic Growth: A Non-Communist Manifesto* (Cambridge: Cambridge University Press, 1960). No page given.
13. Ibid., p. 25.
14. Juan Linz, 'Totalitarian and Authoritarian Regimes', in Fred Greenstein and Nelson Polsby, eds, *Handbook of Political Science. Macropolitical Theory*, volume 3, p. 321 (Reading, Mass.; London: Addison-Wesley, 1975 [reprinted Boulder, Colo., London: Lynne Rienner Publishers, 2000]), pp. 191–357.

15. Juan Linz, 'Some Notes towards a Comparative Study of Fascism in a Sociological Historical Perspective', in Walther Laqueur (ed.), *Fascism: A Reader's Guide* (Harmondsworth: Penguin, 1979), p. 25.
16. Ibid, pp. 43–6.
17. Juan Linz, *Fascismo, autoritarismo, totalitarismo* (Rome: Ideazione, 2003), p. 94
18. Tormey (note 7), p. 168.
19. Ibid., p. 173.
20. In particular, Stanley Payne, *A History of Fascism 1914–1945* (London: UCL Press, 1995), p. 9; G. L. Mosse, *The Fascist Revolution* (New York: Howard Fertig, 1999), pp. xvi, 30–3, 87–8.
21. Tormey (note 7), pp. 180–1.
22. Payne (note 20).
23. Roger Griffin, *International Fascism: Theories, Causes and the New Consensus* (London: Arnold, 1995).
24. I originally explored the implications of an ideal type of fascism based on this approach in *The Nature of Fascism* (London: Pinter, 1991).
25. The heuristic strategy adopted in *The Nature of Fascism* has made me open to the charge in certain quarters of 'idealism', 'culturalism', 'essentialism' and of ignoring the 'praxis' of fascism, as well as its economic and sociological basis, its use of violence, its institutional and organizational structures. However, the actual text of *The Nature of Fascism* makes it clear to those who read it that my one-sentence definition is not presented as a *summum* of the essence of fascism, but as an ideal-typical distillation of a much more complex discursive account of it. Moreover, the rest of the book is concerned with the concrete historical phenomena on which the definition is based, and with the material socio-political conditions which encourage or inhibit its growth.
26. Roger Griffin, 'The Primacy of Culture The Current Growth (or Manufacture) of Consensus within Fascist Studies', *The Journal of Contemporary History*, 37/1 (2002), pp. 21–43.
27. Sven Reichardt, *Faschistische Kampfbünde* (Cologne: Böhlau, 2002). See pp. 19–29.
28. Philip Morgan, *Fascism in Europe, 1919–1945* (London and New York: Routledge, 2003). See pp. 13–14.
29. Angelo Ventrone, *La seduzione totalitaria: guerra, modernità, violenza politica* (Rome: Donzelli, 2003). See pp. 26–46, and section 3, 'The Search for a New Modernity'.
30. Enzo Traverso, *The Origins of Nazi Violence* (New York: The New York Press, 2003). See particularly pp. 93–100, 118–28, as well as pp. 136–48 on 'redemptive violence'.
31. Jay Gonen, *The Roots of Nazi Psychology* (Kentucky: The University of Kentucky Press, 2000).
32. De Grand, *Fascist Italy and Nazi Germany: The Fascist Style of Rule* (New York and London: Routledge, 1995). Contrast pp. 2–3 with pp. 77–81.
33. A. James Gregor, *Phoenix* (New Brunswick, New Jersey: Transaction). See particularly pp. 30–1, 47, 138, 162.
34. Blinkhorn (note 5). See particularly pp. 6, 116–17.
35. Oxford: Oxford University Press, 2002. Passmore distances himself at some length from my own definition and its his own discursive account of fascism on page 31 studiously avoids any reference to rebirth. Yet it is implicit in the opening statement that 'Fascism is a set of ideologies and practices that seeks to place the nation, defined in exclusive biological, cultural, and/or historical terms, above all other sources of loyalty, and to create a mobilized national community', a process that is made possible by 'the advent to power by a new elite'. The approach he adopts is thus fully consistent with the new consensus, even if it naturally contains its own nuances and emphasis on particular features which point away from my variant of it.
36. Marco Tarchi, *Fascismo Teorie, interpretazioni e modelli* (Rome, Bari: Laterza, 2003). The checklist definition Tarchi offers (pp. 153–4) includes the goal of integrating the whole population, of which the fascists from the conscious vanguard, in an organic

national community; reviving traditions which form the basis of national identity to assure the country a glorious future; and educating and mobilizing the population with the aim of establishing a new social and cultural order under the guidance of a leader, all of which directly correlate to 'palingenetic ultra-nationalism'.

37. Robert Paxton, *The Anatomy of Fascism* (New York: Alfred Knopf, 2004). Having attacked the 'static' and 'essentialist' nature of my definition, the one which Paxton provides at the end of the book (p. 218) reads: 'a form of political behaviour marked by obsessive preoccupation with community decline, humiliation, or victimhood and by compensatory cults of unity, energy and purity, in which a mass-based party of committed nationalist militants, working in uneasy but effective collaboration with traditional elites, abandons democratic liberties and pursues with redemptive violence and without ethical or legal restraints goals of internal cleansing and external expansion'.

38. Michael Mann, *Fascists* (Cambridge: Cambridge University Press, 2004). Mann has harsh words for the 'idealism' and lack of concreteness of my approach. Yet his own definition on page 13 characterizes fascism as 'the pursuit of a transcendent and cleansing nation-statism through paramilitarism', and goes onto to describe fascists as revolutionaries pursuing an alternative vision of modernity, both points that endorse the new consensus.

39. Arthur Koestler *et al.*, *The God that Failed. Six Essays in Communism* (London: H. Hamilton, 1950).

40. Robert Waite, *The Psychopathic God: Adolf Hitler* (New York: Basic Books, 1977).

41. Herbert Schneider, *Making the Fascist State* (New York: Howard Fertig, 1968; 1st edn New York: Oxford University Press, 1928), p. 229.

42. Bertrand Russell, *The Practice and Theory of Bolshevism* (London: Allen & Unwin, 1920), p. 16.

43. Cited in W. Michalke (ed.), *Deutsche Geschichte 1933–1945* (Frankfurt am Main: Suhrkamp, 1993), pp. 97–9, downloaded from the Jewish Virtual Library at http://www.us-israel.org/jsource/Holocaust/HimmlerLecture.html (09/07/2004).

44. See, for example, the 'select bibliography' in Michael Burleigh, *The Third Reich. A New History* (London: Macmillan, 2000), pp. 922–3, and in Emilio Gentile, *Le religioni della politica* (Rome, Bari: Laterza, 2001), pp. 220–1.

45. Jean-Jacques Rousseau, *The Social Contract* (Chicago: University of Chicago Press, 1952), book IV, section 8 (1st edn 1762). A major feature of the French Revolution was that a partly spontaneous populist 'civic religion' grew up in the form of a rich body of liturgy and semiotic behaviour that betokened the advent of a new era: see Mona Ouzof, *Festivals and the French Revolution* (Chicago University Press, 1988); L. Hunt, *Politics, Culture and Class in the French Revolution* (Berkeley and Los Angeles: University of California Press, 1981).

46. Plato's *Republic* (Harmondsworth: Penguin, 1987), Book 2, 'The Individual, the State, and Education'.

47. This approach has a deep resonance with the acerbic analysis of fanaticism offered by Emile Cioran in *A Short History of Decay* (Oxford: Basil Blackwell, 1975, original French edition 1949). Cioran spoke as an insider, having been a 'fanatical' believer in the Romanian Iron Guard's promise of cultural rebirth before his conversion to fin-de-siècle decadence as a vantage point from which to observe the human condition in a pose of studiously cultivated cultural pessimism.

48. Hannah Arendt, 'Religion and Politics', in Jerome Kohn (ed.), *Hannah Arendt: Essays in Understanding, 1930–1945* (London: Harcourt, Brace & Co.), pp. 368–91.

49. Jean-Pierre Sironneau, *Sécularisation et religions politiques* (The Hague: Meuton, 1982), pp. 589–91.

50. Hannah Arendt, 'A Reply to Eric Voegelin', in Kohn (note 48), p. 406.

51. A thesis first explored in Eric Voegelin, *Die politischen Religionen* (Vienna: Bermann-Fischer, 1938). His approach has deep affinities with those who see totalitarian ideologies being driven by residues of apocalyptic/eschatological fantasies, in which Fiore

plays a major role. Cf. Norman Cohn, *The Pursuit of the Millennium: Revolutionary Millenarians and Mystical Anarchists of the Middle Ages* (London: Pimlico, 1993 [1957]); James Rhodes, *The Hitler Movement: A Modern Millenarian Revolution* (Stanford, Calif.: Hoover Institution Press, 1980).

52. Barbara Spackman, *Fascist Virilities* (Minneapolis, London: University of Minnesota Press, 1996), pp. 127–8.

53. G. L. Mosse, *The Nationalization of the Masses* (New York: Howard Fertig, 1975, 1999).

54. Cf. note 51.

55. C. Schneider (note 41), p. 220–1: 'fascism takes the old religion into itself, broadens it, vitalizes it, and transforms it into the religion of the future, in which God, Country and Duce become practically indistinguishable'.

56. Michael Burleigh, 'Political Religion and Social Evil', *Totalitarian Movements and Political Religions*, 3/2 (Autumn 2002), pp. 1–17.

57. Karl Popper, chapter 12, 'Hegel and The New Tribalism', in *The Open Society and its Enemies*, Vol. 2, 'The High Tide of Prophecy: Hegel, Marx, and the Aftermath' (London: Routledge & Kegan Paul, 1952; 1st edn 1945), p. 62.

58. J.-Lucien Radel, *Roots of Totalitarianism: The Ideological Sources of Fascism, National Socialism and Communism* (New York: Crane, Russak & Company, 1975), p. 32 (emphasis in the original).

59. Two important contributions by Aron in this context are *Democracy and Totalitarianism* (London: Weidenfeld & Nicolson, 1968) and the essay 'The Future of Secular Religions', in Reimer Yair (ed.), *The Dawn of Universal History: Selected Essays from a Witness of the Twentieth Century* (New York: Basic Books, 2002), pp. 177–203.

60. Burleigh (note 44), p. 18.

61. Payne (note 20).

62. Ibid., pp. 441–61.

63. Stanley Payne, review of Emilio Gentile, *Le religioni politiche: Fra democrazie e totalitarismi*, in *Totalitarian Movements and Political Religions*, 3/1 (Autumn 2002), pp. 122–30.

64. Walter Laqueur, *Fascism Past and Present* (New York: Oxford University Press, 1996).

65. Roger Eatwell, 'Reflections on Fascism and Religion', *Totalitarian Movements and Political Religions* 4/3 (Winter 2003), p. 163

66. Ibid., p. 146. Kershaw makes a similar point in 'Hilter and the Uniqueness of Nazism', *Journal of Contemporary History*, 39/2 (2004), note 25.

67. Burleigh (note 56).

68. Burleigh (note 2). It is clear from the section 'The Brown Cult and the Christians', pp. 252–67, that Burleigh treats Nazism's political religion as a grotesque parody of Christianity. For example, he comments on how a Nazi ceremonial, such as the Commemoration of the Movement's Fallen, engendered only 'quasi-religious emotion', and must have prompted 'nausea in any fastidious rationalist or person of *genuine religious faith*' (p. 264, my emphasis).

69. Burleigh (note 56), Introduction.

70. Ibid., p. 3.

71. In Mosse (note 20).

72. Response to an e-mail by the author. I am grateful to Richard Evans for allowing me to cite it in this article.

73. Kershaw (Note 66), p. 241. Cf the observation in Kershaw (note 7), pp. 41–2 which stresses that 'the uniqueness of specific features of Nazism would not itself prevent the location of Nazism in a wider genus of political systems. It might well be claimed that Nazism and Italian Fascism were separate species within the same genus, without any implicit assumption that the two species ought to be well-nigh identical'.

74. Ibid., p. 247. Cf. his observation in the conclusion of an article written for a German readership on 'Hitler and the Realization of the National Socialist Racial Utopia' that,

'The charismatic rule of Hitler, which as already mentioned displayed unmistakably pseudo-religious features and through its utopian vision of the future awoke expectations of salvation in the population of a modern society, was in many respects atavistic. Nonetheless, it ultimately stemmed from an important characteristic of modernity, namely the conviction, one which had only existed since the end of the eighteenth century, that not God, but humanity itself was in the position to shape the future of human kind and that human happiness as well was no longer primarily to be found in heaven'. [Ian Kershaw, 'Adolf Hitler und die Realisierung des national sozialistischen Rassenutopie', in Wolfgang Hardwig (ed.), *Utopie und politische Herrschaft im Europa der Zwischenkriegzeit*, Schriften des Historischen Kollegs Kolloquien 56 (Munich: Oldenbourg: 2003).] From a political science perspective such passages are an open invitation to locate Nazism fully within a number of processes and phenomena occurring well beyond the narrow confines of German history and make a nonsense of German exceptionalism, however 'unique' the Third Reich was in the destruction the attempts to realize its utopia unleashed.

75. Kershaw (note 66), p. 250.
76. An outstanding example of more 'conventional' scholarship that conflicts with Steigmann-Gall on this point is Uriel Tal, a selection of whose essays on Nazism's relationship to Christianity have been recently published under the title *Religion, Politics and Ideology in the Third Reich* (London: Routledge, 2004) in the series Totalitarian Movements and Political Religions. In 'Structures of German "Political Theology" in the Nazi Era', first published in 1979, Tal states (pp. 87–8) that 'the redemptive character given to *Führer* and Reich was derived from the realm of theology and then transfigured into forms of secularism and politics', citing Carl Schmitt's assertion from his 1934 book *Politische Theologie: Vier Kapitel zur Lehre von der Souveranität* that 'All pregnant concepts of modern political science are secularised theological concepts'. That Tal, in common with Gentile, Burleigh *et al.*, sees a radical distinction between the religion of Christianity and the political religion/political theology of the Nazis can be inferred from his reference in footnote 7 to the 'political use, or rather abuse, of terms rooted in religious tradition during the Nazi era'.
77. For example, Eugen Weber, 'Romania' in H. Rogger and E. Weber, *The European Right* (Berkeley: University of California Press, 1965); Stanley Payne in *Fascism: Comparison and Definition* (Madison: University of Wisconsin Press, 1980). More recently Roger Eatwell has drawn attention to the way the 'conservative mysticism' of Iron Guard poses problems for 'unequivocally including it within the fascist pantheon', and that might warrant the term 'clerical fascism', Eatwell (note 65), p. 154.
78. Cf. Lucretiu Patrascanu, *Sub tre dictaturi* (Bucharest: Editura Socec, 1945), writing in the age of innocence long before the intricate academic disputes over the nature of fascism, who stressed, in Radu's words, that 'the symbiosis between the legionary movement and orthodoxy was simply the subordination of certain religious elements to the commandments of politics'. According to Patrascanu, 'The incorporation of and subordination of orthodoxy to political ends pursued by the Legionary movement are more specific to the Iron Guard than the recognition of a Christian spirituality as a behavioural norm or a source of ethical and social directives'. Cited by Ionid Radu in *The Sword of the Archangel Michael: Fascist Ideology in Romania* (New York: Columbia University Press, Boulder East European Monographs, 1990), p. 140.
79. Cioran (note 47), pp. 3–6. Cf. the 'facetiousness' of Kenneth Toomey, the central character of *Earthly Powers* (London etc.: Hutchinson, 1980), Anthony Burgess's brilliant exploration of the complex relationship between theological and secular spheres of faith. Kenneth Toomey, accused of this vice by a Catholic priest, later to become a candidate for the papacy, tells him (in the 2004 adaptation for BBC Radio 4 by Michael Hastings): 'Ever since this century was born I've watched it commit suicide in a very public way. No other century has killed so many people or committed such atrocious

acts of terror. No other century has offered such inadequate Gods. So I have taken a vow to take nothing very seriously. And if that's being facetious count me in'.

80. Academics would perhaps do well to heed Cioran's sombre pronouncement in *A Short History of Decay* (note 47), p. 7, in the section 'In the Graveyard of Definitions', that 'The idle, empty mind — which joins the world only by the grace of sleep — can practice only by extending the name of things, by emptying them and substituting formulas for them. ... Under each formula lies a corpse'.

81. From the song 'Send Your Love' on the album *Sacred Love* (Polydor, 2003). The song also contains the apposite lines: 'You're climbing down from an ivory tower; You've got a stake in the world we ought to share'.

Fascism, Totalitarianism and Political Religion: Definitions and Critical Reflections on Criticism of an Interpretation

EMILIO GENTILE
Translated by Natalia Belozentseva

To be a historian is to seek to explain in human terms. If God speaks, it is not through him. If He speaks to others, the historian cannot vouch for it. In this sense the historian is necessarily secularist. Yet, with equal force, nothing human is alien to him, and religion, whatever else it may be for true believers, is profoundly human.

Cushing Strout, *The New Heavens and New Earth*

An Interpretation in Three Definitions

Ever since the last decade of the twentieth century, there has been growing scholarly preoccupation with the problem of totalitarianism and political religion. This fact is proved by ever more numerous publications on these subjects, as well as by the founding of the journal *Totalitarian Movements and Political Religions* in 2000. In the first issue of this journal I had the opportunity to expound my interpretation of the relationship between totalitarianism, secular religion and modernity, viewed as the expression of a more general phenomenon I defined as the 'sacralisation of politics'. This term I define as 'the formation of a religious dimension in politics that is distinct from, and autonomous from traditional religious institutions'.[1] As a concrete historical example of the link between totalitarianism and political religion, as well as of the relation between the sacralisation of politics and modernity I also referred to Italian Fascism. For the reasons I explored in depth in my studies on the Fascist ideology, party and regime,[2] I believe that the experience of Italian Fascism – which, as is well known, gave rise to the very concept of totalitarianism – is to be located within the sphere of totalitarian experiments. In the same way, as a result of specific research done in this field, I also believe that fascism belongs to the sphere of modern manifestations of the sacralisation of politics.[3]

My interpretation of fascism as a form of both totalitarianism and political religion has given rise to criticism of various kinds, not confined to reservations about the way these concepts are used in my research. It contests the very validity of these concepts as instruments of analysis in the interpretation of some phenomena within contemporary history. In this sense, a critical reflection on the criticism of my interpretation of fascism as both totalitarianism and a political religion – the subject suggested to me by Roger Griffin as the editor of this special issue of *TMPR* – will hopefully make a useful contribution to the discussion of these questions.

I must stress that my interpretation of fascism as a totalitarian phenomenon does not derive solely from my historical studies, but also from my revision of the concept of totalitarianism via a critical reconsideration of the main theories of totalitarianism appearing after the Second World War. The term 'totalitarianism' can thus be taken as meaning:

> an *experiment in political domination* undertaken by a *revolutionary movement*, with an *integralist conception* of politics, that aspires toward a *monopoly of power* and that, after having secured power, whether by legal or illegal means, destroys or transforms the previous regime and constructs a new State based on a *single-party regime*, with the chief objective of *conquering society*; that is, it seeks the subordination, integration and homogenisation of the governed on the basis of the *integral politicisation of existence*, whether collective or

individual, interpreted according to the categories, myths and values of a *palingenetic ideology*, institutionalised in the form of a *political religion*, that aims to shape the individual and the masses through an *anthropological revolution* in order to regenerate the human being and create the *new man*, who is dedicated in body and soul to the realisation of the revolutionary and imperialistic policies of the totalitarian party, whose ultimate goal is to create a *new civilisation* beyond the Nation-State.[4]

Although this definition may appear to be a lengthy one, it arises from a deliberate choice of how to present the phenomenon. In this way, I intend to highlight the reciprocal connection between all the elements contributing to my concept of totalitarianism, both essential and complementary, so as to represent, in so far as a theoretical definition permits, the historical reality actualised by totalitarian regimes during the twentieth century. In my opinion, this reality cannot be theoretically identified with any of its constituents in isolation from the others. The elements comprising my definition of totalitarianism are the revolutionary party, the monopoly of power, a political religion, the conquest of society, an anthropological revolution and expansionist ambitions. These elements are thus to be considered interconnected, both logically and chronologically, within a dynamic and dialectical relation. This is the reason why my interpretation of totalitarianism differs from those theories that base their definition mainly on the institutional notion of the 'totalitarian regime'. I believe, indeed, that by its own nature totalitarianism is a continuous experiment in political domination, which is why I believe that the very notion of the 'totalitarian regime' has to be viewed essentially from a dynamic, not a static, point of view, and has to be defined bearing in mind specific historical circumstances in which totalitarian experiments were born and put into practice, even when they do not appear 'perfect' or 'completed'.

One of the constituents of my definition of totalitarianism is 'political religion', a term by which I mean:

a type of religion which sacralises an ideology, a movement or a political regime through the deification of a secular entity transfigured into myth, considering it the primary and indisputable source of the meaning and the ultimate aim of human existence on earth.

The essential characteristic distinguishing 'political religion' from 'civil religion' is the extremist and exclusive nature of its historical mission. For example, political religion does not accept coexistence with other political ideologies and movements; it denies the autonomy of the individual while affirming the primacy of the community; it sanctifies violence as a legitimate weapon in the struggle against those it considers internal and external enemies, and as an instrument of collective regeneration; it imposes obligatory observance of its commandments and participation in the political cult; while dealing with traditional or institutional religions, it either assumes hostile behaviour, aiming at their complete elimination, or tries to establish a relation of symbolic coexistence with them in the sense that political religion aims at incorporating a traditional religion in its own system of beliefs and myths, attaching to the latter an instrumental or auxiliary function.

According to this definition, the concept of political religion does not refer solely to the institution of a system of beliefs, rites or symbols; it also relates to other fundamental aspects of the totalitarian experiment, that is, to the conquest of society, the homogenisation of the society formed by the governed, an anthropological revolution, the production of a new type of human being, and even to the ambitious expansion and construction of a new supranational civilisation.

The concepts 'totalitarianism' and 'political religion', understood in the terms outlined above, are two of the constitutive elements of my interpretation of fascism, which I have synthesised in the following definition:

> fascism is a modern political phenomenon, which is nationalistic and revolutionary, anti-liberal and anti-Marxist, organised in the form of a militia party, with a totalitarian conception of politics and the State, with an ideology based on myth; virile and anti-hedonistic, it is sacralised in a political religion affirming the absolute primacy of the nation understood as an ethnically homogeneous organic community, hierarchically organised into a corporative State, with a bellicose mission to achieve grandeur, power and conquest with the ultimate aim of creating a new order and a new civilisation.

The elaboration of this interpretation began in the early 1970s. It has developed during a period particularly conducive to progress in the comparative study of fascism, and has given rise to the topics

and problems that are now at the very centre of historical research
and theoretical discussion, including the current reawakening of
interest in the problem of totalitarianism and political religion. This
progress consists of the continuous enrichment of our empirical
knowledge by means of historical research; of substantial revisions
in our understanding of topics and problems, our methods of analysis, and of our perspectives and interpretations. The renewed
concern with achieving progress in the analysis of fascism has developed within three main fertile periods that we can characterise
according to the type of approach, topics and problems prevailing
in each phase.

The Three Periods of Renewal

The first period, lasting from the mid-1960s to the end of the
1970s, was characterised by extended empirical scholarship and
new attempts to elaborate a general theory of fascism consistent
with the new knowledge produced by empirical research.[5] One of
the most important results, if not the most important, was the gradual tendency to move beyond the traditional representation of
fascism, so prevalent in the early 1960s, which has had a continuing
influence upon both theories and empirical studies of fascism that
persists to the present day.

   According to this traditional representation, fascism did not have
its own historical individuality in the same way as liberalism,
democracy, socialism or communism. Instead, it was a sort of anti-
historical and anti-modern epiphenomenon without culture or
ideology. Everywhere fascism was a movement of violent mercenar-
ies, in the service of the most reactionary part of the bourgeoisie,
led by cynical and opportunistic demagogues who merely subjugated
and led astray the innocent and recalcitrant masses. Based on this
interpretation, the tragic reality of fascism was thus a parenthesis in
the 'authentic' course of contemporary history, as if historians were
performing an act of consolation or exorcism that transformed the
movement into a sort of malign excrescence foreign to the healthy
body of modernity. In consequence, fascists represented something
inhuman, an expression of diabolical madness, or, in the opposite
sense, they were presented as a caricature or in a clownish guise. As
a result, whether demonised or trivialised, fascism was reduced to a
'historical negativity'.[6]

Such interpretations predominated for so long because they were considered the only ones that seemed consistent with a committed political stance of anti-fascism. Thus, this way of conceiving fascism became a kind of 'sacred representation' which could not be discussed in Italy without reopening the deeply contested political question of anti-fascism. Indeed, the interpretation of Italian Fascism as 'historical negativity' led to a serious impoverishment of the cultural anti-fascist tradition itself. In fact, as early as the 1920s, anti-fascist culture produced not only polemical and schematic interpretations, but also gave rise to a more complex and realistic analysis of fascism as a mass movement and a regime which emphasised the ideological, cultural, organisational and institutional character of fascism, as well as its links with modernity and with the transformation of politics under the impact of modernisation and mass society. The researchers who first used the concepts 'totalitarianism' and 'political religion' (although only the first a scholarly neologism) were opponents of fascism, who often became its victims. At the centre of their interpretation of fascism they placed the role of mythic thought, the mobilisation of the masses, the cult of the leader, the single party, the organisation of culture, and grandiose ideas about collective regeneration.[7]

After the Second World War, this important anti-fascist legacy of historical and theoretical analysis was either ignored or almost totally forgotten, whereas the thesis of 'historical negativity' became prevalent. Even if this interpretation appeared convincing, it nevertheless failed to address a fundamental problem of fascism, namely, its novelty as a movement and a political regime, which exerted an attraction on the masses as well as on outstanding intellectuals. The tragic irony of the fascist experience may lie precisely in the 'sincerity' of its irrationalism and in the appeal of its ideology. Fascism was certainly demagogic, but it cannot be accused of disguising its intentions and goals. In a clear and brutal way, fascism proclaimed its disdain for liberty, for equality, for wealth and peace as life ideals; it exalted the power of a minority while imposing blind obedience on the part of the masses; it asserted a fundamental inequality between individuals, classes, nations and races. The militaristic ethics of fascism glorified sacrifice, austerity, a disdain for hedonism, total devotion to the State, discipline and unconditional fidelity, all in order to stand up to the challenge of new wars in the name of grandeur and the power of the nation. All this was not only proclaimed publicly at mass rallies, preached in schools, imprinted on the walls of buildings and along the streets, but was put into practice as the policy of the regime. Despite this 'sincerity', millions of people, both cultured and otherwise, saw in fascism an inspirational movement that was able to provide an answer to questions pertaining to human existence. In addition, many of them considered the totalitarian system an effective solution to the conflicts of modern society, the dawn of a new era of national grandeur, or the birth of a 'new civilisation' destined to last forever.

When presented with evidence of fascism's genuine popularity, the main historiographical schools of the post-war period, inspired by both Marxism and liberalism, either remained silent and indifferent, or limited themselves to presenting these aspects of fascism as marginal or unimportant ones. As Marco Gervasoni has recently observed, Marxist historiography 'despite all of its nuances, remained dumbfounded in the face of the irrational, tending to approach it in a reductionist spirit as a mystification of economic interests', while liberal historiography 'has always felt uneasy when confronted by the accomplishments of mass politics, often ending up explaining totalitarian phenomena on the basis of the psychology of its leaders'.[8] In this way, the problem of fascism's attraction was simply ignored or concealed by interpretations that reduced everything to demagoguery, opportunism and terror. This may be the 'disguising' of the 'appeal of fascism' that Primo Levi, the Jewish intellectual and a victim of fascism, protested against in 1976:

> Everybody knows or even remembers that Hitler and Mussolini, when making public speeches, were believed, applauded, admired, adored as if they were gods. They were 'charismatic leaders' who possessed the secret power to seduce which did not derive from any real credibility or from the justness of the things they said, but from the 'fascinating' way in which those things were said, from their eloquence, their histrionic art, maybe instinctive or maybe patiently exercised and learned. The ideas they proclaimed were not the same all of the time, and were in general aberrant, foolish, or cruel; but still they were cheered and followed by millions of believers until they died. We should remember that those believers, including the diligent executors of inhuman orders, were not born torturers, nor monsters (save few exceptions): they were ordinary people. Monsters do exist but they are not as many as to be really dangerous; the man in the street is much more dangerous, the servant ready to believe

and to obey without arguing, like Eichmann, like Höss, the commander of Auschwitz, like Stangl, the commander of Treblinka, like the French soldiers twenty years later, the slaughterers in Algeria, like the American soldiers thirty years later, the slaughterers in Vietnam.[9]

Understanding the grounds for the appeal that fascism exerted on millions of people between the two world wars was one of the reasons underpinning the first period of renewal in the field of research and interpretation. As we have seen, this period began in the early 1960s, when several historians started studying fascist ideology and culture, and recognised that the success of fascism depended not only on demagogy, opportunism or terror, but also on its capacity to interpret collective aspirations, desires and ambitions; not concealing its brutal and belligerent conception of life and politics but, on the contrary, professing it openly in front of the applauding masses. It is remarkable that it was another Jewish intellectual, George L. Mosse, also a victim of Nazism (but luckier than Primo Levi because he did not go through the hell of the death camps), who became one of the first historians daring to call into question the validity of prevailing presentations of fascism as 'historical negativity'. Mosse was a persecuted man who, being an historian, undertook the task of trying to understand the reasons the spell that his persecutors cast upon millions of people seemed to work, and he went about this by studying the ideology, culture and political style of National Socialism. He considered fascism a phenomenon not at all foreign to the course of contemporary history but, on the contrary, argued that its roots lay deep in the history and society of modern Europe, where it established itself by being able to interpret and represent the aspirations of millions of people, transporting them emotionally into the myths and the rites of a new lay religion.

Symbolically, Mosse can be considered the most representative historian of the first phase of renewal in the study of fascism.[10] The *Journal of Contemporary History*, founded and edited by Mosse and Walter Laqueur in 1966, can be considered as symbolic of this period, and in particular its first special issue on international fascism. Starting from the initial phrase of Mosse's opening article on the genesis of fascism, the distance between traditional interpretations and their presentation of fascism appeared very clear. Mosse wrote: 'In our century two revolutionary movements have made their mark upon Europe: that originally springing from Marxism and fascism'.[11]

We can consider the definition of fascism advanced by Juan Linz in 1976 as similarly symbolising this first period. Linz specified that any definition of fascism could not be based only on its negations, but 'should also consider its new appeal and its conception of man and society'. Linz added that, 'no definition can ignore the importance of its distinctive style, its rhetoric and its symbolism, its chants, ceremonies and shirts that attracted so many young people in the years between the two wars', and further concluded that neither ideology nor style would in any case have been the decisive factor 'without the new forms of organisation and political action'. For all these reasons Linz proposed a multi-dimensional definition which marked a further clear-cut step to move beyond the traditional representation of 'historical negativity':

> We define fascism as a hypernationalist, often pan-nationalist, anti-parliamentary, anti-liberal, anti-communist, populist and therefore anti-proletarian, partly anti-capitalist and anti-bourgeois, anti-clerical, or at least, non-clerical movement, with the aim of national social integration through a single party and corporative representation not always equally emphasised; with a distinctive style and rhetoric, it relied on activist cadres ready for violent action combined with electoral participation to gain power with totalitarian goals by a combination of legal and violent tactics. The ideology and above all the rhetoric appeals for the incorporation of a national cultural tradition selectively in the new synthesis in response to new social classes, new social and economic problems, and with new organizational conceptions of mobilization and participation, differentiate them from conservative parties. The appeal based on emotion, myth, idealism, and action on the basis of a vitalistic philosophy is initially directed at those least integrated into the class structure – youth, students, demobilised officers – to constitute a self-appointed elite and later to all those disadvantageously affected by social change and political and economic crisis against the political system. In a plebiscitarian mobilization of the masses, the fascist appeal is based on an inflation of national solidarity and the rejection of the institutionalization of conflict and cleavages in modern societies and therefore a destruction and/or demobilization of the parties that organize those cleavages, particularly working-class but also clerical parties. Hypernationalism is

reflected in a deep-seated hostility to all organizations and move-ments that can be conceived as international in character – that is communism, even socialism, international finance capitalism, the Catholic Church or at least the Vatican, Freemasonry, the League of Nations, pacifism, and the Jews, even in those move-ments that are not initially anti-Semitic and even less racist.[12]

By the end of the 1970s, the most original and innovative of these new assessments of fascism met with the critical approval of Stanley Payne in his 1980 book, *Fascism: Comparison and Definition*. Payne drew conclusions from the empirical and theoretical disputes of recent years, reworking them into a general definition of fascism, a political phenomenon that he no longer presented exclusively in terms of its negations, but, rather, as combining new and modern features, with its own ideology, culture and revolutionary components blended with traditional and reactionary ones:

> Fascism was after all the only major new ideology of the twenti-eth century, and it is not surprising that a variety of its key features reemerge in radical movements and national authoritar-ian regimes in later times and other regions, even though the profile of the new groups is on balance distinct from the generic European fascisms. A number of these features may be specified:
>
> 1. Permanent nationalistic one-party authoritarianism, neither temporary nor a prelude to internationalism
> 2. The charismatic leadership principle, incorporated by many communist and other regimes as well
> 3. The search for a synthetic, ethnicist ideology, distinct from liberalism and Marxism
> 4. An authoritarian state system and political economy of corporatism or syndicalism or partial socialism, more limited and pluralistic than the communist model
> 5. The philosophical principle of voluntarist activism, unbounded by any philosophical determinism.
>
> In these respects the fascist experience was fundamental to revo-lution and authoritarian nationalism in the twentieth century.[13]

During the second period of renewal in the study of fascism in the 1980s, theoretical elements of the debate weakened considerably, and became, in a way, marginal. In fact, what prevailed among scholars was historical research of singular movements and regimes generally considered fascist, combined with a certain scepticism concerning the possibility of arriving at a theoretical definition of fascism that would meet with the general consent of most scholars. Some, like Karl Bracher and Renzo De Felice, went even further and focused on specific features of single movements and regimes in a way that called into question the very existence of a generic phenomenon that could be termed 'fascism'. During that period, however, research in new fields opened up by the studies of the previous decade continued undeterred by the lack of a consensual definition and made particular headway in examining fascism's political, organisational and institutional aspects, in addition to its ideological ones.

The dawn of the 1990s marked the beginning of a new period characterised by a renewed, major interest in the theoretical aspects of fascism, turning scholarly attention toward its cultural and aesthetic aspects, while also attributing a primary role to ideology and culture in an attempt to give the fascist phenomenon a more precise definition.[14] Roger Griffin's 1991 book, *The Nature of Fascism*, may be considered the most important product of this period. Griffin, a British-born scholar, presented a critical list of the main interpretations of fascism, rejecting those which no longer seemed able to meet the challenge posed by new knowledge and new interpretations that had emerged from the research and discussion of recent decades. By theoretically elaborating the most innovative results produced by the library of existing studies on fascism, Griffin set out a new 'definition of fascism primarily in terms of its "positive" ideological axioms, from which its characteristic style, structures and negations follow',[15] which he condensed into a single phrase: 'Fascism is a genus of political ideology whose mythic core in its various permutations is a palingenetic form of the populist ultra-nationalism'.[16]

The Two Concepts Return

As this third, and current, period of fascist studies got underway, a renewed interest in the problem of totalitarianism and political religion emerged. In fact, we can speak about a 'return' of the historiographical debate characteristic of the 1920s and 1930s As I have already mentioned, this had a fundamental function in the interpretation of fascism by anti-fascist scholars, but during the 1950s it was contested and marginalised within the study of contemporary history, mainly because it was considered an instrument of anti-communist propaganda during the Cold War. By the 1990s, the re-awakening of interest in the subject of totalitarianism coincided with the collapse of the Soviet system that freed the concept of totalitarianism from the ostracism to which it had been condemned, mainly by the communist scholars or, in any case, by those who were not hostile to the Soviet communism.[17] Almost concomitantly, this period also saw a renewal of interest in the question of political religion. One factor that possibly contributed to this, along with the renewed interest in totalitarianism, was the birth – or rather the re-birth – of manifestations of the 'sacralisation of politics' and the 'politicisation of religion' in the modern world. Even if these manifestations cannot be considered residues or variants of the totalitarianism of the twentieth century, they still reintroduce in a new way some of the fundamental features linking the religious dimension, the political dimension and modernity, which were typical of totalitarian phenomena.[18]

Nevertheless, apart from the incidental reasons which provided an impulse to this process, the current debate on totalitarianism and on political religion cannot be understood without bearing in mind that it has been prepared – and made possible by – the renewal of previous interpretations of fascism. To some extent, my own studies and reflections on fascism, totalitarianism and political religion have contributed to this renewal. At the very least I can claim that, contrary to what some critics have asserted, my interpretation of fascism as a totalitarian movement and a political religion predated by several years the current renewal in interest of these themes. As I have already mentioned, my interpretation of fascism was first elaborated during the 1970s, and is rooted in my previous studies on the myth of national regeneration, and in research centred on the emergence of a new lay religion in Italian culture, particularly on the avant-garde movements of the first part of the twentieth century. As a logical consequence, I was led by those studies to re-examine fascism, which, in many aspects, was both a product and an heir of those movements and that culture.

Totalitarianism and Political Religion in the Definition of Fascism

The essential core of my interpretation of fascism as a form of totalitarianism was formulated in an article dating from 1974, in which I stated the following:

the essential element ... of fascist ideology was the *affirmation of the primacy of political action*, that is, totalitarianism in the sense of the total resolution of the *private* into the *public*, and as the subordination of the values which related to the private life (religion, culture, morals, affection, etc.) to the public sphere *par excellence*, namely politics now understood as a form of activism involving the application of naked force, and as the contest of conflicting powers in which the only judge is success. The permanent core of fascist ideology was – as a consequence of totalitarianism – the conception of the State as the implementation of the will to power of an activist minority bent on realising this myth and its *idée-force*. The 'new man' dreamt of by fascists was to have been the product of a class of modern Platos who wanted to build an organic and dynamic State, and considered politics an absolute value, an end in itself. In that respect, the ideology of Italian fascism was *the most complete rationalisation* of the totalitarian State (especially when approached in terms of Gentilean idealism), conceived as a society hierarchically organised and subordinated to a political aristocracy which derived the legitimacy of its power only from the conquest and the perpetuity of its action. Fascism was mainly *the ideology of the State*, whose reality it affirmed to be fundamental and totalitarian. And, as such, it represented the antithesis of communist ideology, which is *the ideology of society*, as it aspires to the realisation of a community of free and equal men, with no divisions of class or hierarchy through the organisation of State power.[19]

The same article outlined an interpretation of fascism as a political religion, viewed as a logical consequence of its totalitarian world view:

The fascist conception of life gave rise to fascist behaviour in the *way* of doing politics, organising social existence, conceiving the overall objectives, not on the basis of logic and persuasion, but by appealing to the instinct, to faith, feeling, and imagination, to the magnetic attraction of the leader. The fascist group was conceived as a group bound by the ties of the faith. A fascist did not choose or discuss doctrine because he was primarily a believer and a fighter. Fascism appeared an escape from all that gave substance and measure to social existence, and hence deprived it of its Romantic, mystic, heroic, and adventurous dimension. Adventure, heroism, the spirit of sacrifice, mass

rituals, the cult of martyrs, the ideals of war and sports, fanatical devotion to the leader – these were the characteristics of
fascist collective behaviour.[20]

From this emotional and extremist conception of politics I inferred
what I defined as fascism's 'essentially *subjective* behaviour toward
politics … an *aesthetic* conception of political life', that manifested
itself in 'transformation of politics into spectacle':

> Rejecting the materialism that, according to fascists, was the
> defining feature of both capitalism and communism, fascism
> extolled the values of the spirit. The materialism of both ideolo-
> gies impoverished the individual, reducing him to a servant
> subordinate to bureaucratic routine, a worker in the service of
> production and machine, a citizen educated according to the
> middle-class morality based on money-making, wealth, and
> indifference to political and social life, trapped in his egoism,
> demoralized by the degrading collectivistic system of labour and
> suffocated by the anonymity of urbanisation. On the contrary,
> fascism presented itself as the political movement that brought
> back the *colour* and the *joy* to social life. In the totalitarian State,
> civil life was a continuous spectacle, where the fascist new man
> was swept away in the flow of orderly collective existence, in the
> re-enactment of rites, in displaying and worshiping symbols, in
> the constant appeal to collective solidarity to the point of mystic
> fusion, at least in peak moments, of psychological and emotional
> ecstasy, of one's own individuality with the unity of the nation
> and the race through the magical meditation of the Leader. Even
> if some of these aspects can still be found in other totalitarian
> regimes, in fascism, they were celebrated as the ideals of civil life
> and represented a considerable factor in its success. Organising
> the consensus of the masses, in fact, was based on these rituals …

In the end these considerations resulted in an overall evaluation of the
significance of fascism in contemporary history; and in particular, as a
modern experience of mass politics:

> A political system based on irrationalism almost inevitably
> reduces political participation, both individual and collective, to
> a mass spectacle. When man is disdained for his rational ideal-
> ism, for his capacity to logically comprehend reality, for his need
> for persuasion and understanding, he is reduced to a cellular

element of the crowd, and as the crowd, becomes easy to influence not through appeal to rational, but solely by means of the
instruments of psychological manipulation and moral violence
imposed through the manipulation of conscience, so that life
becomes reduced to pure superficiality. But by exalting fantasy
and imagination, by fomenting group prejudices, anxieties, frustrations, complexes of grandeur or misery – by all these means
the capacity of the individual to choose and to be critical is
destroyed. Symbols, rites, mass ceremonies and the mythic
consecration of ordinary acts of social life ('The Battle of the
Grain') become the only possible political participation of the
masses, as spectators of the drama that is being performed with
them and on them.[21]

This interpretation of fascism, initially based only on the ideological
and cultural dimensions of its experience, was developed further by
taking into consideration its organisational and institutional aspects,
through a close study of the history of fascist parties and regimes. This
was done in order to verify in which way, by which means, and to what
ends the fascists acted out their totalitarian conception of politics.

In 1982, in a paper given to a conference at the University of
Sydney, I summarised my interpretation of fascism as a totalitarianism
and a political religion by insisting on the links between the fascist
party and the totalitarian experiment under the fascist regime:

The goal of fascism was a revolution that, while leaving the
fundamental pillars of the bourgeois edifice intact, would transform the architecture of the liberal State along the lines suggested
by the myth of the 'new State'. Fascism defined this myth in
terms of a new plan: absolute political supremacy, foreshadowed
by the practical experience of the local power groups formed by
the fascist squads (*squadrismo*). The organisation of the armed
party (*partito milizia*) was the fundamental structure for the new
fascist State.

For many fascists, the squad was an embryonic experience of
totalitarian community, based on the spontaneous support of its
members, who felt that they were united by bonds of elective
affinity and solidarity; they were also united morally by complic-
ity in terrorist ventures, by patriotic fervour, and by the exaltation of war heroes and their dead comrades. The squad formed
a military organisation in order to destroy all adversaries,

whether by physical elimination or by passive obedience imposed through humiliation. The squad also considered itself the armed militia of an integralist and intolerant national religion that fascism sought to impose on all Italians. In this sense, the totalitarian nature of fascism was already present in the squads ... The mixture of politics and religion, the concept of politics as a lay religious experience, was not a fascist invention, but belongs to the history of nationalism after the French Revolution. The lay religion was, nevertheless, an integral factor in fascism mass politics ... It might be said that the totalitarian State, by its very nature, had to assume the character of a lay religious institution, with rituals and symbols, totally enclosing man in his material and moral reality.[22]

Two years later, on the occasion of a conference on Fascism and National Socialism, I tried to synthesise the results of my research in a definition of fascist regime that made use of the expression *totalitarian Caesarism*:

a charismatic dictatorship of the Caesarist type integrated into an organisational structure built on conformity with the totalitarian myth, consciously adopted and concretely operating as a behavioural code and a point of reference for the action and the organisation of the State and the masses.[23]

Totalitarian Caesarism was the institutional aspect of fascism as a modern and revolutionary phenomenon.[24] But its totalitarian nature, in my opinion, preceded the establishment of the regime because it originated before the seizure of power, in the matrix established by the Fascist National Party (PNF) that gave fascism its original characteristics of a 'militia party', something I highlighted in 1989, in the introduction to the first volume of the history of the Fascist National Party:

Fascism's totalitarian orientation emerged with the militia party during the first years of its formation, and consolidated the action of the movement and the regime. During its life as a regime the experiment was carried out on the uneven terrain of the historical and social situation that had been produced in Italy by the first phases of industrialisation and modernisation; it met with obstacles and resistance in the process of its realisation and ended in the catastrophe of the war. Nevertheless, recognising the failure of the totalitarian ambitions of fascism is no reason to minimise or trivialise the seriousness and historical significance of this unique experiment in political dominion, as scholars have tended to do hitherto: for two decades Italy was transformed by the PNF into a huge laboratory that involved millions of men and women, whether they liked it or not, in an attempt to implement a myth of a totalitarian State in order to form a new race of Italians schooled in fascist extremism, in the idolatry of the *primacy of politics* and in the cult of the will to power as the supreme ideal principle.[25]

The concept of 'totalitarianism' seemed to me an analytical instrument useful not only for understanding the historical events of Italian Fascism, but also for the possibility of theoretically linking, in a way firmly based on historical reality, essential components in order to formulate a definition of fascism that would comprise its organisational, cultural and institutional dimensions:

1. A mass movement with a multi-class membership, but where the middle class is prevalent among rank and file and within the leadership, most of whose members are new to political activity; it is organised as a party-militia whose identity is not based on social hierarchy and class origins but rather on the feeling of comradeship, the sense of a shared mission of national regeneration; it considers itself in a state of war against political adversaries, and aims to achieve a monopoly of political power through terror, parliamentary tactics and compromise with ruling elites, so as to destroy parliamentary democracy and create a new regime.

2. An ideology having an 'anti-ideological' and pragmatic character that proclaims itself anti-materialistic, anti-individualistic, anti-liberal, anti-democratic, anti-Marxist, populist and anti-capitalist in tendency; expresses itself aesthetically, more than theoretically, through a new political style and through the myths, rituals and symbols of a lay religion created for the cultural socialisation and integration of the masses, toward faith in the creation of a 'new man'.

3. A culture based on mythical thought and a tragic and activist vision of life conceived as the embodiment of the will to power, on the myth of youth as the creative force of history, and on the militarisation of politics as a life-model and a collective organisation.

4. A totalitarian concept of the supremacy of politics as an integral experience in bringing about the totalitarian State, the fusion of

the individual and the masses into the organic and mystical unity of the nation as an ethnic and moral community by instituting discriminatory and persecutory measures against those viewed as being outside that community, either because they are enemies of the regime or because they are viewed as belonging to races that are considered as inferior, or in any case dangerous to the nation's integrity.

5. A public ethic based on total dedication to the national community, on discipline, virility, comradeship and the warrior spirit.

6. A single party whose mission it is to ensure the armed defence of the regime; to select the leadership cadre and organise the masses within the totalitarian State by involving them in a permanent mobilisation based on faith and emotions.

7. A police apparatus that prevents, checks and represses dissent and opposition, even through the use of organised terror.

8. A political system that organised according to hierarchies of functions appointed from the top down, and crowned by the figure of the 'Leader', who is endowed with a charismatic and sacred nature who leads, orders and directs the activities of the party, the regime and the State.

9. A corporative organisation of the economy that eliminates the freedom of labour unions, broadens the sphere of State intervention seeking to create, according to technocratic- and solidarity-based principles, the collaboration among the 'productive classes' under the regime's control, to reach its power-driven objectives while maintaining private property and divisions among social classes.

10. A foreign policy inspired by the myth of power, national grandeur and the 'new civilization' having imperialistic expansion as its objective.

Despite being subdivided into ten parts, this definition intends to highlight the logical – not merely chronological – connection between the organisational, cultural and institutional dimensions of fascism, viewed as 'one of the first experiments of totalitarian dominion undertaken in the modern age', and as 'a political religion aiming at realising in its institutions a new 'sense of community' on the basis of myth and faith, banishing the liberty of the individual and the masses'.[26]

The idea of the genetic connection between totalitarianism and the 'sacralisation of politics' was consolidated by a deeper understanding, not just of its ideology, but also of the concrete political events of its history. The shift of attention from the ideological dimension to the ritual and symbolic dimension of fascism was stimulated and conditioned by the study of the mass politics enacted by both party and regime, where rites and symbols appeared fundamental elements of a culture based on mythic thought, and central to its policies in the realm of collective organisation and mobilisation.[27] The comparison of the phenomenon of Fascism's 'new politics' with the ritual dimension of National Socialism analysed by Mosse in *The Nationalisation of the Masses*, was, for me, a stimulus to study in depth the peculiarity of the Italian case and its points of contrast with the German one. It is worth stressing that, even if my reflections on fascism as a political religion were influenced by the work of Mosse, who was the first in the new historiography to affirm that 'fascism was a new religion',[28] it is not from his book on the nationalisation of the masses that my interest in the aesthetic, ritual and symbolic aspects of fascism derives.[29] Moreover, it was while reading Mosse's book that I became convinced of the differences between the Italian case and the German one, and, therefore, of the inapplicability of his interpretation of the nationalisation of the masses to the experience of Italian Fascism:

> Even if some of the external and particular aspects of fascism –
> I observed while reviewing Mosse's book in 1975 – correspond to the idea of the 'new politics', in reality, the essential conditions for the elaboration of a national liturgy were missing. The only national political theology was the one elaborated by the tradition associated with Mazzini-Gioberti-Gentile, and this remained purely intellectual. Besides, Italy's historical and social process did not bring about the elaboration of a widespread and shared national liturgy. The only one, which was hardly replaceable, was the Catholic liturgy. In the end, the lay religion of the nation was only the faith of few small groups.

The difference between the various national traditions of Fascism and Nazism was the starting-point for my investigation of the political religion contained in Fascism, which naturally did not have the same background as Mosse had discovered in the case of Nazism. As I pointed out, in 1982, while studying the subject of Fascist religion, Fascism had to produce its own political cult mainly using its own resources:

Fascism invented its political cult by drawing on the traditions of Mazzinianism and socialism, the patriotic ceremonies of the Great War, the rites and the symbols of 'combattentism', of Futurism, of 'arditism' and of 'Fiumanism'. We are speaking about *invention*[30] (but not about improvisation, considering the abundance of existing material which fascism could make use of) because the current state of our knowledge suggests that Fascism was unable to draw on a widespread lay tradition and national liturgy shared by millions of people, similar to the one to which George L. Mosse could trace the origins of the Nazi political cult. This explains the fragility of the Fascist political cult; the sense of the grotesque imposition of empty formulas that it stirred up in so many Italians; the widespread use of the rites and symbols of the Roman world; the predominance assumed, within the limits of new political cult, by a special cult of the *Duce* which ended up absorbing all the other components of the cult and of the Fascist political faith, including the nation and the State. The Fascist political cult, contrary to the Nazi political cult, was not the expression of an advanced process of the nationalisation of the masses, but an instrument to initiate this process. However, from such observations it would be wrong to arrive at the conclusion that the fascist political cult was a ridiculous expedient adopted artificially for propagandistic use and irrelevant to understanding the nature of fascism. As a matter of fact, the political cult, adopted or invented by fascism, was consistent with its totalitarian logic and with its image of man and the masses.[31]

I developed my analysis of the Fascist political cult in the course of the 1980s, along with my research into the history of the Fascist Party and regime, resulting in a later volume on the sacralisation of politics in Fascist Italy published in 1993,[32] the core argument of which was summarised in the article 'Fascism as Political Religion' in the *Journal of Contemporary History* in 1990. The introductory remarks of my interpretation of fascism as a political religion were the reconsideration of the relation between secularisation and sacralisation in modern society. This postulated, instead of a progressive disappearance of the sacred, a constant process of the sacralisation of politics, in the sense that, as I wrote, 'politics has assumed its own religious dimension ... which reached its highest point in the totalitarian movements of the twentieth century'.[33] It is in the context of this process, and as one of its main manifestations in the twentieth century, that the problem of fascism as a political religion acquires its significance. In that sense it is beyond doubt that the 'sacralisation of politics' was a fundamental aspect of fascism from the very beginning, and became increasingly predominant in the course of its development as a political religion that 'placed itself alongside traditional religion syncretically within its own sphere of values as an ally in the subjection of the mass to the State, although it did stress the primacy of politics', because, 'due to its totalitarian nature' and 'to its conception that politics constituted an all-consuming reality, fascism aimed at abolishing the boundaries between the religious and political spheres'.[34]

Criticism as Denigration and the Snare of Presumption

My interpretation of fascism as a totalitarianism and a political religion have been subject to various criticisms. I will limit myself to discussing here the negative criticism related not only to my interpretation, which in itself would be of a little importance, but also to the type which manifests a deep aversion to the very concepts of totalitarianism and political religion, as well as their application to the study of contemporary history.

Criticism is fundamental for the progress of understanding. Renewing the historiography and interpretation of fascism would not have been possible without a solid criticism of the historiography and the more traditional interpretations. But not all criticism carries out a function that promotes progress in understanding. In fact, there is a form of criticism that might appropriately be called denigration because it aims simply at rejecting an interpretation without a cohesive line of argument or any supporting evidence. This is the only sense in which the repudiation of this 'denigrating' criticism is treated here, namely as a contribution to the reflections and the debate on fascism, as well as on totalitarianism and on political religion. I believe it is worth examining the validity of this sort of negative criticism in order to clarify the terms and problems under discussion, even when they are born simply of a hostile prejudice against any approach to fascism that takes issue with its representation as an 'historical negativity', an argument that can even be taken to the point of claiming that the interpretation of fascism as a totalitarianism and a political religion is part of a devious manoeuvre to rehabilitate fascism.

In fact, it was 'denigrating' criticism that my interpretation initially attracted. The first critique of this kind was published 30 years ago, although since then the scholar in question has made amends in a spirit of good faith, claiming to have misunderstood the sense of my historiographical work, and recognising the contribution that my interpretation of Italian Fascism as totalitarianism has made to scholarly research.[35] Twenty years later, the accusation was repeated by those who wanted solely to denigrate my interpretation, defining it as 'anti-anti-Fascist'.[36] This accuser seems to assume he is the sole guardian and authorised interpreter of an authentically anti-Fascist interpretation of Fascism. In reality, the accusation of 'anti-anti-Fascism' levelled at my interpretation reveals a quadruple ignorance: of anti-Fascism, of Fascism, of the current Italian anti-Fascist historiography, and, finally, of my interpretation of Fascism itself. In fact, this interpretation, as anyone who has actually read my writings and has a real, not rhetorical, knowledge of the anti-Fascist tradition, was elaborated in the wake of the interpretations of such anti-Fascists as Luigi Salvatorelli, Giovanni Amendola, Luigi Sturzo and Lelio Basso. Each of these were the first to sense and analyse the newness of the fascist phenomenon as an original experiment in political dominion, acted out by a party organised along military lines, which had conquered a monopoly of political power and was aiming to impose its ideology as a lay religion. It was these anti-Fascist scholars who first invented and spread the concept of totalitarianism, to which other anti-Fascist scholars added the concept of political religion, considering them to be two sides of the same coin.[37] Also, in the current historiography my interpretation of Fascism has obtained the critical approval of many scholars belonging to the Marxist or Marxist-oriented tendency. One of the most weighty exponents of this trend, Giampiero Carocci, in a 1993 review of my book *Il culto del littorio*, declared that he agreed with my thesis that an 'essential aspect of the totalitarian State is its tendency to sacralise politics, to make of it one of the numerous lay religions which, as it is the case of nationalism, characterise modern society'. Thus, Carocci recognised the importance of the central issues, going on to stress that the book filled an important gap in existing scholarship: 'The sources we consulted largely confirm the existence of a Fascist religion, of a "cult of the Lictor", as the fundamental instrument to achieve the goal of making the masses participate in what was or seemed to be the life of the nation'.[38]

To define my interpretation of Fascism as 'anti-anti-Fascist' appears yet more paradoxical, even ridiculous, if we consider that it has been mostly opposed by right-wing thinkers who affirm that Fascism was just an authoritarian regime that never became totalitarian.[39] The denial of the totalitarian character of Fascism, a view expounded mostly by right-wing thinkers, whether neo-Fascist or post-Fascist, is the most explicit expression of a more general tendency that I have called 'the de-fascistisation of Fascism'.[40] This recently resulted in their affirmation that the Fascist regime was a benevolent dictatorship which degenerated only when the alliance with National Socialism infected Italian Fascism with the virus of antisemitism and racism. In the various attacks on my interpretation of Fascism, those who assert that Fascism was not totalitarian, nor even a political religion, without proper supporting evidence, have regularly made use of De Felice's work to do so, frequently citing him out of context in the process. One of these critics wrote that the 'first and the most authoritative of the critics of Gentile's interpretation could be considered his master Renzo De Felice'.[41] In making observations of this kind, the critic's ignorance shows that they have fallen into what might be called the 'snare of presumption', making a partial and distorted use of sources with whom they were not remotely familiar.[42]

My interpretation of fascism as a political religion has also been subject to denigrating criticism of this nature both by some of those who do not deny the importance of studying the ritual and symbolic aspects of fascism in principle,[43] and those who consider these aspects simply irrelevant, and even believe that it is 'ridiculous' to study fascism as a totalitarian movement let alone a political religion.[44] To those just mentioned, we may add critics who categorically reject the possibility of applying the concept of religion to fascism. They either affirm that my interpretation of fascism as a political religion is a product of my ignorance of what religion is,[45] or accuse me of mistaking a metaphor ('fascism is a religion') for reality.[46] It is easy to show, though, that these critics are victims of their own sense of self-importance, because it is evident from their arguments that they have made no attempt to investigate the themes and problems that they claim to address. For instance, when I am accused of not knowing what religion is, such critics ignore the fact that among the first and most important observers of fascism as a political religion were a number of Catholic and Protestant theologians, both lay and religious, with at least one pontiff among them. The fact that members of the clergy and experts in religion like Luigi Sturzo, Paul Tillich, Jacques Maritain, Arthur Keller and Pius XI all shared my ignorance in what religion is – moreover, transmitted their ignorance to me, for it was also their reflections on fascism as a secular religion that helped convince me to study this problem – is not only a personal consolation, but it raises a historical problem of great seriousness, of which religious scholars themselves are certainly aware. It is not by chance that my studies of fascism as a political religion, and of the 'religion of politics' in general, aroused particular interest and frequent approval among Catholic scholars.[47] We may well banish the definition of fascism as a political religion: but the problem of the sacralisation of politics would still remain; a problem which a serious historian cannot avoid taking seriously, which involves investigating the nature of a political phenomenon which, by its use of religious 'metaphors', inspired genuine faith and enthusiasm, while at the same time sowing the seeds of anxiety and terror. To study this problem it is necessary *in the first instance* to study those who produced it; that is, those who were the creators of political religions, by what means they elaborated their ideas and how they institutionalised these religions and put them into practice, investing an enormous amount of energy, money, and constant effort, to turn them into the generators of adoration and instruments of death.

As I wrote in the closing part of my research on fascism as political religion, I think this problem should be treated as the one to be studied as the premise to understanding the process of the sacralisation of politics typical of fascism, and prior to examining other aspects of the same phenomenon, such as its penetration of and effects on the populace:

> Once in power, fascism instituted a lay religion by sacralising the State and spreading a political cult of the masses that aimed at creating a virile and virtuous citizenry, dedicated body and soul to the nation. In the enterprise of spreading its doctrine and arousing the masses to faith in its dogmas, obedience to its commandments, and the assimilation of its ethics and its life-style, fascism spent a considerable capital of energy, diverting those energies from other fields that might perhaps have been more important for the interests both of the regime and of the people. A commitment to the organisation of mass rituals that persisted with obsessive determination for two decades, even when the foundations of the regime were crumbling as a result of defeat in war, is already and of itself a subject worthy of reflection.[48]

This does not mean that we can avoid studying the effect produced by the fascist political religion – and more generally, by the totalitarian experiment – on the life and conscience of the people who were involved, but that we are dealing with a problem which poses considerable methodological difficulties, as I noted in 1988, when dealing with problem of support for the fascist regime:

> We are facing one of the most complex and controversial problems of Fascism: it is difficult to evaluate, because of the lack of specific analysis and of the fluidity of the phenomenon itself, what amounts to 'consensus' in a totalitarian regime, that goes beyond carrying the party card. Any generalisation would be misleading. To exclude the presence of 'consensus' would be as unrealistic and illusory as to presume a lasting and uniform general support. The analysis of 'consensus' should necessarily be divided into different segments, sorted by social condition, place, time, sex, age, and then go on to look at the individual motivations and main sources of this 'consensus' (the myth of Mussolini, the image of fascism, the actions of the party, etc.). In the case of the party we have pointed out some of the aspects of 'consensus' that, with different levels of intensity, were obtained through the monopoly of political activity and the institutionalisation of political professionalism, charity work, entertainment for the masses, and the organisation and mobilisation of youth. However, speaking generally about the relationship between the party and the populace, we must point out that at the end of the 1930s there were many symptoms of growing negative reactions, provoked by party policies, and the more intrusive and oppressive its obsession with organising and mobilising became.[49]

The problem posed by a totalitarian experiment on the general population is of such dimension and complexity that it cannot be solved by mere representations of public opinion, which are often nothing but generalisations taken from limited and questionable sources, carried out with questionable methods, and in many cases inspired by a sort of 'historiographical populism' representing the personal opinion of the author, yet reflected in the opinion of an imaginary people, as a genuine expression of public opinion.

I do not believe that criticism of the nature cited above can detract from the relevance of totalitarianism and political religion to the understanding of fascism. Nor can it in any way contribute to a clarification of the basic issues involved, for it is a form of criticism which, as I have shown with numerous examples, is not able to employ any arguments other than caricature or misrepresentation, and does not provide any rational critique. The intellectual vulgarity and crudeness of the insinuations that often accompany such criticism are aimed at the personality of the scholar, rather than at his or her work, and perhaps do not even deserve to be commented on, corrected or refuted. Time is a resource consumed rapidly and notoriously difficult to manage. It is thus extremely precious, and must be preserved for more serious tasks. Having said this, it was necessary to cite specific examples of this retrograde type of criticism in order to highlight both its dubious scientific reliability and questionable intellectual integrity. Once its lack of substance is recognised it is easier to ignore when encountered again, thus sparing time for reflecting upon more serious questions.

Final Clarifications and Explanations on the Subject of Totalitarianism

Adopting the concept of totalitarianism in defining fascism was a theoretical choice fully consistent with the results of my research into the history of Fascist culture, party and regime, as well as with the history of this concept, its origin and development. As I have already noted, my interpretation of totalitarianism owes much to those scholars who directly experienced life under totalitarian regimes and political religions, and became victims of them. They were the first to start elaborating this concept, almost always linking it to the concept of political religion.[50]

In my interpretation of the totalitarian phenomenon, I clarified some fundamental points which I believe necessary to stress here, for they could help to set the limits in which I consider the concept of totalitarianism a valid analytical instrument, both for the study of international fascism and the study of other contemporary political phenomena, though without making it the exclusive key to interpretation:

1. The use of the concept of totalitarianism in the comparative analysis of single-party political systems created by revolutionary movements does not imply the shared identity of these systems as if they were the branches of the same tree.

2. Totalitarianism, as an experiment in political dominion, does not result from the contingent degeneration or radicalisation of dictatorial power, or from the will of a single individual. Instead, it originates from a revolutionary party with an extremist and palingenetic ideology, craving a monopoly of power in order to conquer society and transform it according to its conception of man and politics.
3. Defining fascism as totalitarianism is not the same as stating that it actually accomplished what it meant by 'totalitarian', nor of stating that Fascism was totalitarian *in the same way* as Bolshevism and National Socialism.
4. The concept of totalitarianism understood as an *experiment of political dominion* does not refer to any 'perfect' and 'completed' totalitarianism in any of its forms. It refers, instead, to a *process* which by its nature can never be considered 'perfect' or 'completed'.

In reference to the last point, which in my opinion is the most important for clarifying the concept of totalitarianism and its application in the study of contemporary history, I cannot but reassert what I wrote in a 1986 article:

> In an historical sense, it can be observed that totalitarianism is always a process and not a complete and definitive form, assuming that connections between institutions and ideology are taken into consideration. The totalitarian integration of society into the State or the party could never be definitive, but would have to be renewed year after year. A complete totalitarian integration would be, paradoxically, the complete realisation of Rousseau's democratic ideal. All totalitarian regimes are therefore 'imperfect' with respect to their ideal of integration; during their existence they all come up against various limits and 'islands of separation'. Historically, one can observe that, even during the lives of those totalitarian regimes which have asserted the supremacy of the party, a 'personalisation' of power has occurred, leading to the political liquidation of the party as a centre in the formulation of choices and decisions, as these become the privilege of the leader. It is, however, precisely the existence of the single party and mass mobilisation which does not allow this 'personalisation' of the fascist regime to be bracketed with traditional personal dictatorships. To reduce Fascism

to 'Mussolinism' is to trivialise the problem of the 'Leader' in the totalitarian system. It not only overlooks the existence and behaviour of the organisation, but also does not take into consideration the fact that without the Fascist organisation, the myth of the *Duce* and the figure himself would have been incomprehensible. Finally, without going into the merits of the debate on the theoretical placing of Italian Fascism within the models of totalitarianism elaborated by the social sciences, one can note that there has been a Fascist conception of totalitarianism, and this cannot be overlooked. Once one attributes a 'totalitarian tendency' to Fascism, which distinguishes it from traditional authoritarian regimes, one then has to study how this tendency originated, how it was formed in reality, and how it operated to modify reality, conditioning the lives of millions of men and women in the process. The failure of fascist totalitarianism is not a proof of its non-existence. The gap between myth and achievement is not an argument against the importance of myths in the politics of Fascism, nor against its conception and mode of organisation of the masses.[51]

Fascism was the 'Italian way to totalitarianism'. Fascist totalitarianism represented a reality in a continuous process of construction which unfolded progressively, taking shape in political culture, education and in the lifestyle of the Fascist regime by means of a complex relationship between the ideology, party and regime which, despite contrasts and contradictions, shows the constant presence of a totalitarian logic peculiar to Fascism, present in both the ideology and the political actions of the Fascist movement/regime. Obviously, the Fascist totalitarian experiment in the course of its implementation encountered numerous obstacles in society: for example, in the apparatus of the old State, and in the Church. Nevertheless, more recent research on these aspects – which I am going to treat widely in a forthcoming article – has confirmed the validity of the interpretation of Fascism as the 'Italian way to totalitarianism', demonstrating how, in the course of its totalitarian experiment, Fascism actually attainted numerous results, so that on the eve of the Second World War, the regime was certainty much more totalitarian than at the end of the 1920s: no opposition within the country seriously threatened the stability and the functioning of the totalitarian laboratory. We should also remember that the end of the Fascist regime was determined by military defeat, not by the monarchy, the Church or popular opposition.

We could certainly agree with those who assert that in Italy fascism did not achieve the condition of a 'perfect' and 'completed' totalitarianism. But I doubt if there exists any possibility of solving the problem posed by Renato Moro; that is, of identifying 'what this missing totalitarian component of the regime actually was',[52] because such a problem, from an historical point of view, does not even arise. If it did, it should be raised in connection with all totalitarianisms, because in the reality of human history, where nothing is perfect, totalitarian regimes are also doomed by their own dynamic and experimental nature to fail to attain complete perfection. Even regimes considered entirely totalitarian, upon closer examination turned out to be imperfect, not only in relation to various theoretical models elaborated by scholars, but also in relation to their totalitarian projects, to the different phases of development of their experiment, as well as to the different historical and social situations in which these regimes were set.[53] However, as Luciano Zani has argued, even

> if, for the sake of argument, it was possible to affirm the accomplishment of a complete and integral totalitarianism on the part of Italian Fascism, there would be substantial elements of contrast not only between Italian Fascism and Stalinism, but also between the various forms of fascism as well, whose common totalitarian conception was not a guarantee of a lasting reciprocal accord and coexistence.[54]

The usefulness of interpreting Fascism as the 'Italian way to totalitarianism' – which, it should be said again, refers not only to the ideology, but also to the policy of the party and the regime – has been continuously confirmed by the research of scholars who explicitly apply it, or reflect it indirectly in their arguments. It is important to mention that Juan Linz, a major authority on these matters in political science, although preferring the term 'failed totalitarianism' instead of 'interrupted totalitarianism' in the context of the Fascist regime, has recently declared: 'It was Gentile who managed to convince me to accept his point of view, according to which Fascism not only had a totalitarian potential, but was evolving towards a totalitarian regime, especially in the Thirties'; while Stanley Payne, who also has been sceptical about the totalitarian character of the Fascist regime, writes that the author of *La via italiana al totalitarismo* 'presents an impressive amount of evidence to bolster his conclusion that during the second half of the 1930s the Italian regime was undergoing a process of totalitarianisation, even though that process was not institutionally complete by the time of Mussolini's downfall in 1943'.[55]

In addition, I believe that the formula I propose, which presents the concept of totalitarianism as an *experiment* and not only as a *regime*, is also effective in interpreting the 'fascist phenomenon'. That is, it permits us to analyse ideas and behavioural types, the dialectics between myth and the organisation of other nationalistic and revolutionary movements, which in the period between the two world wars had characteristics similar to Fascism, because they used the latter as a model in organisation and style, claiming not only to save the nation from Bolshevism or to protect the interests of the bourgeoisie, but to conquer power in order to regenerate the nation and to lead it to a new age of grandeur and power. Those movements shared or imitated the concepts, institutions, motives and behaviour typical of the Fascist synthesis: they opposed rationalism, egalitarianism and the progressive conception of democratic and socialistic ideologies; they disdained the individualism of liberal, middle-class society and parliamentary democracy; they exalted the cult of the 'Leader' and the role of those active minorities who were able to mobilise and mould the masses; they proposed a 'Third Way' between capitalism and communism that was nationalist, totalitarian and corporative, with the objective of creating a new order and a new civilisation. This would be based upon the militarisation and sacralisation of politics, on organisation and mobilisation of the integrated masses, by means of the organisation of the State, into an organic community of a regenerated nation, which would be ideologically and ethnically homogeneous. Apart from the differences, quite profound sometimes, in ideological content and the aims they pursued, what those movements had in common with Fascism was political mysticism, revolutionary dynamism, and an ideological extremism founded on the myth of the nation sacralised as a supreme collective entity, destined to be united and homogeneous, and organised into a state of permanent mobilisation in order to affirm its grandeur, its might and its prestige in the world. All those movements hated and fought against *parliamentary democracy* in the name of the *democracy of the national community*, and dreamt of achieving a 'collective harmony', as Mussolini called it, through the organisation of a new State conceived as the expression of a people's community and the concept of the 'new man'. Therefore, all those movements can be defined as totalitarian, in the sense that all of them were, as Griffin puts it, 'political or social movements driven by a palingenetic vision of the new man which, if implemented, would have created a totalitarian regime'.[56] From this point of view – as Alessandro Campi argues when referring to my interpretation – among the elements which identify the fascist phenomenon, 'there is totalitarianism which cannot be understood only as a regime or a political system (which probably, in the course of history, has never appeared in the complete and perfect form), but also as a general political goal, as a cultural pattern, as a *forma mentis*, as a complete political idea'.

... and on the Subject of Political Religion

Palingenetic myth, the factor that Roger Griffin makes central to his ideal type of fascism, is a crucial element corroborating the totalitarian nature of fascism. It is significant in order to understand the connection between totalitarianism and political religion, because it is a key ideological factor behind the drive to secure a total monopoly of power. Only a monopoly of power, through the subordination of society to the State and the organisation and control of the masses, allows the regime to act out an *anthropological revolution* in order to create a new man and a new civilisation. Palingenetic myth, which already contains a religious matrix and is deeply imbued with religious meaning, contributes by conferring upon fascism the characteristics typical of a political religion with a strong and markedly modern messianic (but not necessarily millenarian) component, because it derives, not from the revival of pre-modern traditions, but from an apocalyptic interpretation of modernity assigning the mission of regeneration to politics.[57]

As to the use of the concept of political religion in the analysis of fascism and totalitarianism, it is necessary to address the more important problems – above all theoretical and methodological ones – raised by some critics of my definition of fascism as a form of sacralisation of politics, especially with respect to the role and concept of political religion for a general interpretation of fascism. Some of this criticism, primarily of my book on the sacralisation of politics in Italy, seems to derive from a misunderstanding of my interpretation which is based solely on a reading of this book, as if I had not written on other aspects

of the Fascist experience, such as the political, organisational and institutional – without taking into consideration my basic definition of
fascism, expressed in the terms of dimensions complementary to
fascist organisations, culture and institutions which I formulated as
long ago as 1990. For instance, this is the case of Simonetta Falasca-
Zamponi, who, while accepting the validity of my approach to fascism
as a political religion, affirms that 'the analytical category of "politics
as religion" does not exhaustively convey the nature of Italian Fascism,
its peculiar cultural content', because 'references to "lay religion"
alone cannot explicate Fascism's unique turn, its original totalitarian
culture'.[58] As a matter of fact, I have never written (nor thought) that
the category of 'political religion' is the only key to the interpretation
of fascism. Above all, I hardly think it reasonable to accuse me, as
Falasca-Zamponi does, of not having taken into consideration in my
studies the 'original totalitarian culture', which, on the contrary, since
the very beginning has played a central role in all my research on
fascism, as, in fact, Robert Gordon recognised in his observation:
'Gentile's approach amounts to nothing less than a redefinition of the
totalitarian project'.[59]

Similarly, I believe that it is a remarkable misunderstanding to
consider my approach to fascism as a political religion as an exclusively 'culturalistic' approach, similar to one which studies fascism as
the 'aestheticisation of politics'. Claudio Fogu, in a review of my book
on the religion of Fascism, remarked: 'Gentile shies away from engaging in any dialogue with either Walter Benjamin's famous thesis or
with the more recent literature on fascist modernism'.[60] Indeed, in my
book neither Benjamin's thesis nor the literature on fascist modernism
is mentioned. This absence, though, was based on a choice, so as to
avoid any possible confusion between the problem of the 'sacralisation
of politics' and the 'aestheticisation of politics'. In my opinion, these
are two substantially different problems, even if they overlap in the
study of rites and symbols. By a curious coincidence, Fogu's review of
my book was published in the issue of a magazine that also included
an article of mine where I explicitly criticised the 'culturalistic'
approach, and the use of Benjamin's thesis in the literature on fascist
modernism:

> Fascist modernism has been especially studied by literary critics
> and historians of art, sometimes with notable results, often draw-
> ing upon Fascism as 'the aestheticisation of politics' which

Benjamin proposed. Yet however suggestive this interpretation, it can also be misleading if it obscures fascism's other important feature, its 'politicisation of aesthetics', which not only inspired fascism's attitude toward avant-garde culture, but lay at the very origin of the encounter between futurism and fascism and of the participation of many Modernist intellectuals in fascism. Such caution might seem excessive, but it is also necessary if we are to avoid letting emphasis on 'the aestheticisation of politics' lead to a kind of 'aestheticisation' of fascism itself, privileging its literary, aesthetic, and symbolic aspects while losing sight of motivations and matrices that are essentially political in nature. To do so risks trivialising the fundamentally political nature of fascism, its culture, its ideology, and its symbolic universe. Even when studying strictly aesthetic manifestations of fascism, such as its political style, its liturgy for the masses, or its copious symbolic production, all of them characteristic and essential elements in the fascist mode of doing politics, it is important not to lose sight of the political dimension of fascist culture.[61]

In my interpretation, the phenomenon of the sacralisation of politics is not to be equated with the 'aesthetisation of politics', nor with the 'new politics' theorised by George Mosse in his study of political symbolism in the nationalisation of the German masses. A gross error is made by those critics who consider my interpretation of fascist religion to be a mechanical derivation, or an application of Mosse's approach to the theme of the 'new politics', which is different from my approach in both the method and the treated themes, as I have explained above. In fact, it is not by chance that Mosse's analysis is based on the concept of the 'aesthetics of politics', while mine avails itself of the concept of the 'sacralisation of politics'.[62] Nor is this difference merely terminological. As Renato Moro observed in a 1995 critique of my book on the sacralisation of politics in Italy, my inquiry went 'in some respects further than the idea of the German-American historian' because of the central position given to the categories of *myth, theology* and *political religion*. Moro added that the centrality of the sacralisation of politics to my analysis of fascism leads to 'a pronounced emphasis on the "theological aspects" of fascist culture and its "religious anthropology"', which goes

> considerably beyond what Mosse asserted concerning its 'liturgical' and 'aesthetic' ones ... And it is perhaps no coincidence that,

with the exception of the deep difference between the two subjects of study under examination, Mosse's work focuses primarily on aesthetic theories and tastes, theatrical experiments, popular festivals and celebrations, gymnastic and choral associations (even widely read novels), while Gentile's rotates constantly around, and ever more closely to, political culture and its theoreticians.[63]

More recently, Roger Griffin has noticed the difference between Mosse's and my approach: 'Gentile seems to have also arrived at his view of fascism as an attempt to sacralise the state largely independently of Mosse'.[64]

I think that these comments fully clarify the substantial difference between my approach and the 'culturalistic' one, which are often confused with one another, as if my interpretation of fascism was confined exclusively to the book on the sacralisation of politics, or was restricted merely to the ideological and cultural dimensions and to the use of the category of 'political religion'.[65] In my first study on fascist ideology in 1974, I expressed my basic convictions on this subject and, in the course of time, have never altered:

> In our narrative we, naturally, have never thought of explaining fascism by making use of its own ideology, even if we consider it one of the elements, and by no means the least important, in the consensus that it won in Italy and abroad. However, history never gives a single answer to questions posed by those who want to understand the past. Therefore, within the limits of our research, we have only tried to reconstruct one of many 'threads' that constituted the fascist phenomenon.[66]

In the same way, a quarter of a century later, I clarified and specified the limits within which I believe the concept of political religion can be legitimately employed, avoiding a general and indiscriminate use of it. In particular, I have stated clearly and unambiguously that the category of political religion does not resolve the problem of fascism, nor the totalitarian phenomenon of which it is a component.

> It should be pointed out, even if it seems obvious, that viewing a political movement as a secular religion does not necessarily suggest that this constitutes the only explanation of its nature and historical significance. Political religion is one element of totalitarianism, not the principal element and not even the most

important in defining its essence. It might be remembered that within the term 'political religion' it is the word 'political' that has dominated history, and should, therefore, prevail in historiographical and theoretical analysis. Drawing attention to the characteristics of totalitarianism as political religion does not signify that one will find the key to understanding the nature of totalitarianism in the sacralisation of politics. This remains a wholly open question.[67]

The superficiality of the 'reductionist' criticism of my interpretation of fascism as a political religion is thrown into relief by those who, although expressing some reservations on the very concept of religion applied to fascism, as Robert Gordon does, nevertheless recognise that my work 'combines a close and shrewd attention to contemporary archive sources with a keen originality of analysis alert to cultural history and histories of attitude and mentality as much as to political and institutional history'.[68] Equally clear is the explanation given by Sergio Luzzatto, who distinguished my approach from the regrettable preoccupation with the 'aestheticisation of fascism' which prevails among the scholars of the 'culturalistic' trend, noticing that 'the dedication and high quality of Gentile's previous research (particularly into the ideological origins of fascism and the internal history of the PNF), prevented the author from falling into a trap of "culturalism" as an end in itself, the tendency to see fascism as a creation of rhetoric and fancy'.[69]

My criticism of the 'culturalistic' approach does not entail criticism of the cultural history of fascism, which, when pursued seriously, has showed itself to be highly productive, delivering insights which extend beyond the cultural dimension because they are also relevant to an understanding of fascism's organisational and institutional dimensions. Instead, it is more accurate to speak of the 'anthropological-cultural' approach, as far as my analysis of fascism as a political religion is concerned, as Giampiero Carocci has recognised in his review on my study of the 'cult of the Lictor':

> Gentile in this book does not write as a scholar of political history, nor of the history of ideas, but as a scholar of anthropological history. The task he sets himself is not to establish if certain acts are or are not congruous to rationality, but to establish to what extent they are congruous to the satisfaction of some human needs, such as security and certainty, needs whose roots go deep into the world of emotions, without touching the sphere of reason.[70]

Another important series of explanations and clarifications concerns the use of the term 'religion' in the definition of fascism. The return of the concept of political religion in the interpretation of fascism, when I re-proposed it at the beginning of the 1990s, initially met with a certain scepticism, not because of any preconceived hostility toward this type of analysis, but due to a certain confusion about the best way to understand the concept of political religion. Griffin, for instance, at first criticised my approach to the study of fascism as a secular religion, putting it alongside the work of other scholars like Eric Voegelin – who applied to the study of National Socialism such concepts as 'millenarianism', 'chiliasm' and 'eschatology' – considering it an 'abuse of religious concepts'. The title of the paragraph where this criticism was expounded left little doubts about Griffin's views: 'Fascism as a Political Ideology, not a Political Religion'.[71] Now, I do not think that the concepts of political ideology and political religion are either antagonistic or exclusive of one other. For example, one need not be a Marxist to solve the presumed antagonism between the two concepts, recognising that religion is, or can become, a political ideology. The history of the two last centuries witnessed frequent manifestations of the political ideologisation of religion in all the reactionary, conservative or democratic movements of Christian or Catholic inspiration in Western Europe, as well as in revolutionary nationalistic movements of the fascist kind, such as the *Falange* or the Iron Guard. Such movements, in my opinion, may already be placed within the dimension of sacralised politics, notwithstanding their exaltation of Catholic or Orthodox Christianity, because their ideology makes the sacralisation of the nation and the State evident, even if through a strongly politicised version of a traditional religion. In turn, movements like the Iron Guard assume, in reality, the character of a political religion in that they become the main factor of legitimation for the sacralisation of the nation, and for the nationalisation of Orthodox Christianity itself, with the exaltation of the 'Romanian God' or by claiming that 'God is a fascist!', a slogan shouted by the Legionary journalist I.P. Prundeni, which, as Radu Ioanid writes, 'succinctly captures the place of mysticism as a distinctive quality of Romanian fascism'.[72] Here, as Lucretiu Patrascanu observes, 'The incorporation and subordination of Orthodoxy to political ends pursued by the Legionary movement are more specific to the Iron Guard than the recognition of a Christian spirituality as a behavioural norm or a source of ethical and social directives'.[73] The Romanian case is a clear example of my theory about the syncretic symbiosis between political religion and traditional religion. The same problem occurs in the case of National Socialism's relationship with Christianity, where the main factor is the sacralisation of politics. It can also be seen in the various attempts at conciliation between National Socialism and Christianity, represented by the 'Aryanisation' of Christ and by his consequent 'Germanisation' and 'Nazification', as many Christian theologians, such as Nathaniel Micklem, warned:

> National Socialism is a movement militant for a new *Weltanscha-uung* or philosophy not derived from Christianity; it is prepared to tolerate only such Christianity as will march in step with the philosophy of Blood and Race and Soil. What Christianity is of this kind, and is it aptly described as 'positive'? ... Any type of religion that is prepared to affirm without qualification the ideals and principles of National Socialism is positive ... It may be politic in public to represent National Socialism as Christianity in action and to declare that the State has no intention of setting up a new Church to replace the old, but the real implication of National Socialism for religion become plain in these official and explicit directions. National Socialism is a new and intolerant religion.[74]

In the case of Italian Fascism, there were Fascist Catholics and Catholic Fascists who, in good faith, did not see any antagonism between Fascism and Catholicism, although it is not a sufficient proof to argue that Fascism was essentially Catholic and that its Catholicism was an impediment to its totalitarianism.[75] To refute this argument, first of all, there was an awareness among the highest ecclesiastical and theological authorities of the Catholic Church, starting with Pope Pius XI, of an incompatibility between Catholic doctrine and Fascist statolatry, which was openly condemned by the Pontiff. We must add to this theoretical condemnation the growing preoccupation with the concrete measures taken by the fascist totalitarian system, which constantly tried to 'privatise' the Catholic faith, using it publicly only to boost its process of absorption into the fascist regime so as to become a 'fascistised' Catholicism, exalted essentially and exclusively as an heir to the Roman universal tradition and a manifestation of the genius of the Italian race. Under these aspects, the problem of the 'syncretic' relationship between political religion and traditional religion, in the terms in which I expressed it in my definition of political religion, is a subject requiring deeper research and reflection.[76]

Nor do I believe it a convincing argument to justify renouncing the concept of political religion to observe that all the ideologies propose an interpretation of the meaning and the final goal of human existence, and all of them have a mythic core and use symbols and rites. Indeed, it is true that all political ideologies contain mythical, ritual and symbolic aspects. It is also true that not all of them avoid institutionalising themselves as a religion and acting accordingly. Benedetto Croce asserted that liberalism was a modern religion, even while denying that fascism was the same. Still, his conception of politics did not embrace the deployment of rites and myths that belonged, in his opinion, to the traditional, not to modern forms of religion. Nevertheless, the fact that some political ideologies, such as fascism itself, visibly emphasise mythic thought, symbolic expression and ritual devotion, is to be seen as a reality specific to its political ideology, which distinguishes it clearly from other movements, such as, for instance, parties inspired by Christianity, which did not have an exclusively rationalistic ideology and belonged to the traditions dominated by the faith, the rite and the symbol. After all, the difference between Mussolini and Luigi Sturzo, between the Fascist Party and the Popular Party, is represented also by a profound and essential diversity in the political style, in their use of rites and symbols, in the attitude toward the Church and Catholicism, and in the behaviour toward adversaries, a fact we have to take into consideration when we place them in a common category of political ideology.

Political religion is certainly an ideology, but, we could say, an ideology with *an extra ingredient*, which makes it *qualitatively different* from other political ideologies. It was this 'extra ingredient', present in Fascism or Bolshevism, that induced some observers of these movements to compare them with phenomena of a religious kind, and to adopt the concept of political religion, since they did not believe the traditional concept of ideology was appropriate. And their use of the concept of religion, in this case, as I have already specified, was not at all metaphoric, nor was it such for religious people and clergymen, who were experts in religion, and who employed it to raise awareness about the threat Fascism posed to Christianity. In the same way, there are contemporary scholars, especially experts in the history of political and religious movements, who consider my interpretation of fascism as a political religion legitimate, and believe that this aspect is an 'essential element of a regime and an ideology, above all a revolutionary one. It acted not only to sacralise politics and to institute a lay religion, but also to precipitate the eclipse of Catholicism',[77] as historian Jean-Dominique Durand put it in his review of my book on the sacralisation of politics in Fascist Italy.

It is evident that, faced with a problem concerning not fascism as political religion but the very legitimacy of the concept of political religion, the definition of what a religion means becomes crucial. Commenting on my article published in the first issue of this journal, Stephen Di Rienzo observed that 'Emilio Gentile ... has not provided a definition for his understanding of what a religion is and the possible antithesis to religious organisation'.[78] Indeed, my article lacked an explicit and formal definition of what I meant by a 'religion'. However, 'my understanding of what a religion is' was expressed in the passage of the article in which I defined the process of the sacralisation of politics:

> This process takes place when, more or less elaborately and dogmatically, a political movement confers a sacred status on an earthly entity (the nation, the country, the State, humanity, society, race, proletariat, history, liberty, or revolution) and renders it an absolute principle of collective existence, considers it the main source of values for individual and mass behaviour, and exalts it as the supreme ethical precept of public life.[79]

According to my point of view, fascism was a political religion, where by religion I understand a *system of beliefs, myths and symbols which interpret and define the meaning and the goal of human existence, making the destiny of an individual and of the community dependant on their subordination to a supreme entity.* This definition is related to an interpretation of religion as a phenomenon that expresses the dimension of the *sacred* as a human experience and, consequently, does not necessarily coincide with the dimension of the *divine*. Therefore, it is quite plausible, in my opinion, to use the term political religion to define the political movements which, predominantly in their culture, organisation and style, appear as manifestations of a sacralisation of politics, that is, in one of the possible manifestations of the sacred in modernity. As the historian of religion, Giovanni Filoramo, observed in connection to my analysis of Fascist political religion,

> the sacralisation of politics and of the State performed by fascism through the cult of the Lictor, far from being a return to the past, constitutes a typical example – which can be used to better

understand the continuous interweaving of politics and religion
which characterises the present era – of the diaspora of the sacred
which characterises the relationship between modernity and religion.[80]

A final point about fascism as a political religion that requires clarification concerns the theme of irrationalism, which is frequently
referred to both in general when fascist culture is discussed, and, in a
more specific way, when fascist culture is recognised as deliberately
and explicitly affirming the primacy of mythic thought, to which its
definition as a political religion is also linked. Now I would like to
state clearly that recognising the irrational and mythic nature of fascist
culture does not mean denying that fascism had its own rationality,
both in structural terms, and in the concrete manifestation of fascism
as an organisation and an institution. 'In this connection', I wrote in
1974, 'we have to observe that the irrationalism of fascist ideology, far
from being a manifestation of blind instincts, was the consequence of
a rational devaluation of reason as a protagonist of history and politics', in the same way that its mass politics, with their emphasis on rites
and the symbols, were not only an expression of mythic thought, but
a consequence of 'a rational use of the irrational', too.[81] We also have
to bear in mind that as far as the irrationality of fascist culture is
concerned, its myths were politically efficient because they were
combined with the rationality of the organisation and the institution.
The organisation and the institution define norms of rational behaviour, formalised and directed in order to achieve a goal. Without the
rationality of the organisation and the institution, without being a
party and a regime, without becoming the ideology of a modern State,
fascism would have probably remained on the fringes of Italy's political culture, confined to the realm of intellectual elitism or marginalised sectarianism. The link between myth and organisation, between
irrationality and rationality, is an inseparable element of fascism, both
as a form of totalitarianism and as a political religion, in the same way
that occurs with other organised religions. This is the link I have
always insisted on in my research, thereby avoiding the trap of transforming the 'rational' irrationalism of fascism into a historiographical
code for the essential irrationality of fascism, and thus relapsing into
the theory of its 'historical negativity'.

Obviously, if we consider that the concept of religion has to be
reserved solely for phenomena which belong to the dimension of the

divine, the problem of political religion is automatically declared irrelevant, simply because it is a problem which does not exist. But even if it were possible, by the general convention and unanimous consensus of all scholars, to ban the use of the concept of political religion in the analysis of political movements, there would still be a need to face the phenomenon of the sacralisation of politics. This dimension still has to be defined whenever it manifests itself in the ideology, organisation and active politics of a movement or a regime. Obviously, we could also negate the existence of this phenomenon as a particular manifestation of the human experience of the sacred, but in my opinion, this could not happen without performing a serious mutilation on our understanding of contemporary history, without surgically removing an important part of its recent past, as much as its present and, probably, its near future as well.

NOTES

I would like to thank Roger Griffin and Robert Mallett for ensuring that as little as possible has been lost in the translation of my article into English.

  1. E. Gentile, 'The Sacralisation of Politics: Definitions, Interpretations and Reflections on the Question of Secular Religion and Totalitarianism', in *Totalitarian Movements and Political Religions* 1/1 (2000), pp.18–55.
  2. E. Gentile, *Le origini dell'ideologia fascista* (Rome and Bari: Laterza, 1975; extended rev. edn., Bologna: Mulino, 1996); idem, *Il mito dello Stato nuovo* (Rome and Bari: Laterza 1982; rev. edn., Rome and Bari: Laterza, 1999); idem, *Storia del partito fascista: 1919–1922: Movimento e milizia* (Rome and Bari: Laterza, 1989); idem, *La via italiana al totalitarismo: Il partito e lo Stato nel regime fascista* (Rome: Carocci, 1995); idem, *La grande Italia: Ascesa e declino del mito della nazione nel ventesimo secolo* (Milan: Mondadori, 1997); idem, *Fascismo e antifascismo: I partiti italiani fra le due guerre* (Florence: F. Le Monnier, 2000); idem, 'Il totalitarismo alla conquista della Camera alta', in *Il totalitarismo alla conquista della Camera alta: Inventari e documenti* (Soveria Mannelli: Rubbettino, 2002); idem, *Fascismo: Storia e interpretazioni* (Rome and Bari: Laterza, 2002); and idem, *The Struggle for Modernity: Nationalism, Futurism and Fascism* (Westport, CT: Praeger, 2003).
  3. E. Gentile, *Il culto del littorio: La sacralizzazione della politica nell'Italia fascista* (Rome and Bari: Laterza, 1993); English translation, *The Sacralization of Politics in Fascist Italy* (Cambridge, MA: Harvard University Press, 1996); and idem, *Le religioni della politica: Fra democrazie e totalitarismi* (Rome and Bari: Laterza, 2001).
  4. Gentile (note 1), pp.19–21 (original emphasis).
  5. The substantial progress achieved in this first period can be seen by comparing the contents, the methods, and the results of two collections of studies on the phenomenon of fascism that appeared in this period: S.J. Woolf (ed.), *European Fascism* (London: Weidenfeld and Nicolson, 1968); and W. Laqueur, *Fascism: A Reader's Guide* (London: Wildwood House, 1976).
  6. See E. Gentile, 'Fascism in Italian Historiography: In Search of an Individual Historical Identity', *Journal of Contemporary History* 21/2 (1986), pp.179–208.
  7. H. Maier (ed.), *Totalitarismus und Politische Religionen: Konzept des Diktaturvergleiches* (Paderborn: F. Schöningh, 1996); and Gentile, *Le religioni della politica* (note 3).

8. M. Gervasoni, 'La storiografia di Emilio Gentile. Politica di massa e miti del XX secolo', *Gli argomenti umani* (February 2002), p.85.
9. P. Levi, *Se questo è un uomo: La tregua* (Turin: Einaudi Tascabili, 1989), pp.347–8.
10. E. Gentile, 'A Provisional Dwelling: The Origin and Development of the concept of Fascism in Mosse's Historiography', in S.G. Payne, D.J. Sorkin and J.S. Tortorice (eds.), *What History Tells: George L. Mosse and the Culture of Modern Europe* (Madison, WI: University of Wisconsin Press, 2004), pp.41–109; and R. Griffin, 'Withstanding the Rush of Time: The Presence of Mosse's Anthropological View of Fascism', in ibid., pp.110–33.
11. G.L. Mosse, 'The Genesis of Fascism', *Journal of Contemporary History* 1/1 (1966), pp.14–26.
12. J.J. Linz, 'Some Notes Toward a Comparative Study of Fascism in Sociological Historical Perspective', in W. Laqueur (ed.), *Fascism: A Reader's Guide* (Harmondsworth: Penguin, 1979), pp.24–6.
13. S.G. Payne, *Fascism: Comparison and Definition* (Madison, WI: University of Wisconsin Press, 1980), pp.211–12. The structure of this book and its conceptual framework were taken up again, but considerably elaborated and brought updated, in S.G. Payne, *A History of Fascism: 1914–1945* (Madison, WI: University of Wisconsin Press, 1995). Another work emblematic of this stage of fascist studies is S.U. Larsen, B. Hagtvet and J.P. Myklebust (eds), *Who Were the Fascists: Social Roots of European Fascism* (Bergen: Universitetsforlaget, 1980).
14. For an essential general outline of the discussion on the fascist phenomenon after 1991, see Payne, *A History of Fascism* (note 13); R. Griffin (ed.), *International Fascism: Theories, Causes and the New Consensus* (London: Arnold, 1998); J.A. Mellon (ed.), *Orden, Jerarquía y Comunidad: Fascismos, Dictaduras y Postfascismos en la Europa Contemporánea* (Madrid: Tecnos, 2002); and A. Campi (ed.), *Che cos'è il fascismo: Interpretazioni e prospettive di ricerca* (Rome: Ideazione, 2003).
15. R. Griffin, *The Nature of Fascism* (London: Pinter, 1991), p.14.
16. Ibid., p.26.
17. As examples of productivity in this field I will cite only some of the works that have appeared during the last decade: J. Taylor, *The Rise and Fall of Totalitarianism in the Twentieth Century* (New York: Marlow, 1993); S. Tormey, *Making Sense of Tyranny: Interpretations of Totalitarianism* (Manchester and New York: Manchester University Press, 1995); Gentile, *La via italiana al totalitarismo* (note 2); A. Gleason, *Totalitarianism: The Inner History of the Cold War* (New York and Oxford: Oxford University Press, 1995); H. Maier and M. Schafer (eds.), *Totalitarismus und Politische Religionen Konzepte des Diktaturvergleichs* Vol. I and II (Paderborn: F. Schöningh, 1996–97); 'Dictature, Absolutisme, et Totalitarisme', *Revue Française d'histoire des idées politiques* 6/2 (1997); A. Söllner, R. Walkenhus and K. Wieland (eds.), *Totalitarismus: Eine Ideengeschichte des 20 Jahrhundert* (Berlin, Akademie Verlag, 1997); W. Wippermann, *Totalitarismustheorien: Die Entwicklung der Diskussion von den Anfängen bis heute* (Darmstadt: Primus, 1997); M. Florese (ed.), *Nazismo, fascismo, comunismo: Totalitarismi a confronto* (Milan: Mondadori, 1998); A. Siegel (ed.), *The Totalitarian Paradigm after the End of Communism: Towards a Theoretical Reassessment* (Amsterdam and Atlanta: Rodopi, 1998); K.D. Henke (ed.), *Totalitarismus* (Dresden: Hannah Arendt Institut für Totalitarismusforschung, 1999); J. Klotz (ed.), *Schlimmer als die Nazis: 'Das Schwarzbuch des Kommunismus' und die neue Totalitarismusdebatte* (Cologne: PapyRossa Verlag, 1999); B. Bruneteau, *Les Totalitarismes* (Paris: A. Colin, 1999); 'Totalitarismus und Liberalismus', *Prokla* 2 (1999); E. Jesse (ed.), *Totalitarismus im 20 Jahrhundert: Eine Bilanz der internationalen Forschung*, 2 edn. (Baden-Baden: Nomos, 1999); M. Helberstam, *Totalitarianism and the Modern Conception of Politics* (New Haven, CT, and London: Yale University Press, 1999); J.J. Linz, *Totalitarian and Authoritarian Regimes* (London: Lynne Rienner, 2000); S. Courtois (ed.), *Quand tombe la nuit: Origines et emergence des régimes totalitaires en Europe 1930–*

1934 (Paris: L'Âge d'homme, 2001); F. Budi Hardiman, *Die Herrschaft der Gleichen* (Frankfurt am Main: Peter Lang, 2001); E. Traverso, *Le Totalitarisme* (Paris: Seuil, 2001); and J.J. Linz, *Fascismo, autoritarismo, totalitarismo: Connessioni e differenze* (Rome: Ideazione, 2003).

18. In this case I again limit myself only to some of the works that have appeared over the last decade: Gentile, *Il culto del Littorio* (note 3); A. Piette, *Les religiosités séculières* (Paris: PUF, 1993); H. Maier, *Politische Religionen: Die totalitären Regime und das Christentum* (Freiburg: Herder, 1995); S. Behrenbeck, *Der Kult um die toten Helden: Nationalistische Mythen, Riten und Symbole 1923 bis 1945* (Neuburg a.d. Donau: SH-Verlag, 1996); A.J. Klinghoffer, *Red Apocalypse: The Religious Evolution of Soviet Communism* (Lanham, MD: University Press of America, 1996); H. Maier (ed.), *Totalitarismus und Politische Religionen* (Paderborn: F. Schöningh, 1996); H. Maier and M. Schäfer (eds.), *Totalitarismus und Politische Religionen: Konzepte des Diktaturvergleich* (Paderborn: F. Schöningh, 1997); P. Berghoff, *Der Tod des politischen Kollektives: Politische Religion und das Sterben und Töten für Volk, Nation und Rasse* (Berlin: Akademie Verlag, 1997); Y. Karow, *Deutsches Opfer: Kultische Selbstauslöschung auf den Reichsparteitagen der NSDAP* (Berlin: Akademie Verlag, 1997); M. Ley, *Apokalypse und Moderne: Aufsätze zu politischen Religionen* (Vienna: Sonderzahl, 1997); M. Ley and J.H. Schoeps (eds.), *Der Nationalsozialismus als politische Religion* (Bodenheim: Philo Verlagsgesellschaft, 1997); C.E. Bärsch, *Die politische Religion des Nationalsozialismus* (München: W. Fink, 1998); M. Huttner, *Totalitarismus und Säkulare Religionen: Zur Frühgeschichte totalitarismuskritischer Begriffs- und Theoriebildung in Großbritannien* (Bonn: Bouvier, 1999); K.G. Riegel, 'Transplanting the Political Religion of Marxism-Leninism to China: The Case of the Sun Yat-Sen University in Moscow (1925–1930)', in K.H. Pohl (ed.), *Chinese Thought in a Global Context* (Leiden, Boston and Köln: Brill, 1999), pp.327–58; H. Maier (ed.), *Wege in die Gewalt: Die moderne politischen Religionen* (Frankfurt am Main: Fischer Verlag, 2000); M. Cristi, *From Civil to Political Religion: The Intersection of Culture, Religion and Politics* (Waterloo, Ontario: Wilfred Laurier University Press, 2001); and Gentile *Le religioni della politica* (note 3).

19. E. Gentile, 'Alcune considerazioni sull' ideologia del fascismo', *Storia contemporanea*, 5, 1 (1974) pp.120–1.

20. Ibid., p.123.

21. Ibid. pp.123–4. I would like to point out that when I wrote this article I was not aware of Walter Benjamin's thesis on the 'aestheticisation of politics', nor Mosse's unpublished book on the nationalisation of the masses, where he adopted the concept of the 'aesthetics of politics'; the latter came out a year later. By this clarification I intend to underline the fact that my interest for the aesthetic, ritual and symbolic aspects of fascist politics as well as for fascist political religion derived directly and, I would say, spontaneously from the study of the fascist phenomenon itself rather than from Benjamin's or Mosse's influence.

22. E. Gentile, 'Italian Right-Wing Radicalism: Myth and Organisation', in R. Bosworth and G. Rizzo (eds.), *Altro Polo: A Volume of Italian Studies* (Sydney: Frederic May Foundation for Italian Studies, 1983), pp.17–30, reprinted in Gentile, *The Struggle for Modernity* (note 2), pp.77–88.

23. E. Gentile, 'Partito, Stato e Duce nella mitologia e nella organizzazione del fascismo', in K.D. Bracher and L.Valiani (eds.), *Fascismo e nazionalsocialismo* (Bologna: Il Mulino, 1986), p.265, reprinted in Gentile, *Fascismo* (note 2), pp.147–70.

24. E. Gentile, 'Il fascismo fu una rivoluzione?', *Prospettive settanta* (October–December 1997), pp.590–6, reprinted in Gentile, *Fascismo* (note 2) pp.265–308; idem, 'Il fascismo', in F.M. Agnoli, F. Cardini, E. Gentile and L. Morra, *L'Europa del XX secolo fra totalitarismo e democrazia* (Faenza: 1991), pp.101–10; and idem, 'La modernità totalitaria', new introduction to *Le origini dell'ideologia fascista* (Bologna: Il Mulino, 1996), pp.3–49.

25. Gentile, *Storia del partito fascista* (note 2), p.vii.

26. Ibid., p.x.

27. Gentile, *Il mito dello Stato nuovo* (note 2), pp.249–52.

28. G.L. Mosse, 'E. Nolte on Three Faces of Fascism', *Journal of History of Ideas* 4 (1966), pp.621–5.

29. On the influence Mosse's book had on my elaboration of the interpretation of fascism as political religion, see below pp. 68–69.

30. As far as the expression 'the invention of the political cult' is concerned, it is necessary to specify that it precedes the publication of Eric J. Hobsbawm and Terence Ranger (eds.), *The Invention of Tradition* (Cambridge: Cambridge University Press, 1983), and, therefore, does not derive from it.

31. Ibid., p.251.

32. Gentile, *Il culto del littorio* (note 3).

33. E. Gentile, 'Fascism as Political Religion', *Journal of Contemporary History* 25 (1990), p.229.

34. Ibid., pp.230–1.

35. G. Santomassimo, 'Le matricole del libro e moschetto', *Il manifesto*, 15 June 2003: 'The whole course of Emilio Gentile's research – initially misunderstood by many who willingly make amends – has tended to outline in the first place the culture, the symbology, the rituality of Italian fascism as a totalitarian phenomenon, and then, in the closing stages, to provide a more concrete examination of the construction and the consolidation of an authoritarian regime which *wanted* to be totalitarian'.

36. Foremost among them is Richard Bosworth. He asserts that my interpretation of Fascism could be characterised by 'its almost anti-anti-Fascism', Bosworth, *The Italian Dictatorship* (london: Arnold, 1998), p.22. This author claims to be a critic of my ideas on fascism, but what he presents as my interpretation is nothing but distortion, even misrepresentation of my thought, in order to make me seem 'the leading figure among the new generation of neo-Rankean anti-anti-Fascists', ibid., p.21. To confirm this allegation, Bosworth discusses what he claims to be my thesis, through omissions and arbitrary extrapolations of quotations, attributing to me assertions which are his pure invention. For instance, Bosworth writes that 'In 1995 Gentile felt confident enough to come up with his own definition of Fascism', ibid., pp.21–2; and presents as a 'definition of Fascism' my definition of 'totalitarian Caesarism', which instead refers solely to the fascist political system, and in doing so makes a mistake in the date of its formulation, namely 1986. Similarly, Bosworth comes up with a distorted version of my ideas when, about my book *La grande Italia* (note 2), he writes: Gentile 'argued the provocative and curiously nostalgic case that popular identification with the Italian nation reached its apogee in 1911', ibid., p.24; while in the same book I clearly state that this 'popular identification' in 1911 was only an apparent one, something I extensively demonstrate in the chapter deliberately entitled 'Le Italie dell'Italia monarchica'. Neither is it true that my interpretation of Fascism 'as a "political religion" squared the circle against traditional Marxist claims that Fascism expressed a class reality and a class purpose', ibid., p.24. Actually, in my studies on the origins of the fascist ideology and in my history of the Fascist Party, its class nature is widely discussed. In a similar way the class dimension of Fascism is also present in my definition of fascism, given in the *Enciclopedia italiana* (Roma: Istituto della Enciclopedia Italiana, 1992), yet Bosworth does not quote it. Another distortion is to allege that, from my history of the Fascist Party, 'The PNF's real character, it emerged, was cultural', ibid., p.128, which is simply not true. One more distortion is the manipulation of a quotation of mine, for which my affirmation 'Fascism always felt itself to be a *movement* and a *militia*', becomes in Bosworth's text: 'this was an organisation which was 'always *a movement and a militia*', ibid. Once again Bosworth distorts my interpretation when he writes that 'we have Gentile's assertions that the Italian "people" had, to a considerable degree, became Fascist true believers', ibid., p.131, because such an assertion cannot be found in any of my writings, while there are many which express a judgement entirely different from the

one Bosworth attributes to me. Again, it is simply untrue that I support the thesis of the 'genuineness of Fascism's claims to have forged a totalitarian Italian society', ibid., p.235, because in all the writings where I discuss the Fascist totalitarian experiment I clearly state that it ended up in failure. Apart from these distortions, and by way of a confirmation of the poor scholarship that characterises Bosworth's book on the interpretations of Italian fascism, it should be sufficient to quote some additional simple examples. For instance, Bosworth affirms that I had secured a 'place in the editorial boards of *Storia Contemporanea* and the *Journal of Contemporary History*', ibid., p.21, ignoring the fact that the magazine *Storia Contemporanea* has never had an 'editorial board' and that for this magazine I had been merely a contributor, and not even a regular one. Equally misleading is his statement that 'Gentile has duly received the applause of his academic faction. Non-De Feliceans, however, retain many doubts', ibid., p.129. Indeed, this affirmation is rendered absurd by the mainly positive judgements that most 'non-De Feliceans' expressed on my work, in particular, regarding my interpretation of totalitarianism and the sacralisation of politics in Fascism, as is known by anyone who has at least a superficial knowledge of the Italian historiography on fascism of the last few decades. With the same factual ignorance, Bosworth affirms that 'leading figures ... in the Catholic Church' participated in Mussolini's first government, ibid., p.41; locates Rieti, a town in the Lazio region of central Italy, in the south of Italy, ibid., p.134; and defines as 'an anonymous preface', ibid., p.200, n.143, the preface to the volume by R. De Felice, *Mussolini l'alleato 1940–1945: La Guerra civile 1943–1945* (Turin: Giulio Einaudi, 1997), signed by the historian's wife, Livia De Felice. Finally, as conclusive proof of the superficiality and unreliability of Bosworth's book as a general critical survey of the interpretations of Fascism, it is sufficient to observe the conspicuous absence of references and comments on the interpretations of Fascism proposed by more serious and authoritative exponents of Italian Marxist or left-wing historiography, like Giorgio Candeloro, Enzo Collotti, Ernesto Ragionieri, Enzo Santarelli and Piergiorgio Zunino, to name but a few. These historians, indeed, have provided interpretations of Fascism entirely different from Bosworth's, which replicates the thesis of 'historical negativity', and this may be the reason why the works of these historians do not even appear in the bibliography of his book.

37. Gentile (note 1), The point is explored further in Gentile *Le religioni della politica* (note 3) 2001, pp.50–5, 70-102; see also Gentile, 'Fascism in Power: the Totalitarian Experiment', in A. Lyttelton (ed.), *Liberal and Fascist Italy* (Oxford: Oxford University Press, 2002), pp. 139-141.

38. G. Carocci, 'Antropologia del fascismo', *Lettera dall'Italia* (July–September 1993), p.40.

39. The thesis of an authoritarian and not totalitarian Fascism which became a dictatorship not by vocation, but merely as an unwanted circumstantial consequence, was the interpretation of the Fascist experiment put forward by neo-Fascists like the *Movimento sociale italiano* (MSI): 'Fascism', we read in an article published on 14 December 1986 in *Secolo d'Italia*, the official organ of the MSI, 'became a dictatorship by force of circumstances, rather that through inclination. This dictatorship was theorised *a posteriori*, but was not programmed by the fascism–movement. Even when the need to theorise the dictatorship came, fascism conceived it as a transitory phase, determined by historical contingencies, neither ineluctable nor inalienable. It had nothing in common with the Leninist dogma of the "dictatorship of the proletariat". Besides, as far as the dictatorship is concerned, the fascist regime was authoritarian, not totalitarian. After conquering the monopoly of political power – which became transformed into a real participatory and active consent, therefore, into legitimation – the regime did not attempt to do the same in the fields of economics and culture. This has nothing whatsoever to do, again from this point of view, with the real modern totalitarianism which is communism, that systematically and programmatically subjugates politics, culture, economics over which it gains exclusive and coercive control'. This thesis finds its

support in interpretations of Fascism as an 'authoritarian regime of mobilisation', and therefore not a totalitarian one. This interpretation is provided by an expert in political sciences, Domenico Fisichella, a prominent member of the *Alleanza Nazionale*, which grew out of the *Movimento sociale italiano*. Fisichella categorically and repeatedly rejects my interpretation of Fascist totalitarianism, without ever citing either my definition of totalitarianism or my definition of fascism, and without discussing the facts and arguments supporting it. Following closely the historiographical knowledge of Fascism of 30 years ago and refusing to take into consideration a considerable amount of new knowledge on the reality of the fascist regime, provided by the new historiography, Fisichella resorts to an evident deformation of my research and my interpretation when he asserts that the 'thesis of an "Italian way to totalitarianism" and of "totalitarisation" of the regime lies essentially on the basis of analysis of proclamations and doctrinal and propagandistic proclamations and sometimes even on normative precepts', which are not complemented by concrete facts. D. Fisichella, *Totalitarismo: Un regime del nostro tempo* (Rome: 2002), p.10. As a matter of fact, my works on the history of the Fascist Party, on the Fascist regime and on the institutions of the monarchical State, such as the Senate, deal with concrete actions and structures and not only with ideology and proclamations. For a synthesis of the result of this studies, see E. Gentile, 'Fascism in Power: The Totalitarian Experiment', in A. Lyttelton (ed.), *Liberal and Fascist Italy 1900–1945* (Oxford and New York: Oxford University Press, 2002), pp.139–74.
40. Gentile, *Fascismo* (note 3), pp.vii–viii.
41. M. Tarchi, *Fascismo: Teorie, interpretazioni e modelli* (Rome and Bari: Laterza, 2003), p.130.
42. Marco Tarchi, an expert in political science and a Right-Wing intellectual, quoted De Felice in order to refute my interpretation of fascism as a totalitarianism and a political religion. In the first case, Tarchi writes peremptorily that, 'The conviction that what developed during those twenty years was an authoritarian regime of the classical type "albeit black-shirted", strongly conditioned by its supporters, built on a compromise with traditional institutions, whose "most typically modern demagogic-social dimensions" are not sufficient to consider it, despite the declared aspirations, a real totalitarianism, which was expressed by De Felice in the entry, written in the mid-1970s for the *Enciclopedia del Novecento*, still remains relevant', Tarchi (note 41), p.132. However, Tarchi omits to let the reader know that De Felice's phrase concerning the Fascist regime is preceded by a conditional statement. In the following paragraph, referring to the definition of the Fascist regime, quoted by Tarchi, De Felice specifies that 'such a superficial and factual vision would be, however, partial', R. De Felice, 'Fascismo', in *Enciclopedia del Novecento* (Rome: Istituto dell'Enciclopedia italiana, 1977), p.915. On the subject of Fascism as a political religion, Tarchi asserts that De Felice, in *Intervista sul fascismo* (Rome and Bari: Laterza, 1975), 'declared himself to be contrary to the hypothesis that during the *Ventennio* in Italy there ever existed any form of political religion', Tarchi (note 41), p.130. But in this case, De Felice himself refutes Tarchi, who quotes De Felice badly: indeed, in the above quoted encyclopaedia entry, De Felice affirmed that Fascism, in the same way as National Socialism, set a completely new goal 'to transform the masses by organising them in a political movement with the characteristics of a lay religion', De Felice, 'Fascismo', p.920. Finally, as for De Felice's judgement on my interpretation of fascist totalitarianism, Tarchi blunders again when he neglects to refer to what Mussolini's biographer wrote in 1982 specifically about my definition of fascist totalitarianism: 'Emilio Gentile has penned the definitive statement on this matter, which also helps explain the essence of Fascist totalitarianism and its deep difference from the Nazi and Stalinist ones', R. De Felice, 'Introduction', in R. De Felice and L. Goglia (eds.), *Storia fotografica del fascismo* (Rome and Bari: Laterza, 1982), p.xix. Faced with such 'glitches', I do not intend to set myself the problem of whether this is a case of accidental ignorance or accidental bad faith. It is interesting, though, to note that Tarchi's book quoted above appeared with the same publishing house and in the

same series as my critical essay on De Felice: E. Gentile, *Renzo De Felice: Lo storico e il personaggio* (Rome and Bari: Laterza, 2003). This essay illustrates with extensive quotations the evolution of his interpretation of the Fascist regime, which culminated in the conviction that Fascism was a totalitarian regime.

43. For instance, this is the case of Mabel Barezin in her review of the Italian edition of Gentile, *Il culto del littorio* (note 3), attributing to me affirmations and ideas which are simply false. It is not true that, as Barezin asserts, Gentile 'assumes that representation of power equals realities of power' and, 'never directly confronts how symbols and rituals contribute to political practice' and 'fails to make an analytical distinction between the producer of the ritual and the Italian populace as audience of symbolic practices. In short, Gentile fails to differentiate between movement and regime, party and people', Mabel Barezin, *Journal of Modern Italian Studies* 1/3 (1996), pp.470–2. As I clearly set out in the introduction to my book, the subject matter and the aim of my work was mainly that of 'singling out and analysing the origin, the motivations, the forms and the goals of the "cult of the Lictor"'; consequently I turned 'chiefly toward the promoters and the propagator of the "cult of the Lictor"', Gentile, *Il culto del littorio* (note 3), p.viii. However, within the framework of the book I also expounded my considerations on the political function of the 'cult the Lictor', as well as on the reaction of the populace, when it was possible to record them, ibid., pp.189–95; 292–7. And in the closing part I clearly expressed my overall evaluation of the effects of the 'cult of the Lictor': 'The totalitarian experiment of the Fascist political religion failed amid the ruins of a disastrous military defeat in a war both Fascism and anti-Fascism lived and combated as a "war of religion". Probably, the reasons for the failure lie in the very nature of the experiment, conducted in the euphoria of a voluntarism which believed enduring what was ephemeral, mistook emotions for conviction, the enthusiasm of success for confession of faith, the physical mass, as being similar to ocean waves, for the conscious body of the nation. But the same happened to the other experiments in secular religion', ibid., p.313.

44. This is the case of Tobias Abse, who, in an article dedicated to the English translation of *Il culto del littorio*, tried to denigrate my interpretation of fascism as a totalitarianism, presenting it in a caricature that generated the same effect as distorting mirrors in a funfair. Indeed, without *ever citing anything* of what I had been writing for years on the theories of totalitarianism, on the diversity and on the necessity of the differentiation between Fascism, Communism and National Socialism, as well as on the limits, the failures and the defeat of the Fascist totalitarian experiment, Abse peremptorily asserts that my 'theoretical framework is totally dependent on reviving the completely bankrupt notion of Italian Fascism constituting a totalitarian regime to be ranked alongside Nazism and what Gentile quaintly calls "Bolshevism". It is revealing that Gentile writes as if the concept of totalitarianism was unproblematic in the Russian and German instances, but this apparent ignorance of well-known debates about Nazism and Stalinism in not crucial to an argument about Fascist Italy', T. Abse, 'Italian Fascism: Political Religion, Political Ritual or Political Spectacle. Emilio Gentile and his Critics', *South European Society and Politics* 3/2 (1998), pp.142–50. Also in this case misrepresentation prevails over critical argumentation, as when Abse affirms that 'Gentile seems to have regressed to the antiquated political science clichés of a Germino', making reference to the book by Dante L. Germino, *The Italian Fascist Party in Power* (Minneapolis: University of Minnesota Press, 1959), as if I myself did not express towards Germino's book a critical judgement, similar to the one I expressed toward the other theories on totalitarianism elaborated by political science. For that purpose I refer back to what I wrote in Gentile, *Il mito dello Stato nuovo* (note 2), pp.255–6 (1999 edn., pp.xvii–xviii); and Gentile, *La via italiana al totalitarismo* (note 2), pp.65–9.

45. It is Abse again who distinguishes himself, repeating his criticism of my book on the fascist political religion, by referring to what he calls my 'distance from the Catholic tradition': 'a distance that some might argue has had a negative effect on Gentile's understanding of what constitutes a religion', T. Abse, 'The History of Italian Fascism',

in K. Flett and D. Rendon (eds.), *The Twentieth Century. A Century of Wars and Revolutions?* (London: Rivers Oram, 2000), p.160. But this is again a glaring example of how Abse has fallen into the 'snare of presumption', an easy trap for those who speak of things they ignore. As a matter of fact, it was Catholic scholars who were the first and the most original interpreters of Fascism as a political religion and some of them, like Igino Giordani and Luigi Sturzo, are cited in the same book that Abse criticises.

46. This is what Barbara Spackman asserts in *Fascist Virilities: Rhetoric, Ideology and Social Fantasy in Italy* (Minneapolis and London: University of Minnesota Press, 1996), pp.127–9. Spackman begins by giving me an 'elementary lesson in metaphor', ibid., p.128, using Benedetto Croce's quotation, taken from the 'Manifesto degli intellettuali antifascisti' of 1925, where the philosopher defines as an 'abuse' the definition of Fascism as a religion, given by Giovanni Gentile. Also in this case, before giving elementary lessons, one should follow the elementary rules of scholarship. Indeed, it is not enough to quote an occasional phrase of Croce's in order to disprove the interpretation of fascism as a political religion. The mere fact that Croce, the anti-Fascist, denied his former friend and Fascist Gentile (who was also a philosopher of religion) the right to define Fascism as a religion, should not cause surprise, considering that Croce asserted that it was not even an ideology. But anyone who has read some pages of Croce's other writings on religion, for instance at least the two first chapters of his *Storia d'Europa nel secolo decimonono* on the 'religion of freedom' and on the 'opposite religious faiths', knows that his concept of religion, with reference to the political movements, legitimises, and not in the metaphorical sense, the definition of fascism as a political religion.

47. See, for example, D. Veneruso, 'Nel fascio al posto della Croce il simbolo di un'ideologia fallimentare', *L'Osservatore Romano*, 13–14 April 1993; R. Moro, 'Religione e politica nell'età della secolarizzazione: riflessioni su un recente volume di Emilio Gentile', *Storia contemporanea* 26/2 (1995); D. Veneruso, 'La democrazia non può essere una nuova edizione di "religione secolarizzata"', *L'Osservatore Romano*, 14 July 2000; and A. Zaccuri, 'Il secolo del Leviatano', *Avvenire*, 25 October 2001.

48. Gentile, 'Il fascismo fu una rivoluzione?' (note 24), p.159.

49. Gentile (note 6), p.197.

50. Cf. Gentile, *Le religioni della politica* (note 3), chs.3 and 4.

51. Gentile (note 6), p.201.

52. In this context I would like to point out that the criticism levelled at my interpretation of fascism as a form of totalitarianism by Robert O. Paxton is equally unjustified. He argues that 'Even Emilio Gentile, most eager to demonstrate the power and success of the totalitarian impulse in Fascist Italy, concedes that the regime was a "composite" reality in which Mussolini's "ambition of personal power" struggled in "constant tension" with both "traditional forces" and "Fascist Party intransigents" themselves divided by "muffled conflict" [*sorda lotta*] among factions', R.O. Paxton, *The Anatomy of Fascism* (New York: Knopf, 2004), p.120. He goes on to state that 'Emilio Gentile … admits that the totalitarian experiment was incomplete', and at the same time, contradicting himself, reproaches me for being 'less interested in the problem of how the Fascist project was altered and subverted in the process of its integration into Italian society', ibid., pp.229–30. Clearly such judgements point to a superficial and biased reading of my book on Fascist totalitarianism, especially of the concluding chapters which focus on various aspects the effect that the totalitarian experiment had on Italian society, the various sources of resistance to it, the obstacles and barriers it came up against, and the disappointments and frustrations that its limited realisation caused to Fascists themselves. It is equally clear that Paxton misunderstands my interpretation when he states that I would be 'most eager to demonstrate the power and success of the totalitarian impulse in Fascist Italy', given that I actually have no intention at all of 'demonstrating' its power, but rather of 'showing and understanding' an empirical reality, namely the progressive expansion of Fascist power that is fully documented in my studies and in recent historiography. As for the internal conflicts and tensions within

Fascist totalitarianism, and its composite and incomplete character, Paxton mistakenly takes as a 'concession' or 'admission' what is actually a constitutive component of my interpretation of Fascism and the totalitarian experiment as a whole, which maintains that not just Fascism, but all totalitarian experiments are necessarily 'imperfect' and 'incomplete' when compared with a theoretical model of a 'perfect' totalitarian society. Besides, without explicitly acknowledging it, Paxton in fact echoes much of the interpretation that I presented in *La via italiana al totalitarismo* (note 2), especially when he states that 'One must concede that Mussolini's regime, eager to "normalize" its rapport with a society in which the family, the Church, the monarchy, and the village notable still had entrenched power, fell far short of total control. Even so, Fascism regimented Italians more firmly than any regime before or since. But no regime, not even Hitler's or Stalin's, ever managed to pinch off every last parcel of privacy and personal or group autonomy', Paxton, *The Anatomy of Fascism*, p.211.

53. Speaking about the diversity of totalitarianisms, Adrian Lyttelton, in a recent discussion of my interpretation, aimed to 'introduce a distinction between a "hot totalitarianism", characterised by a great institutional instability, by the use of terror and high level of ideological mobilisation, and a "cold totalitarianism", marked by a relatively stable institutional order, by substitution of terror with an all-prevailing apparatus of surveillance, by the climate of conformism', which would be the case of Italian Fascism, A. Lyttelton, 'La religione della patria', *L'indice* 7/8 (2003), p.22.

54. L. Zani, 'Famiglie politiche e modernità totalitaria: Il partito unico nel fascismo italiano', in idem, *Les familles politiques en Europe occidentale au XX siècle* (Rome: École Française de Rome, 2000), p.118.

55. Linz, *Fascismo, autoritarismo, totalitarismo* (note 17), p.35; S.G. Payne, Foreword to Gentile, *The Struggle for Modernity* (note 2), pp.xv–xvi.

56. R. Griffin, 'The Palingenetic Political Community: Rethinking the Legitimation of Totalitarian Regimes in Inter-War Europe', *Totalitarian Movements and Political Religions* 3/3 (2002), p.37. As regards the validity of the application of the concept of totalitarianism to the fascist phenomenon, see the introduction to the volume edited by Alessandro Campi (note 14), pp.xxxix–xliii.

57. For the apocalyptic interpretation of modernity in the sense explained above, that is, as one of the characteristics typical of totalitarian movements after the First World War, see E. Gentile, 'Un apocalisse nella modernità: La Grande Guerra e il Mito della Rigenerazione della politica', *Storia contemporanea* 26/5 (1995), pp.733–87.

58. S. Falasca-Zamponi, *Fascist Spectacle* (Berkeley, CA: University of California Press, 1997), p.7.

59. R. Gordon, 'Fascism', *Patterns of Prejudice* 32/1 (1998), p.70.

60. *Modernism/Modernity* 1/3 (1994), pp.235–7.

61. E. Gentile, 'The Conquest of Modernity: From Modernist Nationalism to Fascism', *Modernism/Modernity* 1/3 (1994), p.57. For my criticisms of the 'culturalist' approach to Fascism, see also Gentile (note 33), pp.60–1.

62. We might point out that in Mosse's work, as far as I understand it, the expression 'sacralisation of politics' appears only after publication of my book on the fascist religion: G.L. Mosse, *The Fascist Revolution: Towards a General Theory of Fascism* (New York: H. Fertig, 1999), p.xiii.

63. Moro (note 47), pp.310–12.

64. Griffin (note 10), p.130 n.42.

65. See, for example, D. Atkinson, 'Enculturating Fascism? Towards Historical Geographies in Inter-War Italy', *Journal of Historical Geography* 25/3 (1999), pp.393–400.

66. Gentile, *Le origini dell'ideologia fascista* (note 2), p.ix.

67. Gentile (note 1), p.51.

68. Gordon (note 59), p.69.

69. S. Luzzatto, 'The Political Culture of Fascist Italy', *Contemporary European History* 8/2 (1999), p.323.

70. Carocci (note 38), p.40. However, Carocci believed it 'reductive to study the myth if we confine ourselves to observing the awareness that its followers had of it', but added: 'Since Gentile is a scholar who is too shrewd not to know this fact, there is nothing else to do but to take cognisance of his refusal to emphasize what the scholars have noticed, mainly in Nazism, but in the second place also in Fascism, that is, the decadent, mortuary, nihilistic aspects of fascist activism in its behaviour deriving from Dannunzianism and from Arditism'. As a matter of fact, the refusal Carocci referred to derives from the fact that my analysis was primarily aimed at studying the function of the myth in mass politics, which, in my opinion does not involve the aspects pointed out by Carocci, which were typical of certain fascist groups involved in Dannunzianism or in Arditism.
71. Griffin (note 15), p.30. More than ten years later this criticism came up again, without new arguments, from Roger Eatwell's side. Though recognising the utility of the approach proposed by me, he still reasserts that 'fascism was a political *ideology* rather than a political *religion*', R. Eatwell, 'Reflections on Fascism and Religion', *Totalitarian Movements and Political Religions* 4/3 (2003), p.163. The gulf dividing ideology and religion, presented as an argument to refute the concept of political or secular religion, was already put forward by Hannah Arendt in the debate with Jule Monnerot, who had defined communism as a secular religion in his book *Sociologie du Communisme* (Paris: Gallimard, 1949); see H. Arendt, 'Religion and Politics', *Confluence: An International Forum* 2/3 (1953); Monnerot's objection, ibid. 2/4 (1953); and Arendt's reply, ibid. 3/3 (1954).
72. R. Ioanid, *The Sword of the Archangel: Fascist Ideology in Rumania* (New York: Columbia University Press, 1990), p.140.
73. Ibid.
74. N. Micklem, *National Socialism and the Catholic Church* (London: Oxford University Press, 1939), pp.39–40, 52, 194–5.
75. For a more extensive treatment of this argument, I refer the reader to my article in the next issue of *Totalitarian Movements and Political Religions* 6/1 (Spring 2005).
76. Gentile (note 1), pp.23–4; Gentile, *Le religioni della politica* (note 3), pp.210–11.
77. *Archives de Sciences sociales des religions* 92 (1995).
78. S.R. Di Rienzo, 'The Non-Optional Basis of Religion', *Totalitarian Movements and Political Religions* 3/3 (2002), p.75.
79. Gentile (note 1), pp.18–19.
80. G. Filoramo, *Le vie del sacro* (Turin: Einaudi, 1994), p.26.
81. Gentile, *Le origini dell'ideologia fascista* (note 2), pp.426–8.

Nazism and the Revival of Political Religion Theory

In the last ten years, totalitarianism theory has experienced a major comeback. Whether the end of the Cold War indicates the triumph of the First World or the implosion of the Second, it has brought with it a renewed triumphalism in academic circles that would likely have pleased Hannah Arendt. Once again fascism and communism are conjoined as symptomatic of a lack of 'Western' liberal democracy in their native societies. This is evident not only in new scholarship, but in a new journal devoted solely to this subject – namely this one – and in the new *Hannah Arendt Institut für Totalitarismusforschung* in Dresden, a scholarly St Patrick committed to reviving totalitarianism theory after the collapse of social-historical Marxist historiography.[1] Directly connected with the resurgence of totalitarianism theory is a renewed interest in theories of fascism as a 'political religion'. This has been especially apparent lately in the historiography of Italian Fascism; here the political religion angle has to some degree been informed by a more innovative interest in aesthetics and identity formation.[2] By contrast, recent German scholarship has tended to be a more conventional affair of intellectual history, more inclined to re-centre the Nazi 'neo-pagans' as the locus of Nazi ideology, insisting that Himmler's or Rosenberg's attempts to create a new *Religionser-satz* to replace Christianity really were important after all.[3] In this essay, I will attempt two things: first, to survey some of the lineages of political religion scholarship, assess its theoretical and conceptual qualities, and suggest ways in which Nazism might better be under-stood as a 'religious politics'; second, I will turn to the historical record, to investigate exactly how the Nazis conceived their move-ment as potentially religious.

The complementarity of 'totalitarianism theory' and 'political reli-gion' theory is self-evident. Totalitarianism theory, at its most elemen-tal, suggests that the form of twentieth-century dictatorships counted more than the content; style is emphasised over substance. A milita-rised society, one-party state, suppression of the public sphere, a supreme leader with some degree of charisma or at least personality cult – these are the focus of attention. By contrast, the different poli-cies these regimes pursued, their contrasting ideologies, what their societies actually looked liked – are all given secondary consideration.[4] According to totalitarianism theory, atomised 'mass man', deprived of the moral compass of *Gemeinschaft* and hurled into the anomie of *Gesellschaft*, found a *Gemeinschaft* once again, this time writ large. 'Political religion theory', by comparison, also insists on the centrality of the rootless 'mass man'. Here, the totalitarian subject suffers – espe-cially in the German case, we are told – from a Nietzschean 'death of God', leaving him de-Christianised and therefore vulnerable to 'blind enthusiasms'. Nazism allegedly served to sacralise the collectivity once again. Like totalitarianism theory, political religion theory emphasises Nazi form (the hypnotic power of a new charismatic faith) over Nazi content (the message of that religion and to whom it appealed). Among the original representatives of this view were Eric Voegelin and Gerhard Ritter, who both argued that Nazism had been primarily a moral disease originating in the Enlightenment, and who both prescribed a simple 'return' to Christian values as the best antidote. This argument complemented the politics of conservatives like Voege-lin and Ritter, by obviating the need to seek the social roots of Nazism's popularity – thereby refuting suggestions that Hitler was more than an aberration in the course of German history. This strain of argumentation was reinforced by a strong orientalising tendency in contemporary Christian apologia, whereby the rectitude of Germany's Christian culture was contrasted with an alleged 'Islamic' quality to the Nazis' political culture. This attempt to put a prophylactic around Germany, thereby casting Nazism and its historical precedents as alien infections, was particularly sneering. As Karl Jung put it in 1939: 'We do not know whether Hitler is going to found a new Islam. He is already on the way; he is like Mohammed. The emotion in Germany is Islamic, warlike and Islamic. They are all drunk with a wild man'.[5] In these varied ways, the 'moral dimension' of post-war scholarship, as Ian Kershaw calls it, served as the historical counterpart of the totalitarianism theory then being developed by political scientists like Arendt. By pointing to instances of Christian alterity to Nazism, this scholarship helped erect a potent symbol of national regeneration, the *Stunde Null* – thereby refuting those scholars of the victorious Allied powers who claimed that Nazism was a disease encompassing *all* Germans.

This was a popular argument outside of academia as well. Some of the most prominent public intellectuals of the post-war period made it part of the intellectual landscape of the post-war period. Hannah Arendt herself, the 'philosophical counterpart' to Gerhard Ritter,[6] allowed for no ambiguity when she argued:

> Nazism owes nothing to any part of the Western tradition, be it German or not, Catholic or Protestant, Christian, Greek or Roman ... Ideologically speaking, Nazism begins with no traditional basis at all, and it would be better to realise the danger of this radical negation of any tradition, which was the main feature of Nazism from the beginning.[7]

The immediate post-war context for this 'moral dimension' has disappeared, but its enduring popularity is still in evidence today.

'Political religion theory', then, finds a multi-layered connection with totalitarianism theory; it is equally reliant upon, and in many ways intertwined with, theories of nationalism. For instance, George Mosse suggested almost 30 years ago that nationalism as such was literally a 'new religion', in which the secularist wine of personal charisma and racialism filled the old bottles of piety and spirituality left empty by modern apostasy.[8] Fritz Stern's study of three proto-Nazi intellectuals similarly argues that apostate academics created a Germanic religion 'which hid beneath pious allusions to ... the Bible a most thoroughgoing secularisation. The religious *tone* remained, even after the religious faith and the religious canons had disappeared'.[9] These arguments presume that nationalism brought with it, and in fact was a leading cause of, secularisation. As with political religion theorists, what mattered for this school were the religious idioms, not the ideology. However, unlike many forms of secularisation theory, which suggest that modernity witnesses a decline in religiosity *per se*, the variety most associated with the literature on Nazism suggests that de-Christianisation did not lead to agnosticism or atheism, but rather left a spiritual yearning, a void waiting to be filled with another content. A recent echo of this view is found in the recent work of Michael Burleigh, who asserts that with Nazism, Christianity's 'fundamental tenets were stripped out, but the remaining diffuse religious emotionality had its uses'.[10] Amongst those arguing that Nazism was a form of Nietzschean secularisation, the most surprising was Detlev Peukert. Renowned for his unique contributions to Nazi historiography and refusal to toe party lines, Peukert nonetheless suggested:

> we view the roots of modern racism as lying in the problem of legitimation in a secularised world. A secularised world no longer provided final answers: it had no way of pointing beyond itself. Once the facade of non-transcendent everyday mythology had been shattered by crisis, the search was on for 'final solutions'.[11]

This claim is all the more surprising coming from someone whose politics were so at odds with Ritter's. Both Peukert and Ritter intersected in this case, however, in the importance they placed on the apparent de-Christianisation of Germany, and Christianity's replacement with Nazism. At the end of the day the most recent works on political religion and totalitarianism theory offer little new beyond Voegelin's earlier theories, heavily reliant as they are on complimentary concepts like charisma.[12]

The many scholars who have employed political religion theory are correct in claiming to see a religious dimension in Nazism. For 'totalitarian' regimes in general, the use of physical space and prophetic language was indeed often consciously derived from religious sources. Hitler himself freely admitted that the model for Nazi night rallies came from his own Catholic upbringing.[13] There was an undeniable, highly emotionalist quality to Nazi performance, which historians generally assume supplied a growing demand in the German public for a spiritual politics. But was this the actual linchpin of Nazi social success? As descriptive as this concept is, how useful is it as a category of analysis? How far does performance and choreography go in explaining the Nazi appeal? The political religion thesis presumes the attraction to Nazism was based on emotion instead of idea, on form instead of content. Whatever the Nazi 'platform' may have been is deemed irrelevant, or at best secondary. The 'religion' of political religion theory becomes the act of believing, not *that which is believed*.

However appealing and self-contained this theory seems, it cannot sustain itself empirically. Such a focus ignores the findings of social historians who, in the last 20 years, have provided very detailed analyses of who did and did not join, or vote for, the NSDAP. To a striking degree, such analyses have demonstrated a predictability of Nazi attraction based on factors like class, region, geography and – most importantly – confession. What these studies demonstrate rather clearly is that however dramatic Hitler's display of personal charisma may have been, however emphasised by the Nazis' own propaganda, it played little if any role in actually shaping the Nazi electorate. The attraction to Nazism was instead determined by the factors that governed electoral choice between Germany's other political parties: calculated self-interest.[14] And, while functionalist interpretations have often held sway, defining that self-interest in material 'pocketbook' terms, there are provisional indications that a culturalist definition of self-interest, drawing upon intangible aspects of the Nazi appeal – like the promised renewal of morality and 'honour' – may reveal deeper insights. A culturalist interpretation would certainly take us much further towards understanding the overwhelmingly Protestant nature of the Nazi electorate than would a purely materialist interpretation.[15] Regardless of which approach is taken, the social-historical approach definitively undermines the 'political religion' presumption that their *style* earned the Nazis their electoral success. As David Blackbourn has argued, fascist ritual was successful primarily when it played to an audience receptive to the message; that is, 'where it went with the grain of particular experiences and interests'.[16] This argument has been born out by specialists of the 1933–45 period such as David Welch, who has proven Blackbourn's assertion correct *vis-à-vis* Nazi propaganda; it succeeded with those already 'converted' to the Nazi message, and largely failed to win over those who before 1933 had yet to be convinced.[17]

Nazi propaganda may have portrayed Hitler as a kind of Holy Roller, mesmerising his audience at the night rallies and 'converting' it to his cause. And the historical record is full of testimonials of Hitler's charismatic power working its magic on sceptics reluctantly dragged by friends to the rally at the Zeppelin field, only to be won over in a wave of religious fervour. But while this image of Hitler as mass hypnotist reveals a good deal about the *ambitions* of Nazi propagandists, it tells us very little about the realities of audience reception or the degree of actual social consent which the Nazis were so anxious to secure. Several studies have pointed to the Nazis' deep concern with public opinion and consensus building as a precondition for their activities.[18] Robert Gellately has demonstrated how the Gestapo, perhaps the most infamous symbol of totalitarianism in the popular imagination, was in fact heavily dependent on public participation for its success.[19] Recently Gellately has explored this theme further, demonstrating the ways in which social consensus was erected and disrupted, with little emphasis on Hitler's charisma or other quasi-religious aspects of Nazi performance.[20] The work of Nathan Stoltzfus, among others, has shown how it was possible to mount popular resistance in Nazi Germany in clear defiance of Hitler's hypnotic powers.[21] Among other things, these studies reveal that the Nazis ultimately put little store in their own charismatic gifts, their ability to 'sacralise the collectivity' through a *Religionsersatz* when attempting to form a national consensus. The Nazis knew, in other words, that their state was less than totalitarian. Significantly, some of the first STUDIES to question the totalitarian quality of Nazi rule were examinations of churches written by non-church historians – significant because historians of church and state under Nazism were generally some of the most consistent proponents of totalitarianism theory.[22]

In spite of the findings of these scholars, 'political religion' theorists have by and large been able to carry forth with remarkably little consequence. The latest example of this is the synoptic narrative by Michael Burleigh, titled *The Third Reich: A New History*, which represents the latest and most prominent attempt, not only to resuscitate political religion theory, but also to restore it to the more influential position it once enjoyed. Recapitulating the earlier theories of Mosse and Stern, Burleigh contends that 'sacralised collectivities, such as class, nation or race, had already partly supplanted God as objects of mass enthusiasm or veneration'. He agrees with a prior generation of scholars that this political religion was 'self-consciously pagan and primitive', that in spite of its claim to be scientific, Nazism had 'one foot in the dark irrationalist world of Teutonic myth'.[23]

As self-confident as this scholarly revival seems to be at the moment, it still needs to solve the basic deep-seated problems plaguing a prior generation of 'political religion' and totalitarianism theorists. What exactly constitutes 'religion', such that both Christianity and Nazism can be considered two equally valid examples of it? By what means can we demonstrate that one form of identity – being national-istic – must necessarily impinge upon and usurp another form of iden-tity – being Christian? If Nazism can be seen as a religion, then cannot all politics potentially be seen in this light? Can politics be *religious* without being *religion*? As powerful as the allure of political religion theory is for a new generation of scholars, they largely leave these questions unanswered. At its most basic, political religion theory presumes a static 'zero sum' model of identity formation. The possibil-ity that one can be national *and* religious, not national *or* religious, is not considered. Also overlooked is the historical record of nationalism in modern Europe, which frequently demonstrates not an opposition between national and religious feeling, but more often an affinity. This is seen not only in the cases of Poland and Ireland, where a structural overlap of religious and linguistic identity can be explained in geo-cultural terms, but also in countries precisely like Germany, where Christian clergy – especially Protestant – played a leading role in constructing and shaping a movement which has most often been regarded as secular.[24]

Equally unsubstantiated is the common insistence that Christianity has gone into decline in the modern age. In the last 15 years or so, a great deal of historical investigation has taken place to demonstrate the continued power and influence of Christianity in Europe, not only among an intellectual élite, but among larger social strata as well. Aside from a select number of intellectuals whose social impact has still to be measured, there is little evidence to show that German soci-ety as a whole experienced a 'Death of God' before Nazism; or more to the point, that those who were attracted to Nazism (either at the polling station or membership office) were apostate Christians. Only those who *wish* the modern era had seen the decline of Christianity – either to dissociate it from an historical record they abhor or to asso-ciate its decline with one they esteem – can any longer argue this was so.[25]

If there is indeed no 'zero sum' relationship between national and religious identity, and if the modern age has not in fact been secular in the sense of being de-Christianised, then in what sense can we still say that Nazism contained a religious dimension? Given the profoundly political character of fascism, it is less interesting – and ultimately less fruitful – to know whether it can be qualified as religion in a phenomenological sense than to identify its relationship with the extant religions that had long been part of the societies that went fascist. And here the same scholarship that valorises style can often make telling, though frequently inadvertent, references to a substantive relationship as well. Returning briefly to the historiography on Italian Fascism, we can see this reflected in Mabel Berezin's work. On the one hand, she suggests that in Fascist Italy 'everyone participated in Catholic practices that were *independent* of doctrine or belief and shaped Italian fascist and public consciousness'. The religious form is emphasised here; Berezin speaks of a 'fascist transposition' of Catholic idioms, such as the catechism, which aided the forming of Fascist political culture. On the other hand, however, Berezin points to a substantive connection to Catholicism. She speaks of ideological 'affinities', especially with regard to Fascist social theory: 'In a direct borrowing from *Rerum Novarum*, corporations, Fascist unions that encompassed the entire workforce, were the organising vehicles that concretised the state–individual relation'.[26] Berezin admittedly argues this was simply a 'borrowing' – Catholicism in her view was a pool of ideas to be siphoned off, not the ontological root of fascism *per se*. But the 'borrowing' is nonetheless comprehensive. Elsewhere Berezin points out that 'as an ideology, Fascism was anti-democratic, anti-liberal, anti-socialist, and anti-Masonic' – all components of a platform that was recognisably Catholic in certain places at certain times.

What we have is not a borrowing so much as wholesale adaptation. Rather than 'political religion', what we have is something that could be called 'religious politics', whereby a political-secular movement takes on the temporal teachings of an established religion. While a theory of 'religious politics' has yet to be developed, such a concept would place far greater emphasis on the content of a religion's message – particularly with regards to the social order – than the form of that religion's ritual. In the German case, it would emphasise the ways in which the Nazis carved out a constituency of particular religious interests. In this sense, a fruitful point of comparison would be with the Centre Party and, after the war, the Christian Democrats, both of whom undertook a type of cross-class, religious representation and hence can be classified as a religious politics, albeit of a radically different substance.[27] In the case of Nazism, the overwhelming attraction among Germany's Protestants, similarly cutting across class lines, would justifiably qualify the NSDAP as a Protestant Centre Party, fulfilling a long-held ambition to rally together a disparate Protestant electorate around an ideological *Volkspartei*.

Immediate insights are gleaned when applying the religious politics concept to historical fascism. As Berezin intimates in the Italian case, the social attraction to fascism would be explicable not through its ability to recreate religious ritual, either physical or discursive, as though the message of fascism were secondary. The key, rather, would be the ways in which fascism promised to remould state and society, and the types of social milieus regarding such a message as attractive or unattractive. In German historiography there are examples of a similar conceptual tension between style and substance. Without stating so explicitly, Burleigh suggests that Nazi *ideology*, and not just Nazi choreography, contained a religious element. While it appropriated for itself a scientistic sheen, this ideology was not just about applied biology,

> but the expression of eternal scientific laws, revealed by God and in turn invested with sacred properties ... This was politics as a biological mission, but conceived in a religious way ... Armed with his religious science, Hitler [was] God's partner in ordering and perfecting that part of mankind which concerned him.[28]

Interwoven into his analysis of Nazi political religion, Burleigh provides evidence that Nazism derived its ideology from a particular interpretation of theology. The distinction is vitally important, even if not fully drawn out in this instance. Instead of a religion with a political dimension, what we might witness in Nazism is a politics with a religious dimension.

Other scholarly voices (albeit from a distinctly functionalist rather than intentionalist standpoint) suggest that whatever the ontological sources of Nazism, at the level of ideas a 'borrowing' from Christianity similar to Italian Fascism was taking place. For example, Martin Broszat suggested that: 'A considerable part of this ideological rhetoric which the NSDAP had sucked up from all available sources, was indeed itself derived from Christian convictions'.[29] The telling expression 'sucking up' reveals a typically functionalist understanding of ideology as secondary within the Nazi movement. But Broszat opens up the possibility that more than just isolated instances of 'borrowing' from Christian tradition is taking place. It is precisely *here* where the overwhelmingly Protestant composition of the Nazi social base becomes so revealing. Instead of a political religion in which Hitler's voters rushed to the movement in a tide of emotion, might Nazism have been seen as a religious politics in which these voters dispassionately reflected on the ideological platform of Nazism, believing they saw in it a Christian platform?

Nazism cannot represent both a 'destructive mimesis of Christianity'[30] and simultaneously derive its ideology from Christian convictions. The question becomes: which was it? Did the Nazis view themselves as a replacement for Christianity, or as its restorer?

* * *

Whether the Nazis felt themselves to be a 'political religion' is best investigated by exploring the efforts of some in the movement to create a literal *Religionsersatz*. Those who uphold 'political religion theory' most strenuously usually point to 'neo-pagans' like Rosenberg and Himmler, implying that their esoteric religious ideas were hegemonic within the movement. It is then often inferred that Hitler himself subscribed to their mysticism. For instance, Philippe Burrin maintains that 'Hitler remained devoted to the idea of a religious reform of the Germans. And if he abstained from preaching this in public, it was Himmler who undertook this task by making the SS the force that was to add religious reform to political renewal'. Burrin goes further, suggesting that 'Hitler and his men ... satisfied their [religious] fascination through speculative theories that they considered scientific such as the "glaciation cosmogony"'.[31] Less well known, but equally revealing, was another attempt to turn Nazism into a religious movement by the sectarian Christian Artur Dinter. While he had no interest in Wotan or other Nordic legends, Dinter was at least as committed as the paganists to turning the party from a secular into a religious movement.

Rosenberg's paganist opus, *The Myth of the Twentieth Century*, is the most obvious attempt among the Nazis to forge a new political religion. As he wrote:

> The men of the coming age will transform the heroes' memorials and glades of remembrance into the places of pilgrimage of a new religion; there the hearts of Germans will be constantly shaped afresh in pursuit of a new myth ... Today a new faith is awakening: the myth of blood, the faith that the divine essence of

mankind is to be defended through blood; the faith embodied by the fullest realisation that Nordic blood represents the mystery which has supplanted and surmounted the old sacraments.[32]

This new religion would place the highest value in the idea of racial honour: 'The idea of honour – national honour – is for us the beginning and end of all our thoughts and deeds. It can endure no equivalent centre of power of any type, neither Christian love nor freemasonic humanism nor Roman dogmatism'.[33] This Christian 'brotherhood of man' was nothing more than an attempt to allow Jew and 'Turk' to take precedence over the European. In the name of Christian love, Europe was besieged by unrest and chaos: 'Thanks to preachings on humanity and the equality of all peoples, every Jew, Negro and Mulatto can be a full citizen of a European state'.[34] When the Nordic states of Europe were overwhelmed by the Roman south, the concept of honour was overtaken by that of Christian love: 'Christianity ... did not know the idea of race and nationality, because it represented a violent fusion of different elements; it also knew nothing of the idea of honour, because in pursuance of the late Roman quest for power it subdued not only the body, but also the soul'.[35]

It is voices such as Rosenberg's and Himmler's which are invoked when historians argue that Nazism was a political religion seeking to replace Christianity. However, these voices constituted a minority within their own movement. One need look no further for proof of this than Hitler himself. Though Hitler was known for tailoring his remarks to please his audience, even in Rosenberg's presence he was less than enthusiastic about paganism. Before publishing it, Rosenberg asked Hitler for his opinion of *Mythus* (six months after receiving the manuscript, Hitler still had not read it). Hitler coolly replied: 'It is a very clever book; only I ask myself who today is likely to read and understand such a book'.[36] It was a reflection of the insecurity of Rosenberg's position that he replied by asking whether he should suppress it or even resign party office. Hitler said 'no' to both, maintaining that Rosenberg had a right to publish his book since it was his intellectual property.[37] However, on later occasions Hitler would express regret that Rosenberg had written the book in the first place. According to Albert Speer, Hitler referred to it as 'stuff nobody can understand', written by a 'narrow-minded Baltic German who thinks in horribly complicated terms ... A relapse into medieval notions!'[38] Hitler was even more dismissive in his 'Table Talk', stating privately:

I must insist that Rosenberg's *Myth of the Twentieth Century* is not to be regarded as an expression of the official doctrine of the Party ... It is interesting to note that comparatively few of the older members of the Party are to be found among the readers of Rosenberg's book, and that the publishers had, in fact, great difficulty in disposing of the first edition.[39]

Himmler's mysticism fared no better. As Hitler told his circle of confidants: 'What nonsense! Here we have at last reached an age that has left all mysticism behind, and now he wants to start that all over again ... To think that I may some day be turned into an SS saint!' Whereas Himmler attacked Charlemagne as the subjugator of ancient pagan-Germanic tribes, Hitler declared: 'Killing all those Saxons was not a historical crime, as Himmler thinks. Charlemagne did a good thing in subjugating Widukind and killing the Saxons out of hand. He thereby made possible the empire of the Franks and the entry of Western culture into what is now Germany'.[40] Hitler even approached Himmler himself, fully rejecting the foundation of a new religion, calling it a 'chimera'.[41] There is ample evidence that Hitler had no time for Himmler's anti-Christian neo-paganism; but even among the party's other paganists, Himmler's religious views were regarded as bizarre. Himmler unwittingly acknowledged this, warning his underlings that no polemics against such theories would be tolerated.[42] The particular obsession with 'glaciation cosmogony' was too much even for Rosenberg, who sent a circular to all NSDAP offices assuring them that 'adherence to these theories was no part of being a National Socialist'.[43]

These were admittedly private expressions. But Hitler did not spare his paganist colleagues in the party from public derision. As he wrote in *Mein Kampf*:

The characteristic thing about these people is that they rave about old Germanic heroism, about dim prehistory, stone axes, spear and shield, but in reality are the greatest cowards that can be imagined. For the same people who brandish scholarly imitations of old German tin swords, and wear a dressed bearskin with bull's horns over their bearded heads, preach for the present nothing but struggle with spiritual weapons, and run away as fast as they can from every Communist blackjack.[44]

He disdained 'those German-*völkisch* wandering scholars whose positive accomplishment is always practically nil, but whose conceit can scarcely be excelled'.[45] Any attempt at making Nazism a religious movement came in for total reproach:

> Especially with the so-called religious reformers ... I always have the feeling that they were sent by those powers which do not want the resurrection of our people ... I shall not even speak of the unworldliness of these *völkisch* Saint Johns of the twentieth century or their ignorance of the popular soul.[46]

This last statement could have applied as equally to Artur Dinter, who sought to transform Nazism from a secular party into an explicitly religious movement. Dinter would ultimately be expelled over his growing rift with Hitler on this issue; the grounds upon which he would be removed provide us with further insight into Hitler's own thinking on religion. As this episode reveals, if Hitler believed his movement was *religious*, he entirely rejected the idea that it should be a *religion*.

Like many in the Nazi leadership, Dinter held Martin Luther in high regard, esteeming him as a nationalist figure who, among other things, had invented the German language. And among many Nazis there was an admiration for Luther's *religious* struggle as well.[47] Dinter was among them, but he took his admiration to extreme ends, going so far as to formulate a platform for 'completing' the Reformation in Germany. Luther had failed to unite all Germans under the banner of 'true' Christianity: it would now be the responsibility of the Nazi Party to complete the process. Dinter enunciated this vision in 1926 through his *197 Thesen zur Vollendung der Reformation* (197 Theses for the Completion of the Reformation), in which he declared that the only path to German political renewal was through a religious revolution. The following year in Nuremberg he established his own organisation, the Christian-Spiritual Religious Association (*Geistchristliche Religionsgemeinschaft*), and a periodical, *Das Geistchristentum* (Christianity of the Spirit).

Owing to Hitler's disinterest in his proposal, Dinter grew increasingly opposed to Hitler's leadership. In return, Hitler had Dinter expelled from the NSDAP. A few weeks after Dinter's expulsion, Hitler gave a speech in Passau:

> We are a people of different faiths, but we are one. Which faith conquers the other is not the question; rather, the question is whether Christianity stands or falls ... We tolerate no one in our

ranks who attacks the ideas of Christianity ... in fact our movement is Christian. We are filled with a desire for Catholics and Protestants to discover one another in the deep distress of our own people.[48]

Hitler unequivocally wished to cast Nazism as a religious politics rather than a political religion; while the movement would be informed by religious ideology, it would not assume the form of a religious movement. Furthermore, Hitler contended that the religious ideology in question would be Christian – and therefore closer in content to Dinter – not anti-Christian, as the paganists had hoped.

Most of the Nazi élite joined with Hitler in rejecting these political religions, especially Rosenberg's and Himmler's paganism. As Goebbels noted in his dairy, Göring complained that if Rosenberg had had his way, there would be 'only cult, *Thing*, myth, and that sort of swindle'.[49] In 1939 Göring confronted Rosenberg point blank, asking him: 'Do you believe that Christianity is coming to an end, and that later a new form created by us will come into being?' When Rosenberg said he did think this, Göring replied he would privately solicit Hitler's view.[50] No record exists of Göring asking Hitler this question, but there is little doubt Hitler would have rejected Rosenberg's contention. Goebbels's views on paganism closely matched Göring's; his estimation of Rosenberg's abilities were summarised in his reference to him as 'Almost Rosenberg': 'Rosenberg almost managed to become a scholar, a journalist, a politician – but only almost'.[51]

Hitler rejected attempts to turn Nazism into a political religion, seeing his movement instead as a religious politics – in conformity with Christian precepts, not opposed to them. In a party gathering at Munich's Bürgerbräukeller in 1922, he dealt with the question of whether one could be both antisemitic and Christian:

> I say my Christian feelings point me to my Lord and Saviour as a fighter (tumultuous, prolonged applause). They point me toward the man who, once lonely and surrounded by only a few followers, recognised these Jews and called for battle against them, and who, as the true God, was not only the greatest as a sufferer but also the greatest as a warrior ... as a Christian and a human being, I read the passage which declares to us how the Lord finally rose up and seized the whip to drive the usurers, the brood of serpents and snakes, from the Temple (tumultuous applause)![52]

In this speech, delivered in front of a mostly Nazi audience, Hitler referred to Jesus as 'the true God'. He made it plain that he regarded Christ's 'struggle' as direct inspiration for his own. For Hitler, Jesus was not just one archetype among others, but, as he said on another occasion, was 'our greatest Aryan leader'.[53] While emphasising Jesus's human qualities, in this instance Hitler also alluded to his divinity. It should be pointed out that Hitler said these words publicly: what did he say behind closed doors?

At a private meeting with his confidants from the *Kampfzeit*, in which he explained why economics must be subordinate to politics, Hitler again spoke of a connection between Nazism and Christianity, one deeper than a simple 'borrowing':

> Socialism is a political problem. And politics is of no concern to the economy ... Socialism is a question of attitude to life, of the ethical outlook on life of all who live together in a common ethnic or national space. Socialism is a *Weltanschauung*!
>
> But in actual fact there is nothing new about this *Weltanschauung*. Whenever I read the New Testament Gospels and the revelations of various of the prophets ... I am astonished at all that has been made of the teachings of these divinely inspired men, especially Jesus Christ, which are so clear and unique, heightened to religiosity. *They* were the ones who created this new world view which we now call socialism, they established it, they taught it and they lived it! But the communities that called themselves Christian churches did not understand it! ... they denied Christ and betrayed him![54]

Hitler claimed that where the churches failed in their mission to instil a Christian ethic in secular society, his movement would take up the task. Hitler not only read the New Testament, but professed to be inspired by it. As a consequence, he also claimed that the substance of Nazi social theory is 'nothing new'.

Whatever Hitler's own personal religiosity – which certainly cannot be described as Christian in the conventional, ecclesiastical sense – it contained a Christian element. Until the end of his life he esteemed Christ, so much so that he decided it was necessary to rescue Christ from his own Jewishness. Even while Hitler's anti-clericalism grew, his opinion of Jesus remained high. As he said to his confidants in October 1941: 'The Galilean, who later was called the Christ, intended something quite different. He must be regarded as a popular leader who took up his position against Jewry ... He set Himself against Jewish capitalism, and that is why the Jews liquidated Him'.[55] In Hitler's eyes, Jesus's status as an Aryan remained unquestioned: 'It is certain that Jesus was not a Jew'. However much Hitler claimed to be an enemy of organised religion, this conception of Jesus displayed a clear limit to his apostasy, and the retention of a specifically Christian dimension to his beliefs.

More than just Hitler, others in the Nazi movement exhibited a similar commitment to Christianity. One was the *Gauleiter* of East Prussia and eventual Reich Commissioner of Ukraine, Erich Koch. In addition to being *Gauleiter* Koch served in 1933 as the elected president of the provincial Protestant church synod. Contemporaries of Koch, including those against the Nazified 'German Christians', confirmed that his Christian feelings were sincere. According to the leader of the East Prussian Confessing Church, Koch spoke 'with the deepest understanding of our church' and consistently dealt with 'the central themes of Christianity'. In his post-war testimony, taken by a public prosecutor in Bielefeld in 1949, Koch would insist: 'I held the view that the Nazi idea had to develop from a basic Prussian-Protestant attitude'.[56]

This Protestant orientation among the Nazi Party élite, evident even in Hitler's estimation of Protestantism as the 'national religion' of the Germans,[57] matched the party's own heavily Protestant social base. Hans Schemm, *Gauleiter* of Bayreuth, Bavarian *Kultusminister* and head of the National Socialist Teachers' League (NSLB) further illustrates this correlation. During the *Kampfzeit*, Schemm was known for his slogan, 'Our religion is Christ, our politics Fatherland!' His speeches were designed to cast Nazism as a religious politics: as a police report stated, Schemm spoke 'like a pastor' and often ended his deliveries with the Lutheran hymn, 'A Mighty Fortress is our God'.[58] In one of these speeches, he spoke of God in Nazism's conceptual universe: 'Our confession to God is a confession of a doctrine of totality ... To give ultimate significance to the totalities of race, resistance and personality there is added the supreme totalitarian slogan of our *Volk*: "Religion and God". God is the greatest totality and extends over all else'.[59] Here Schemm makes specific reference to the 'totalitarian' nature of Nazism. But he makes it clear that the totalising claims of Nazism as a *Weltanschauung* did not preclude the possibility that such a *Weltanschauung* could have been based on a variety of Christianity. Far from conflicting loyalties, for Schemm Christianity and Nazism went hand in hand:

we are no theologians, no representatives of the teaching profes-
sion in this sense, put forth no theology. But we claim one thing
for ourselves: that we place the great fundamental idea of Christianity in the centre of our ideology [*Ideenwelt*] – the hero and
sufferer, Christ himself, stands in the centre.[60]

Schemm also dealt with the issue of the sanctification of racial
science, which many political religion theorists consider central. In
doing so, however, Schemm insisted that racialism was consistent with
– indeed stemmed from – a Christian attitude. As he told a meeting of
Protestant pastors:

We want to preserve, not subvert, what God has created, just as
the oak tree and the fir tree retain their difference in a forest. –
Why do the trees in the forest not interbreed? – Why is there not
only one type of tree [*Einheitsbaum*]? Why should our concept
of race suddenly turn into the Marxist concept of a single type of
human? We are accused of wanting to deify the idea of race. But
since race is willed by God, we want nothing else but to keep the
race pure, in order to fulfil God's law.[61]

Political religion theorists argue that the Nazis' 'theology of race' was
religious but anti-Christian; however, the Nazis themselves claimed
that it was Christian. Again, these were public pronouncements, and
as such might be called into question. But in private, Schemm retracted
none of his professions. In party correspondence regarding the sectarian Protestant League (*Evangelischer Bund*), a leading voice of politicised Protestantism seeking active political cooperation with the
Nazis, Schemm stated: 'The Protestant League stands very close to the
NSDAP. It is consciously German and, through moral religious
energy, wants to contribute to the building up of the German
people'.[62]

The racial dimension to Schemm's religion, while apparently so at
odds with the message of Christianity, had in fact a rather impressive
theological lineage. Within Germany, a generation of Protestant theologians had been erecting a theology of *Schöpfungsglaube*, which sanc-
tified the *Volk* as an order of God's creation. These were not marginal
eccentrics, or sycophants aping contemporary political trends, but
some of the most respected Christian thinkers of the day. Their theology carried with it a message of race separation and superiority notice-
able for its parallels with the efforts of contemporary American and

South African theologians to erect similar theologies of race.[63] The sanctification of race qualifies Nazism not as a political religion, but as a religious politics.

We cannot here give a comprehensive overview of the religious views of all Nazis.[64] But what is clear is that, by their own account, most Nazis did not believe their movement was a political religion. Actual efforts at making Nazism a political religion were notable for their singular failure. Other Nazis not only provide evidence of the ridicule with which paganism was received, but also demonstrate how a Christian world view could be retained. Religious qualities to Nazism were certainly apparent, but there is much evidence to suggest that these qualities added up to a religious politics. Such a suggestion admittedly contravenes much of our inherited thinking about the movement and its ethos. The totalising quality of Nazism, its attempt to nestle itself into every aspect of the individual as well as the collective, certainly could argue for its 'totalitarian' nature, but hardly qualifies it as a religion. Unless, of course, we suggest that all totalitarian regimes are political religions – in which case this particular analytical device loses its ability to account for differences between systems that not only opposed liberal democracy, but also opposed each other. If the bloodiest war in Russian – and world – history is any indication, then content should take precedence over form in the investigation of the religious dimension of Nazism.

NOTES

1. Some works sponsored by this new institute include Achim Siegel (ed), *Totalitarismustheorien nach dem Ende des Kommunismus* (Köln: Böhlau, 1998); and Klaus-Dieter Müller, Konstantin Nikischkin and Günther Wagenlehner (eds.), *Die Tragödie der Gefangenschaft in Deutschland und in der Sowjetunion 1941–1956* (Köln: Böhlau, 1998). Of course, any attempt at revival or reintroduction also brings with it a good amount of change. We do not see in the Institut a two-dimensional return to the *status quo ante* in totalitarianism scholarship circa 1950s–1960s, but rather an attempt to update it while retaining basic fundaments from its Cold War heydays.
2. See, for instance, Emilio Gentile, *The Sacralization of Politics in Fascist Italy* (Cambridge, MA: Harvard University Press, 1996); and Mabel Berezin, *Making the Fascist Self: The Political Culture of Interwar Italy* (Ithaca, NY: Cornell University Press, 1997).
3. Cf. Michael Ley and Julius Schoeps (eds.), *Der Nationalsozialismus als politische Religion* (Bodenheim: Philo, 1997); and Hermann Lübbe, *Heilserwartung und Terror: Politische Religionen des 20. Jahrhunderts* (Düsseldorf: Patmos, 1995).
4. See the excellent article by Ian Kershaw, 'Totalitarianism Revisited: Nazism and Stalinism in Comparative Perspective', *Tel Aviver Jahrbuch für deutsche Geschichte* 23 (1994).
5. Carl Jung, *The Collected Works of C.G. Jung* (Princeton, NJ: Princeton University Press, 1970), Vol.10, p.281.

6. Steven Aschheim, 'Hannah Arendt and Karl Jaspers: Friendship, Catastrophe and the Possibilities of German–Jewish Dialogue', in idem, *Culture and Catastrophe: Germans and Jewish Confrontations with National Socialism and Other Crises* (New York: New York University Press, 1996), p.112.

7. Quoted in ibid., p.112.

8. George Mosse, *The Nationalisation of the Masses* (New York: Howard Fertig, 1975).

9. Fritz Stern, *The Politics of Cultural Despair: A Study in the Rise of the Germanic Ideology* (Berkeley, CA: University of California Press, 1974), p.xxv (original emphasis). While Stern's conventional intellectual approach came under attack from a later generation of social historians, the secularisation theory underpinning it went unchallenged.

10. Michael Burleigh, *The Third Reich: A New History* (New York: Hill and Wang, 2000), p.256.

11. Detlev Peukert, 'The Genesis of the "Final Solution" from the Spirit of Science', in Thomas Childers and Jane Caplan (eds.), *Reevaluating the Third Reich* (New York: Holmes and Maier, 1993), p.247.

12. One of the most prolific scholars of political religion is Hans Maier, who has recently edited two invaluable volumes on the topic: Hans Maier (ed.), *'Totalitarismus' und 'politische Religionen': Konzepte des Diktaturvergleichs*, 2 vols. (Paderborn: Schöningh, 1996–97). See as well the highly theoretical analysis of Claus-Ekkehard Bärsch, *Die politische Religion des Nationalsozialismus* (Munich: Wilhelm Fink, 1999), who pays closer attention to a Christian element but claims this is confined to a discursive appropriation of tropes like the Trinity. A good introduction, emphasising theory, is Philippe Burrin, 'Political Religion: the Relevance of a Concept', *History and Memory* 9 (1997), pp.321–49.

13. Adolf Hitler, *Mein Kampf*, trans. Ralph Manheim (Boston: Houghton Mifflin, 1962), p.475.

14. See, for instance, Thomas Childers, *The Nazi Voter: The Social Foundations of Fascism in Germany, 1919–1933* (Chapel Hill, NC: University of North Carolina Press, 1983); Jürgen Falter, *Hitlers Wähler* (Munich: C.H. Beck, 1991); and Richard Hamilton, *Who Voted for Hitler?* (Princeton, NJ: Princeton University Press, 1982). A more recent intervention, which emphasises material considerations to the exclusion of the cultural, is William Brustein, *The Logic of Evil: The Social Origins of the Nazi Party, 1925–1933* (New Haven, CT: Yale University Press, 1996).

15. Hartmut Lehmann, 'Hitlers evangelische Wähler', in idem, *Protestantische Weltsichten: Transformationen seit dem 17. Jahrhundert* (Göttingen: Vandenhoeck and Ruprecht, 1998), pp.130–52; Wolfram Pyta, *Dorfgemeinschaft und Parteipolitik, 1918–1933: Die Verschränkung von Milieu und Parteien in den protestantischen Landgebieten Deutschlands in der Weimarer Republik* (Düsseldorf: Droste, 1996); and Richard Steigmann-Gall, 'Apostasy or Religiosity? The Cultural Meanings of the Protestant Vote for Hitler', *Social History* 25 (2001), pp.267–84.

16. David Blackbourn, 'The Politics of Demagogy in Imperial Germany', reprinted in idem, *Populists and Patricians: Essays in Modern German History* (London: Unwin Hyman, 1987), p.218.

17. David Welch, *The Third Reich: Politics and Propaganda* (London: Routledge, 1993).

18. Path-breaking in this direction is Ian Kershaw, *Popular Opinion and Political Dissent in the Third Reich: Bavaria, 1933–1945* (Oxford: Oxford University Press, 1983).

19. Robert Gellately, *The Gestapo and German Society: Enforcing Racial Policy 1933–1945* (Oxford: Oxford University Press, 1990).

20. Robert Gellately, *Backing Hitler: Consent and Coercion in Nazi Germany* (Oxford: Oxford University Press, 2001).

21. Nathan Stoltzfus, *Resistance of the Heart: Intermarriage and the Rosenstrasse Protest in Nazi Germany* (New York: W.W. Norton, 1996).

22. Cf. Jeremy Noakes, 'The Oldenburg Crucifix Struggle of November 1936: A Case of Opposition in the Third Reich', in Peter Stachura (ed.), *The Shaping of the Nazi State* (London: Croom Helm, 1978).

23. Burleigh (note 10), pp.10–12.
24. For similar observations with regard to the *Kaiserreich*, see Peter Walkenhorst, 'Nationalismus als "politische Religion"? Zur religiösen Dimension nationalistischer Ideologie im Kaiserreich', in Olaf Blaschke and Frank-Michael Kuhlemann (eds.), *Religion in Kaiserreich: Milieus – Mentalitäten – Krisen* (Gütersloh: Chr. Kaiser, 1996), pp.503–29. Walkenhorst also provides a good summation of current work on the specifically Protestant-Christian content of 'secular' German nationalism.
25. Some of the strongest arguments for secularisation have come from committed believers. As Steve Bruce points out, this is quite relevant: 'Contrary to what one might expect from closet secularists, in their different ways [secularisation theorists] all have made it clear that they expect a secular world to be rather unpleasant ... [David] Martin has a clear conservative dislike for the hedonism and liberality of the modern secular world and he adds a further reason for finding the secular world uncongenial: he is an ordained Anglican ...', See Steve Bruce (ed.), *Religion and Modernisation: Sociologists and Historians Debate the Secularisation Thesis* (Oxford: Oxford University Press, 1992), p.2.
26. Berezin (note 2), pp.350–1 (emphasis added), p.60.
27. See Stathis Kalyvas, *The Rise of Christian Democracy in Europe* (Ithaca, NY: Cornell University Press, 1996), which attempts a theory of the relationship between religious cleavage, identity and party formation. Of course Christian Democracy, while originally inimical to parliamentary democracy, parted company with totalitarianism in its gradual acceptance of liberal political form.
28. Burleigh (note 10), pp.13–14. See as well Saul Friedländer, *Nazi Germany and the Jews* (New York: Harper Collins 1997).
29. Martin Broszat *The Hitler State* (London: Longman, 1981), p. 224.
30. Burrin (note 12), p.338.
31. Ibid., p.336. Burrin relies on Brigitte Nagel, *Die Welteislehre: Ihre Geschichte und ihre Rolle im 'Dritten Reich'* (Stuttgart: GNT, 1991). See as well Jost Hermand, *Old Dreams of a New Reich: Volkish Utopias and National Socialism* (Bloomington, IN: Indiana University Press, 1992), p.193, who maintains that Hitler subscribed to this teaching, which incidentally linked the 'flood of Genesis and the destruction of the Teutonic kingdom of Atlantis to "gravitational catastrophes" supposedly unleashed when the Earth "captured" a moon in its orbit'.
32. Alfred Rosenberg, *Der Mythus des 20. Jahrhunderts: Eine Wertung der seelisch-geistigen Gestaltenkämpfe unserer Zeit* (Munich: Hoheneichen, 1930), p.114.
33. Ibid., p.514.
34. Ibid., p.203.
35. Ibid., p.155–6.
36. Quoted in Robert Cecil, *The Myth of the Master Race: Alfred Rosenberg and Nazi Ideology* (London: Batsford, 1972), p.100.
37. Ibid., p.101.
38. Albert Speer, *Inside the Third Reich* (New York: Avon, 1970), p.96. For Goebbels's views on and relationship with Rosenberg, see ibid., pp.122–5; and Ralf Reuth, *Goebbels* (New York: Harcourt Brace, 1993), pp.201–5.
39. Adolf Hitler, *Hitler's Table Talk 1941–1944: His Private Conversations*, trans. Norman Cameron and R.H. Stevens, intro. Hugh Trevor-Roper (London: Weidenfeld and Nicholson, 1953), p.422 (11 April 1942). *Mythus* was published as a private work, never becoming an official guide to Nazi thinking like *Mein Kampf*. It never received the official stamp of the NSDAP, nor did the party's official publisher publish it. Hitler occasionally considered sanctioning the book, but never did. However, *Mythus* was occasionally banned lower down the ranks of the party, for instance by the Breslau branch of the National Socialist Teachers' League (NSLB): Bundesarchiv Berlin-Lichterfelde (hereafter BAB), NS 22/410 (8 September 1935: Breslau).
40. Speer (note 38), p.94.

41. Josef Ackermann, *Heinrich Himmler als Ideologe* (Göttingen: Musterschmidt, 1970), p.90.
42. Hermand (note 31), p.64.
43. Cecil (note 36), p.119.
44. Hitler (note 13), p.361.
45. Ibid., p.360.
46. Ibid., pp.361, 363. Given Hitler's utter contempt for Himmler's endless mysticism and pseudo-religious babble, not to mention Rosenberg's own rejection of it, it is extremely unlikely that Hitler approved of *Welteislehre*, as Hermand and Burrin both suggest.
47. Richard Steigmann-Gall, '*Furor Protestanticus*: Nazi Conceptions of Luther, 1919– 1933', *Kirchliche Zeitgeschichte* 12 (1999), pp.274–86.
48. BAB, NS 26/55 (27 October 1928: Passau).
49. Elke Fröhlich (ed.), *Die Tagebücher von Joseph Goebbels: Sämtliche Fragmente* (Munich: K.G. Saur, 1987), entry for 13 April 1937. *Thing* refers to the 'Thing' places, sites set up by Nordic paganists for their religious ceremonies.
50. Hans-Günther Seraphim (ed.), *Das politische Tagebuch Alfred Rosenbergs* (Göttingen: Musterschmidt, 1956), entry for 22 August 1939.
51. Alfred Krebs, *Tendenzen und Gestalten der NSDAP: Erinnerungen and die Frühzeit der Partei* (Stuttgart: Deutsche Verlags-Anstalt, 1959), p.166.
52. *Völkischer Beobachter*, 13 April 1922.
53. Eberhard Jäckel (ed.), *Hitler: Sämtliche Aufzeichnungen 1905–1924* (Stuttgart: Deutsche Verlags-Anstalt, 1980), p.635.
54. Henry Ashby Turner (ed.), *Hitler: Memoirs of a Confidant* (New Haven, CT: Yale University Press, 1985), pp.139–40.
55. Hitler (note 39), p.76 (21 October 1941).
56. *Institut für Zeitgeschichte*, MC 1 (interview of 15 July 1949).
57. Turner (note 54), pp.19–21, 210; Seraphim (note 50), entry for 19 January 1940.
58. Franz Kühnel, *Hans Schemm, Gauleiter und Kultusminister* (Nuremberg: Stadtarchiv Nürnberg, 1985), pp.134–5.
59. Gertrud Kahl-Furthmann (ed.), *Hans Schemm spricht: Seine Reden und sein Werk* (Bayreuth: Gauverl. Bayerische Ostmark, 1935), p.124.
60. Walter Künneth, Werner Wilm and Hans Schemm, *Was haben wir als evangelische Christen zum Rufe des Nationalsozialismus zu sagen?* (Dresden: 1931), p.19.
61. Ibid., pp.19–20.
62. BAB, NS 12/638 (6 March 1931: Berlin).
63. For an exploration of *Schöpfungsglaube* and its theological origins, see Robert Ericksen, *Theologians under Hitler* (New Haven, CT: Yale University Press, 1985); and Wolfgang Tilgner, *Volksnomostheologie und Schöpfungsglaube: Ein Beitrag zur Geschichte des Kirchenkampfes* (Göttingen: Vandenhoeck and Ruprecht, 1966). On race and religion in South Africa, see T. Dunbar Moodie, *The Rise of Afrikanerdom: Power, Apartheid, and the Afrikaner Civil Religion* (Berkeley, CA: University of California Press, 1975); and Leonard Thompson, *The Political Mythology of Apartheid* (New Haven, CT: Yale University Press, 1985). For the United States, see Michael Barkun, *Religion and the Racist Right: The Origins of the Christian Identity Movement* (Chapel Hill, NC: University of North Carolina Press, 1994); and Leo Ribuffo, *The Old Christian Right: The Protestant Far Right from the Great Depression to the Cold War* (Philadelphia: Temple University Press, 1983).
64. For a broad analysis of the religious views of the Nazi élite, see Richard Steigmann-Gall, *The Holy Reich: Nazi Conceptions of Christianity, 1919–1945* (Cambridge: Cambridge University Press, 2003).

The British Union of Fascists as a Totalitarian Movement and Political Religion

THOMAS LINEHAN

A nation biologically unhealthy will die, unless revified ...

E.D. Randall

This article will consider the concepts of totalitarianism and political religion in the context of inter-war Britain's premier fascist movement, the British Union of Fascists (BUF).[1] It will begin by looking at the classic model of totalitarianism and suggest that it had weaknesses which constrained its heuristic and empirical value for studying important aspects of fascist reality and experience. Nevertheless, despite these drawbacks the concept of totalitarianism retains some validity as a means of probing important aspects of fascism, not least in terms of fascism's utopian (dystopian) vision of life and its invasive attempt to penetrate the realm of total experience and being.

It is a self-evident truth that knowledge, rather than being transparent or 'immediate', has irreducibly representational and discursive aspects. All knowledge of the past has to be filtered through an articulated system of concepts and there can be no meaningful, direct encounter with the primary sources unless mediated through a conceptual framework.[2] It follows that knowledge of the fascist past can only be inferred by recourse to conceptual schema. One conceptual model that has enjoyed wide circulation in the post-war decades among historians and social scientists, seeking to recover the historical reality of fascism, has been that of 'totalitarianism'. The term has undergone a number of permutations since it was first uttered in 1925 by Mussolini to describe the structural characteristics and ideological aims of his new fascist state.[3] In scholarship, the most thorough definitions began to appear during the 1950s, while the most systematic, and the one that has served as something of a template for many scholars who have drawn on the totalitarian concept since then, was that promoted by Carl J. Friedrich and Zbigniew K. Brzezinski in 1956.[4] Essential characteristics of totalitarianism, according to Friedrich and Brzezinski, are an elaborate and officially prescribed ideology, a monolithic and hierarchical one-party arrangement led by a single individual, a bureaucratically centralised and planned economy, and a near monopoly of military power. Other features are total control of mass communication and reliance on coercion and terror, either through the party or the secret police.

There were some strengths in this early classical definition of the concept. For example, it points out the strong modernist impulse driving fascism through highlighting the *technological* dimension of coercion and control. Another strength, particularly in its stress on the terroristic aspects of totalitarian states, was that in the classical rendering of the concept, the term 'totalitarianism' became densely overwritten with negative signification and meaning. As a result, it conjured up the appropriately nightmarish Kafkaesque and Orwellian imagery that serves as a constant reminder to the present of the dangers to human freedom and individual rights from particular types of political experimentation and forms of political organisation. There were deficiencies in the classical paradigm, however, which constrained its heuristic and empirical value for studying crucial features of fascism. First, it tended to address the circumstances of regime fascisms and had limited application to the study of fascism in its movement phase. At times, too, the model's methodology was descriptive rather than analytical, tending to preoccupy itself with classification and description of the external identities and features of different totalitarian systems.[5] There was a sense, also, that with the classical paradigm one was inhaling the rarefied air of pure abstraction, and as such, the approach tended towards the ahistorical. In this vein, some scholars have concluded that the model failed to fit the historical circumstances of Mussolini's self-styled 'totalitarian' state, nor even those of Nazi Germany, the former regime in particular conforming to a more 'semi-pluralist institutional system' rather than a full-blown totalitarian dictatorship.[6]

Additionally, the classical account was at times over eager in assuming a convergence of perspective, method and goals between fascism and communism, a charge that has been frequently levelled by its detractors, with some justification. According to one assessment, classical totalitarian theory, and subsequent interpretations influenced by it, 'assume that similarities in the exercise of power in communist and fascist states are more characteristic of their essential nature than far more crucial differences in socio-economic structure and ideological goals'.[7] Some of its critics viewed the theory as a sub-text of the Cold War and detected an effort to smear post-war communism with the stain of fascism. In its attempts to couple communism with fascism, in its efforts to compile a checklist of doctrinal and structural commonalities thought to exist between them, the classical model of totalitarianism has been placed within the parameters of a liberal outlook and historiography that is itself acutely ideological.[8]

The *political* side of fascism was also over-determined in the classical definition, particularly in its stress on political power when attempting to specify the means by which fascism exercised control over its subjects. This latter point highlights a further problem with the traditional paradigm. Totalitarian control was almost exclusively defined in terms of external coercion, implying that a mass manipulation method of control was being deployed. Rather, as we will see below, although external political coercion was obviously a feature, the exercise of fascist rule operated on other planes and was subtler than was recognised in traditional totalitarian theory.

The totalitarian concept, despite the weaknesses of the old model – the question of its application to communism apart, which is not the subject of this study – if applied less schematically, remains useful as a means of exploring vital aspects of the fascist ideological and political project, as well as the fascist experience. As Michael

Burleigh has written recently *apropos* Nazism and totalitarianism, 'the "total" part captures most strikingly the insatiable, invasive character of this form of politics'.[9] If we turn to the BUF, the 'total' part also captures, most tellingly, crucial aspects of its 'form of politics'.

The BUF held a totalising perspective on reality, which stemmed from its organic view of life and culture. The Mosleyites believed that civilisations, nations and cultures were biological organisms with their own evolutionary life cycles, like other life forms in nature. To the BUF, a melancholy prognosis that owed much to the philosophy of Oswald Spengler, Britain was nearing the end of its evolutionary life cycle of creative development. The biological organisms of nation and culture were apparently exhibiting signs of acute 'physical' enfeeblement, ill-health and degeneracy, manifested in a variety of decadent and morbid features in national and cultural life. According to the BUF, the prevailing political and philosophical orthodoxies of the day – philosohical Liberalism, Bolshevism, Rationalism and Positivism in the main – spawned the decadent and morbid, as did an assortment of contemporary cultural doctrines and forms, particularly intellectual modernism in the arts. In relation to the latter, the following response to artistic modernism by Edwin C. Cornforth was typical. 'The squalid staleness of "modern" art, a product of the spiritual indigence of Liberal-Democratic thought, amounts to a disease', he wrote in the BUF press in 1934. In modern music, for example, unlike the music of Schubert, which 'expressed moonlight and romance', and the 'great passion' to be found in Beethoven's work, the 'grovelling materialism of Liberal-Democratic culture has deprived most modern composers of the inspiration necessary to emulate the achievements of the past'.[10] Similarly, Cornforth thought the buildings of modernist architecture, the artistic design of which did not go beyond an elementary sense of balance and proportion, 'destitute of character and atmosphere' and representative of 'the ugly bareness of liberal culture'.[11]

Repudiating Spengler's fatalism, the BUF was convinced that the physical laws of nature could be defied; death could be cheated and virile evolution could continue under fascist aegis and direction. The BUF's totalitarian enterprise thus represented a 'defiance of impending fate', a renunciation of the 'death in life' of political and cultural decadence, and an aspiration setting itself against the seemingly iron law of biological determinism. A new cycle of organic development would begin once the corporate organisation of national life had been established, a *total integration* of economic, social, political and cultural activity that would bring a *totality of purpose* to national life. A leading BUF ideologue, E.D. Randall, explained this corporate purpose: 'Biologically, Fascism is right to begin with, believing that the secret of a nation's true greatness is the harmony of its organic life, discarding the selfish futilities of individualism for the sublime entity of the Corporate nation'.[12] It was believed that the corporate integration of life would rescue the nation from the supposed blight of 'decadence' and rekindle a national 'life force'. The 'life force' was imagined as an enigmatic Bergsonian or Shavian inner source of vital and irrational energy, a 'vital flame', which the fascists believed was the wellspring of the regenerative urge that would expedite the nation's transition to a higher state of evolution.

In a related sense, the BUF's totalitarian project also represented a revolt against evolutionary and biological *time*. This was not an eschatological project. Unlike the Marxist eschatological vision of politics and the world, which embraced the belief in an end to (pre-) History, the BUF's conception of biological and historical time, following Spengler, was cyclical. This entailed not closure, nor the immanence of the final goal, but a ceaseless struggle in nature, life, culture and history for survival and domination.

British fascism, then, would act as the midwife in bringing to birth a new organic form, one fully integrated and 'harmonious', an organic model which accords with Roger Griffin's conception of fascism as a form of 'palingenetic ultra-nationalism', with its stress on the fascist obsession with decadence and the myth of rebirth.[13] That this corporate and 'evolutionary' goal comprised an unambiguously totalitarian project was recognised by the BUF Leader, Oswald Mosley, almost at the inception of his movement, when he stated in 1933 that 'without Fascism the achievement of the totalitarian and Corporate State is impossible'.[14] The BUF liked to visualise its evolutionary and totalitarian mission through metaphor. Fascism 'is the floodgate through which the evolution of man is pouring', stated a BUF writer, 'massing hourly, flinging its freshets into the streams, and down the rivers to the ocean of a Fascist creation'.[15]

The BUF's totalitarian project operated on other registers. Participation in the Mosley mission would amount to a 'total' way of life and self-referential world for fascist recruits, an all-consuming enterprise that extended beyond conventional notions of political engagement. The social and cultural became important sites of ideological manipulation and integration, which would aid the process of binding BUF initiates into a community of believers and activists. In the cultural field, members would receive regular guidance on matters of aesthetic taste and consumption from the BUF press.[16] BUF members were vigorously engaged in other fields, too. They joined fascist football teams and fascist rowing teams, where they would acquire healthy physiques, learn the lesson of group cohesion behind leadership elements, and engage in virile athleticism – all of which received the seal of approval from fascist ideologues. In relation to the latter, Cuthbert Reavely of the BUF could write that: 'the fresh air of athleticism enables the spiritual flame to burn more brightly'.[17] Members also participated in inter-branch boxing bouts, attended 'keep fit' tuition classes run by the branch, and went cycling and hiking with their fascist comrades along England's country lanes.

This lively social and cultural existence was an index of the 'totalising' experience of membership and the fascist life. Like their generic fascist counterparts in other countries, the BUF aimed at creating conditions of 'organic wholeness', or organic totality, at the level of the individual and the group. Fascism, it was claimed, would transcend forms of alienation, atomisation, fragmentation and discord thrown up by 'mass society' and liberal capitalist modernity, and restore a state of harmony to the individual. This would be accomplished, in one sense, by inviting individuals to dissolve their individual identity into the collective whole of the Mosley movement, and experience the psychic sensation of what BUF official Robert Gordon-Canning called the 'sublime spirit of mystic comradeship'.[18] This fusing of part and whole had an insidiously seductive aesthetic dimension. The voluntary dissolution of self into the mass experience of the fascist drama is characterised by generating sublime feelings of aesthetic harmony and wholeness in the individual. Personal feelings of alienation dissolve into what Susan Sontag called 'ecstatic feelings of community', a state where abdication of individual autonomy and personal freedom takes the form of pageantry and theatre, and submissiveness and subjugation to authority is rhetorically cast by fascist propaganda as communal service for the national good.[19] This fascist 'aesthetic' paralleled the ornamental totality of the 'Mass Ornament', a phenomenon observed by Siegfried Kracauer in relation to modern forms of entertainment, which seemed to replicate the increasingly Taylorised process of modern work.[20] In the Mass Ornament, individuals merge into ornamental arrangements wherein their individual identities disappear as they become absorbed into the depersonalised and geometrical formations of the ornament. As Kracauer famously put it in his comment on the 'indissoluble girl clusters' of the ornamental Tiller Girls: 'The hands in the factory correspond to the legs of the Tiller Girls'.[21] In the Mass Ornament, with its pleasurable illusion of aesthetic harmony and the seamless integration of individuals into a totality, we can, following Kracauer in relation to the Nazi state aesthetic, observe some key ingredients of the fascist aesthetic.[22]

In its craving to forge totalities and view individuals as solely elements of the whole – as in the Mass Ornament, a process that was to be acted out on the grand stage of state and nation as well as in the ranks of the fascist party – fascism reduced people to objects. Fascist writers would frequently conceal this repressive act of dissolution behind pious and grandiloquent language, or flights of incredible romantic fantasy. Rather than accurately depicting individuals as submissive subjects succumbing to authoritarian control, they would instead be turned into aspects of romantic nature visualised through metaphor. 'As the raindrops fall upon a hillside, collect and form a rivulet and many rivulets join to make a river', fantasised the BUF's Robert Gordon-Canning:

> and several rivers join into one great river to sweep onward through and over all barriers until it arrives at its destination and merges into the ocean, so the individual member of the British Union coalesces and unifies himself in the great fundamental political-social element of National Socialism, his individual journey completed, but his individual force still active and more than ever intensified and magnificent within the ranks of the British Union.[23]

The Mosleyites spoke of restoring the 'whole man' in another sense. They proclaimed that they would eliminate the artificial division between mind and body, a state of being which supposedly characterised the human condition in the era of liberal modernity. By privileging the realm of vitalistic intuition and the irrational, fascism, they stated, would eradicate divisions between Cartesian rationalism and subjectivity, logical calculation and spontaneity, and more generally, intellect and emotion. Attacks on the 'anaemic intellectualism' of the age were also rampant in the BUF press. Deriding the 'cultured intellectuals' with their 'soft lily-white hands' and 'scented bodies', a Mosleyite charged that there 'seems to be no escape from the monster of perverted thought and insipid affection that saps vitality and good sense and kills the instinctive manful appreciation of life'.[24] Fascism, of course, elided traditional boundaries and embraced paradox, between that of traditionalism and modernity, pessimism and optimism, past and present, demagogic populism and élitism, the individual and the collective, part and whole, aesthetics and politics and, so too, between rational mind and inner emotion.[25]

As we have seen in the examples above, the BUF's integralist, totalitarian mission was frequently expressed through metaphor. A particular favourite was the body metaphor. In the new fascist corporate order, declared Mosley in 1939, 'a nation emerges organised in the divine parallel of the human body as the name implies. Every organ plays a part in relation to the whole and in harmony with the whole'.[26] It was the image of the youthful, healthy body that was usually favoured, which communicated the preferred image of national life as a healthy athlete tirelessly keeping at bay the forces of biological deterioration. The repressive, and potentially murderous, aspect of fascism's organic and totalitarian project becomes all too apparent through the imagery of the body, for, as Claude Lefort has pointed out, the integrity of the totalitarian 'body' can only be assured through constant vigilance against parasitical elements and expulsion of its waste matter.[27] As Jorian Jenks, a romantic 'blood and soil' agrarian fascist – the BUF's equivalent of Walther Darré – observed, it 'is essential to model national life upon the natural lines of human physiology … [and] if any organ or member behaves at variance with the rest of the body, then the system is clearly disordered and abnormal'.[28] The message concerning the obligation of compliance behind Jenks's musings on the BUF's totalitarian project and the body, and his equating internal disturbance and dissidents with bodily abnormalities is not too difficult to discern. No wonder, then, that A.K. Chesterton, a member of Mosley's high command, striking up another graphic set of biological metaphors, could equate the forces of so-called 'decadence' with invading armies of typhus germs, or a disease akin to a bubonic plague.[29]

Robert Gordon-Canning preferred to draw on a variation on the image of the 'gardening state' when thinking about threats to the fascist community, or body politic, and the necessity of excising them. The 'gardening state' image, predicated on the notion of the beautiful garden and the need to uproot pestilential 'weeds' disfiguring it, featured with some frequency in political discourses seeking to articulate planned, statist visions of better, 'purer' societies following the carnage and destruction wrought by the Great War. The BUF warrior must be possessed of a 'militant urge to annihilate evil causes', declared Gordon-Canning, adding further that 'evil, like weeds, if tolerated, will crush out good, as once green pastures succumb to the thistle'.[30] In contrast to the imagery of pestilential weeds, the 'evil causes' that were imagined to blight national life, and the BUF's mission to bring forth 'the renewal of national life', brought to Jorian Jenks's mind 'the bursting of the bud and the uprush of the young leaf-blades' of glorious spring.[31]

Moreover, the BUF's acts of cultivation, biological engineering and political prophylaxis would be accomplished with the aid of modern science. The Faustian idea of creation-destruction lies close to the heart of the totalitarian grand narrative of BUF leader Oswald Mosley. He was possessed of the Faustian aspiration toward domination of the environment, driven as he was by the belief in technology's potential to subdue the world of nature, creating a world 'reborn through science'. This Faustian association points up a key aspect of the BUF's palingenetic and totalitarian aspirations, a generic trait it shared with its sister fascist parties on mainland Europe between the two world wars, that is its revolutionary, anthropological experiment to bring to 'birth' a new biological and cultural type.[32] Like the mythical figure of Faust, the new 'Blackshirt man' of the BUF would transform himself into a person of a new kind, a 'will-to-achievement' type restlessly asserting himself and in communion with his creative nature, which was to be found, somewhat cryptically, as we have seen above, in the realm of inner sensory emotion. Indeed, it was through this tireless, endless self-expansion that this new biological and cultural type would define himself and become himself.

The BUF's Faustian dimension highlights a problem with some versions of the totalitarian model, which claim that fascist and Nazi totalitarianism sought to impose closure on the dynamic openness of modern life and its ever-present threat to dissolve traditional forms. The image of the Faustian 'Blackshirt man', and indeed fascism's preferred image of the nation as a healthy athlete engaged in restless activity to hold the forces of biological deterioration in check, both suggest that there was an alternative dynamic at work in the BUF's totalitarian project. This was a dynamic that favoured relentless, open-ended revolutionary expansion, a creative-destructive impulse pre-figured in the tragedy of Goethe's *Faust*. If we consider our earlier discussion, it was the activism of ceaseless self-expansion and aggressive fascist revolutionary engagement that would assist the 'Blackshirt man' in his quest to achieve the 'aesthetic experience of wholeness' and arrive at the desired state of organic completion. In terms of the BUF's revolt against linear time also – cyclical rather than eschatological, reflecting Spengler – it entailed a ceaseless struggle in life, politics and culture for survival and domination. Passive disengagement from life and politics was simply not an option. One suspects that Mosley had a more open-ended vision in his thoughts, rather than passive closure, when he remarked in 1939 that modern science will enable man to 'soar beyond the restraint of time and circumstance'.[33]

To confine one's understanding of the BUF's totalitarian project to this belief in the Promethean power of science, however, would be to know it one-dimensionally and partially. We have already looked at some of the ingredients making up this project: the BUF's organic and corporate revolt against the destiny of evolutionary and biological time; the complex dialectic of pleasure and submissiveness that comprised the quest for 'organic wholeness'; and the Mosleyite suspicion of Cartesian rationalism and the related notion of the primacy of mind over more abstract metaphysical sources of knowing. To focus just on the allure of scientific panaceas for Mosley, then, would be to misunderstand profoundly the BUF and the elements constituting its revolt. There is also another ingredient to consider, another dialectic in play, which involved a further resolution of seeming paradoxes and an eliding of traditional boundaries. This was the dialectic of science and faith, because the scientific was infused with the spiritual, as indeed were all secular aspects of the BUF's project. The BUF's revolutionary strivings had their basis in a creative fusion of science and faith, of the secular and the sacred, the material and the spiritual. Almost at the point of the BUF's formation, in 1933, Mosley announced that 'Fascism comes to politics with the force of a new religion'.[34] In the years that followed, religious language and symbolism were always present in the BUF's engagement with British politics and life. In this sense, the BUF's fascism can also be understood as a form of 'political religion', and indeed, as Emilio Gentile has shown, the sacralisation of politics was an essential element of the fascist totalitarian experiment.[35]

Fascist nationalism, declared the Mosleyite James Drennan, 'is a sacred passion – a mass communion – which symbolises the devoted sense of organic being within the nation'.[36] 'The creed we serve', wrote

E.D. Randall in 1934, 'teaches us that struggle is ennobling and that its action on the soul of man imparts a sacramental strength'.[37] To take another of many such examples, Jorian Jenks believed that 'Fascism mobilises and gives expression to those spiritual qualities of service and sacrifice which should be the basis of all religion', and saw in the fascist spirit 'the fiery ardour of a religious revival'.[38] Robert Gordon-Canning, too, equated 'the basic principles of religion' – service and love according to him – from 'which there was no material and selfish reward but only an inward light of infinite radiance', with the 'militant and mystic forces' animating the BUF's national socialism.[39] Not content with drawing on such sanctimoniously nebulous rhetoric, Gordon-Canning proclaimed that fascism recalled the warrior spirit of the Christian knights during the Crusades, and that the fascist life 'should be that of the perfect knight', epitomised by Sir Philip Sidney, 'of Christian chivalry'.[40]

Alexander Raven-Thomson, another senior BUF figure, struck the same pious note, believing that the modern age had discovered in fascism a new faith which shared many of the characteristics of religious belief. The fascist outlook, to Raven-Thomson, found a natural harmony with the religious instinct in man. 'The moral code which has been laid down by religion is also the basis of fascist ethics', he stated.[41] According to him, fascism, like Christianity, 'recalls mankind to spiritual faith'.[42] Additionally, and as has been perceptively observed by Leslie Susser, the BUF spin on British history recalled the archetypal Christian myth of grace, fall and redemption; the Elizabethan 'age of achievement' so revered by the Mosleyites cast as Eden, the ensuing age of Whig parliamentary liberal democracy and *laissez-faire* materialism as Sin, and the coming Fascist Corporate State as the new Jerusalem.[43] We can observe other characteristics of a political religion in Mosley's movement. As with organised religion, the BUF provided its followers with certainty in place of doubt, the promise of salvation rather than the fall into perdition or apocalyptic catastrophe, as well as grand explanation and meaning to counter the confusion of contemporary life and modernity. In Oswald Mosley, the new Mosleyite political religion had its charismatic founder, whom the BUF propaganda machine deified as a cult object of veneration and dedication for the fascist faithful. Similarly, Mosley's apocalyptic and palingenetic diagnosis of ailing, late-imperial Britain, *The Greater Britain* (1932), functioned as a sacred text and source of inspiration for fascist devotees, while its intrinsic message was a call to faith around a supposedly redemptive, regenerative mission to bring into being the new fascist 'Jerusalem'.[44]

The BUF also created its own liturgy. Mosley's Blackshirts participated in solemn collective rituals, some of which functioned to confirm party unity, while others served to transmit myths that the party held dear, such as that of the heroic Great War sacrifice and accompanying spirit of the war-dead generation. The latter was one of the most revered myths of Mosley's movement, which aimed to preserve in its political discourse and in its rituals and symbolism the spirit of terrible sacrifice and heroism generated by the trench experience. Each Armistice Day on 11 November, while the BUF remained in existence, its activists staged the ritual of an anniversary march to honour the fallen of the war generation. The BUF's Hackney Branch in East London, for example, a locality of BUF strength, engaged in an annual Armistice Day pilgrimage to the site of the local War Memorial to pay homage to the war dead of the district. On Armistice Day 1934, an ordered assembly of Hackney Blackshirts, with their ex-servicemen members in the van, conducted a simple solemn ceremony at the War Memorial, replete with bemedalled uniforms and paramilitary fascist salutes.[45] On Armistice Day 1935 the ritual was re-enacted, with some 300 local BUF members and supporters marching to St Luke's Church in Hackney, whereupon a Hackney Blackshirt war veteran, a Military Medalist, laid a wreath at the church's War Memorial.[46] These commemorative processions to sites of remembrance and mourning were deliberately solemn affairs that seemed to evoke a religious sense of feeling in those who participated. Such cherished Mosleyite myths as the transcendent spirit of the war-dead generation also enabled the BUF's activists to unify around the potent national symbol of the Great War sacrifice that the party leadership had astutely appropriated.

There were other Mosleyite myths, drawn from the British past and imperial experience, which similarly aimed to evoke an almost religious sense of feeling in BUF members, and around which were created other collective rituals. 'Our colonies', declared the BUF writer E.D. Hart, 'are indeed a sacred trust'.[47] The dominant grand narrative of a glorious and beneficent English national past and imperial heritage, reinforced by a glut of contemporary jingoistic adventure novels and the carefully choreographed pageantry of theatrical 'events' associated with empire occasions, a narrative absorbed uncritically by many beyond the ranks of fascism, supplied Mosleyite propagandists with an abundant stock of heroes and heroic tales of derring-do with which to excite the membership. The BUF had its own pantheon of heroes, drawn from this narrative, that included Walter Raleigh, Humphrey Gilbert, Cecil Rhodes, Warren Hastings, Clive of India, Horatio Nelson and T.E. Lawrence.[48] Of course, this embrace of British imperial 'heroes' spoke to a key tenet of the Mosleyites' ideology, that is, their élitist belief in the stoic, decisive, 'will-to-achievement' leader-figure prepared to dare all for nation, race and empire. Falasca-Zamponi has suggested that fascist myths are narratives or texts, serving to enhance its self-identity and manufacture its own preferred history of itself.[49] In a similar way, fascist histories, including the BUF's reverential eulogies to British imperial heroes, were mythic inventions. The BUF's histories were fictionalised texts imposed on the flux of history, for the purpose of aligning the recipient of the message with its unashamedly celebratory, triumphalist and extremely partial version of the national past.

Encouragement of the collective ritual of the solemn, studied rendering of the National Anthem at party gatherings by the BUF leadership, and other such overt displays of patriotism, served to transmit these myths of the British past and imperial experience to the party faithful, instilling in them love of country and pride in empire. The appropriation of other traditional patriotic rites and symbols by the BUF would serve the same purpose. Members were urged to celebrate Empire Day with due reverence and solemnity. The Union flag, the supreme symbol of British imperial authority, was in evidence at all official, and many informal BUF, events. Its presence alongside the fascist flag emblazoned with the *fasces*, the fascist totem of unity and authority, signified the supposed harmony between the nation's patriotic tradition and fascism. The joint presence of the Union Jack and the fascist flag, along with other fascist motifs, would transform one of the calendar's traditional rites of passage into a fascist ceremonial form. The August 1935 marriage of Patrick Owen-Burke, credited with founding the first of the BUF's East End branches, was a full-blooded fascist ceremonial, complete with a watching assembly of members in full fascist regalia, snapped-out fascist salutes, and a Blackshirt guard of honour holding aloft the fascist flag and Union Jack as the bride and groom left the church.[50] The transformation of this most traditional of Christian ceremonies into a fascist celebratory ritual was even more stark higher up the chain of the BUF's command. When Ian Hope Dundas, then BUF Chief of Staff, married in December 1933, Mosleyite personnel and symbols were everywhere in evidence.

Besides the usual paramilitary uniforms, fascist salutes and 'Fascist Guard of Honour', the BUF Leader was in attendance as the best man, senior BUF officers assisted as ushers, and the collar of the bride's dress was trimmed with golden *fasces*.[51] Even the custom of cutting the wedding cake was 'fascistised', with the fascist bride – herself the sister of a prominent BUF figure – cutting the cake with an axe, while the approving groom looked on holding the *fasces*.

That most sacred rite of passage in the Christian calendar, the funeral, also melded into fascist liturgy. In 1934, the premature death at the age of 40 of a west London fascist due to wounds sustained during the Great War was marked by the solemn ritual of the Fascist Funeral. While a squad of Blackshirts gave the full fascist salute over the grave, the daughter of the deceased laid a wreath of daffodils on the grave in the shape of the *fasces*.[52] Evoking the spirit of the war-dead generation, and as if challenging death itself, the message on the wreath read: 'He still marches in spirit with us, and urges us on to gain the Fascist state'.[53] In performing the rites of death in this way, the BUF conceived death as an affirmation of the immortality of stricken Blackshirts, who remained in communion with those fascists left behind.[54] Death was thus read as an affirmation of the power of life and rebirth.

Such rituals served the purpose of initiating BUF recruits into the strange 'total' world of British fascism, binding them into a community of believers. There were other collective rituals that performed the same function, such as the celebratory ritual of the mass march to commemorate the anniversary of the movement's formation. Of course, the most memorable of these specifically Mosleyite annual rites, designed to point up the BUF's foundation as an event of major political significance, was that of 4 October 1936 at Cable Street in London's East End, which was spectacularly thwarted by a massive anti-fascist counter-mobilisation.[55] The carefully choreographed pageantry of the BUF mass rally developed a recognisable ritual structure. In evidence at most large meetings was a liturgical structure: a sea of patriotic and fascist flags; a fascist processional; a rendering of patriotic and fascist community songs; the Leader's grand entrance amidst great fanfare; and then the 'sermon' read to the faithful, to complete the transformation of the gathering into a liturgical mass.[56]

The BUF also produced its own equivalent of clerical fascists, who sought to propagate the notion that fascism was compatible with Christian beliefs and that the spiritual interests of Britain's multitude of Christians would be best served if they aligned themselves with the BUF. One of the most outspoken clerical fascists, the Reverend H.E.B. Nye, tried to claim, in a piece written in early 1939, that fascism was the guarantor of the survival of traditional religion and Christian civilisation. In an analysis informed by Spengler's grand fantasies concerning the evolutionary life-cycles of cultures and civilisations, the fascist cleric argued that religion, or an Age of Faith, always underpinned the creative culture phase of a civilisation because it provided the indispensable ingredient of spiritual direction.[57] So it was, according to Reverend Nye, during the West's creative phase of culture, broadly spanning 18 centuries, which preceded the modern age of 'decadent' democracy. Religion was the 'foster mother of our Civilisation', he wrote, and all defenders of Western civilisation should have no hesitation in declaring their allegiance to Christ, and hostility to those forces that threatened religious faith. Not surprisingly, Reverend Nye was a bitter anti-communist, believing atheistic communism to be the 'Anti-Christ'; that in seeking the destruction of religion, it would bring about the death of civilisation itself. Nye's anti-communist rhetoric provides a window into his apocalyptic imagination. Communists were referred to as 'veritable beasts of prey', 'insane fanatics', 'vultures who scent the corpse of humanity from afar', 'the cancer that causes the death of every civilisation', while fascism is cast in heroic and mythic terms as 'the modern Saint George, and the killer of the Dragon of Communism'.[58]

This extreme, apocalyptic frame of mind, reinforced by a pessimistic Spenglerian perspective, would induce in Nye an ambivalent attitude towards the Church of England. On the one hand, the Church was viewed as an indispensable bulwark of traditional religious belief, and thus civilisation, while on the other, some of its prelates and lower clergy were accused of fellow-travelling with 'the potential destroyers of the Christian Church', the communist Left. In typically chilling language, Nye warned that in the 'Red Day of Wrath' the 'Red clerics' will 'expiate with their own blood their careless guardianship of the Faith delivered unto them to defend'.[59] This accusation would be a common refrain in BUF discourse on religion. Reverend Nye had earlier, in an article in the BUF press in August 1936, accused some priests of being 'notorious communists'.[60] In a similar vein, in a later piece, Nye attacked Victor Gollancz's Christian Book Club for its 'strong socialistic bias', its anti-fascist and anti-German stance, and its propensity 'for sowing the seeds of hatred under the sacred banner of

Christ'.[61] At issue here, to Nye's mind – an ironic disposition given his outspoken adherence to fascist political doctrine – was the belief that the Church of England, or at least many of its clergy, was abusing its high spiritual office by meddling in politics and the affairs of state. It is the fascist conception, pronounced the fascist Reverend, 'that the Church should concentrate on spiritual things', and the name 'Christian' should not be desecrated by prefixing it to any club or society 'whose self-avowed object is the perpetuation of hate and misunderstanding'.[62] Another BUF member, writing in 1936, was even more forthright. 'It is the Church's job to save souls through spiritual and not political means', and 'we do not expect the Church to interfere in politics', he asserted.[63] Another clerical fascist, the Reverend E.C. Opie, struck a similar note in the BUF press. Writing in 1936, he shamelessly condoned Nazi Germany's imprisonment of some members of the Lutheran and Roman Catholic Church on the grounds that by dabbling in politics – the domain of the state – and identifying with left-wing causes, they had themselves invited retribution by transgressing the supposedly inviolable laws of the new Germany.[64] Jorian Jenks took a similar line. In a clear warning to the established Church in England, he wrote that 'if men occupying responsible positions as Ministers of God deliberately take part in political controversies, they are likely to be regarded as camouflaged politicians and treated accordingly'.[65]

Clashes between the BUF and the established Church flared up in other areas as well, such as on birth control and eugenics. Like many fascist groups, the BUF's outlook on politics and life was partly informed by harsh, uncharitable Nietzschean ideas concerning power, virility and the 'superman', a disposition which inclined it towards favouring society's so-called healthy, stronger elements at the expense of the 'weak'. In *Fascism: 100 Questions*, issued in 1936, Oswald Mosley suggested that the so-called 'unfit' should be given the choice of voluntary sterilisation or segregation. Mosley would reiterate this eugenic position on other occasions, a stance that brought censure from the Catholic Church and its press organs, which was opposed to such thinking.[66] On other occasions, though, as in response to events arising from the Spanish Civil War, the BUF and the Catholic Church found common cause, with the former eager to act as the champion of the latter's interests and well-being. The Spanish conflagration, from July 1936, unleashed a wave of pent-up, often ideologically driven, anti-clerical sentiment and violence against Church property and personnel that appalled the BUF. Usually ignoring the Anarchist dimension to the anti-clerical violence, and leaping to the Catholic Church's defence, the BUF described Republican Spain as atheist 'Moscow's Spanish Church-burning branch'.[67] Left-leaning elements within the English Church also became the target of the BUF's ire regarding the Spanish events. A cartoon in the BUF press carried the message that behind the Christian Book Club were the 'Spanish Church burners' and 'bloodthirsty' Bolshevism.[68]

The alliance between fascism and Catholicism over the Spanish Civil War issue may have had as much to do with shared outlook as with expediency. Reference has been made to the reactionary moral agenda evident in fascism and Catholic socio-political theory, such as the emphasis on prescriptive regulations governing the organisation of sexual and family relations, and the advocacy of piety in social and private life.[69] A pro-fascist Catholic contributor to the *Westminster Cathedral Chronicle* in January 1937 wrote approvingly that, like Catholicism, fascism stood for the family as the prime unit in the social order.[70] Fascist and significant strands of Catholic political thinking both favoured the hierarchical and 'organic' organisation of society, according to the principles of the corporate state as a means supposedly to transcend class antagonisms. Both loathed and feared the communist 'Anti-Christ', too, of course. Fascist propagandists would also evoke the edicts of papal encyclicals and cited universal Catholic principles and Catholic philosophers as a justification for fascist political behaviour. In an article in the BUF press entitled 'Catholic Doubts and the Corporate State', which cited Catholic philosophy, the BUF's philosopher, Alexander Raven-Thomson, referred to the 'divine purpose' behind political life and the organic state's march towards some mysterious, spiritual goal. The order of the march, however, continued Raven-Thomson in the same mystical language, 'is never a mere end in itself, but always something much more vast, made up of all life's elements, and therefore instinctive with the full mystery of life'.[71] It should come as no surprise that the clerical fascist, Reverend H.E.B. Nye, favoured the revival of a strict Catholic faith in continental Europe as the best means of ensuring the stability of polity and nation.[72]

The Mosleyites' defence of established religion, in the form of the Roman Catholic Church during the Spanish conflict, however, was not enough to offset the more numerous points of tension between them and the established Church at home during the mid-to-late

1930s. Even the Anglican Church's longstanding association with the liberal state came in for attack. The Reverend Nye, for example, thought that the form of religious teaching and belief practised in the liberal state ran contrary to the purpose of authentic religion which, to his mind, should proclaim a single, authoritative and unchanging dogma and teach an unchanging, revealed truth, all of which would be disseminated by a duly authorised, unified and disciplined priest-hood.[73] The ultimate purpose of such definite teaching of an authoritative dogma by a unified clergy would be to promote unity within the state while instilling a respect for leadership, discipline and authority, all cherished fascist principles. Religious liberalism, on the other hand, or liberal churchmanship as he termed it, with the acceptance of the doctrine of private judgement at its core, led to modernist doubts, moral anarchy and ever-widening dissension within the nation.[74]

Although the BUF was forever claiming an affinity between fascist principles and Christian beliefs, it is important to recognise that the 'spiritualism' of Mosleyite fascism was of a different order to that of the established Church, or to traditionally organised religion. In terms of understanding it as a political religion, the BUF always engaged in an overwhelmingly 'this-worldly' enterprise that lacked a conventionally understood religious-transcendent quality. As ever, Robert Gordon-Canning expressed the essential aspects of the BUF approach. 'While the religious mystic believes in withdrawal from this world and a contemplation upon God', he explained, 'the National Socialist believes in an active participation in life; while the religious mystic believes in meditation as the path to God, the National Socialist believes in action with his fellow human beings as the true path to pursue towards the attainment of Paradise'.[75] Alongside its persistent sniping at the Church, as we have seen, and despite its claim that there was an essential affinity between fascism and Christianity, the BUF also spurned many of the key tenets of traditional Christian thought. Again, as mentioned, the Christian doctrine of egalitarianism and protection for the weak was repudiated in favour of the stark Nietzschean idea of exalting and encouraging the strong. 'The Christian ideal that all men are created equal', complained Major-General John Frederick Charles Fuller, just prior to his enrolment in the BUF, is the foundation of both democracy and socialism, which promote humanitarianism and social philanthropy. While humanitarianism was 'founded on the fallacy that all lives must be saved', continued the eugenicist Fuller, 'social philanthropy ruins the strong'.[76] Pursuing his eugenic rant, he chastised humanitarian democracy for its efforts to prevent the 'inefficient and worthless' from starving. Not surprisingly, Fuller was an advocate of enforced segregation and sterilisation for certain categories of the so-called unfit. Oswald Mosley's Faustian thinking on sin, positing as it did the notion that evil was sometimes necessary and should be released so as to attain good, also diverged from Christian doctrine.

This is not to say that there was not a mystic, transcendent element in the BUF's outlook and political philosophy. Rather, this could be located in the BUF's attempt to infuse its political mission with what it believed to be the spirit of past generations. BUF writers frequently summoned the spirit of their ancestors to animate their political venture. 'There is a song of England', wrote Edwin C. Cornforth in the party press in 1934, 'that wanders in the wind', and in it resided the 'British racial spirit' handed down over the centuries.[77] It was the goal of a fascist art, continued Cornforth, to impart this 'British racial spirit' to the 'jaded modern Englishman', so that he should 'feel, throbbing down the ages, the thrill that Drake and Raleigh and the great Elizabethans knew, and the spirit of high adventure will come to him to face the problems of the present age'.[78] These elemental sources were thought to transmit genuine power, for 'tapping the source of this exalted patriotism the Fascist Movement will inspire a new culture and a new way of life'.[79] 'Fascism in our will and spirit', wrote Oswald Mosley in a similar tone in 1933, 'bridges the gulf of ages. The romantic traditions of the past are linked to the scientific realities of the future'.[80] In this instance, the elemental spirit wandering down the ages was that of 'Merrie England', another of the BUF's cherished myths of the English past. 'Our minds travel back to the Christmases of "Merrie England" at the dawn of our nation's greatness', continued Mosley, 'then forward to the Christmases of the future, to a nation reborn, revitalised and clad in the glittering panoply of a period in which the will of man and the genius of modern science have triumphed over material environment'.[81] 'Fascists stand where stood the heroes of our past', continued Mosley.[82] Such sentiments recurred in BUF writing, as in Mosleyite rhetoric on the Great War. Our fathers 'died that we live', stated the Blackshirt Doreen Bell, 'and in living grasp the torch they flung to us'.[83] In the mystic reaches of the British fascist imagination, and in a variation on the theme of rebirth and regeneration, not only did past and present fuse, but also the spiritual and the corporeal, the dead and the living.

NOTES

1. The BUF was formed in October 1932 by a renegade Labour Party figure, Sir Oswald Mosley. At the height of its political success, in mid-1934, it accumulated a membership of 40,000. See Thomas Linehan, *British Fascism, 1918–1939: Parties, Ideology and Culture* (Manchester: Manchester University Press, 2000).
2. See Brian Fay, 'The Linguistic Turn and Beyond in Contemporary Theory of History', in Brian Fay, Philip Pomper and Richard T. Vann (eds.), *History and Theory: Contemporary Readings* (Oxford: Blackwell, 1998), pp.1–12.
3. See Stanley Payne, *A History of Fascism 1914–45* (London: UCL Press, 1995), pp.121–3.
4. Carl J. Friedrich and Zbigniew K. Brzezinski, *Totalitarian Dictatorship and Autocracy* (Cambridge, MA: Harvard University Press, 1956). See also Hannah Arendt, *The Origins of Totalitarianism*, 2nd edn. (London: Allen and Unwin, 1958).
5. Bernt Hagtvet and Reinhard Kühnl, 'Contemporary Approaches to Fascism: A Survey of Paradigms', in Stein Ugelvick Larsen, Bernt Hagtvet and Jan Petter Mykelbust (eds.), *Who Were the Fascists? The Social Roots of European Fascism* (Oslo: Universitetsforlaget, 1980), pp.26–51.
6. Payne (note 3), pp.121–2, 206. With regard to the Mussolini state, this is the conclusion of many of the contributors to David Forgacs (ed.), *Rethinking Italian Fascism: Capitalism, Populism and Culture* (London: Lawrence and Wishart, 1986).
7. Hagtvet and Kühnl, (note 5), p.35.
8. Forgacs (note 6), p.3. For a recent example of this critique, see Slavoj Ziek, *Did Somebody Say Totalitarianism? Five Interventions in the (Mis)Use of a Notion* (London: Verso, 2001).
9. Michael Burleigh, *The Third Reich: A New History* (London: Macmillan, 2000), p.14.
10. *Blackshirt*, 2 November 1934, p.8.
11. Ibid.
12. *Fascist Week*, 19–25 January 1934, p.4.
13. See Roger Griffin, *The Nature of Fascism* (London: Routledge, 1993), pp.32–6. See also Griffin's 'General Introduction' to his reader, Roger Griffin (ed.), *Fascism: Oxford Readers* (Oxford: Oxford University Press, 1995), pp.1–20.
14. Oswald Mosley, *Blackshirt Policy* (London: BUF Publications, 1933), p.74.
15. *Blackshirt*, 8 February 1935, p.6.
16. On culture, aesthetics and British fascism, see Julie V. Gottlieb and Thomas Linehan (eds.), *The Culture of Fascism: Visions of the Far Right in Britain* (London: I.B. Tauris, 2004).
17. *Blackshirt*, 30 August 1935, p.9.
18. Robert Gordon-Canning, *The Inward Strength of a National Socialist* (London: Greater Britain Publications, c.1938), p.3.
19. Susan Sontag, 'Fascinating Fascism', in Brandon Taylor and Wilfried van der Will (eds.), *The Nazification of Art: Art, Design, Music, Architecture and Film in the Third Reich* (Hampshire: Winchester Press, 1990), p.214. Sontag's essay first appeared in 1974 and was later reprinted in Susan Sontag, *Under the Sign of Saturn* (New York: Farrar, Straus and Giroux, 1980).
20. Siegfried Kracauer, *The Mass Ornament: Weimar Essays* (Cambridge, MA: Harvard University Press, 1995).
21. Ibid., p.79.
22. Siegfried Kracauer, *From Calgari to Hitler: A Psychological History of the German Film* (Princeton, NJ: Princeton University Press, 1947), p.302.
23. Gordon-Canning (note 18), p.4.
24. *Blackshirt*, 3 August 1934, p.6.
25. For an intelligent study of fascism's propensity to overcome boundaries, see Alice Kaplan, *Reproductions of Banality: Fascism, Literature, and French Intellectual Life* (Minneapolis: University of Minnesota Press, 1986).

26. Oswald Mosley, *Tomorrow We Live* (London: Greater Britain Publications, 1939), p.54.
27. Claude Lefort, *The Political Forms of Modern Society: Bureaucracy, Democracty, Totalitarianism* (Cambridge: Polity Press, 1986), p.287.
28. Jorian Jenks, *Spring Comes Again* (London: The Bookshelf, 1939), p.75.
29. *Fascist Quarterly* 11/1 (January 1936), pp.58–67.
30. Gordon-Canning (note 18), p.3.
31. Jenks (note 28), p.80.
32. Emilio Gentile, 'The Sacralisation of Politics: Definitions, Interpretations and Reflections on the Question of Secular Religion and Totalitarianism', *Totalitarian Movements and Political Religions* 1/1 (2000), p.18.
33. Mosley (note 26), p.79.
34. Mosley (note 14), p.7.
35. Gentile (note 32), p.19.
36. James Drennan, *BUF, Oswald Mosley and British Fascism* (London: John Murray, 1934), pp.218–19.
37. *Blackshirt*, 27 July 1934, p.6.
38. Jenks (note 28), pp.60, 58.
39. Gordon-Canning (note 18), p.2.
40. Ibid.
41. *Fascist Week*, 9–15 February 1934, p.4.
42. Ibid.
43. Leslie Susser, 'Fascist and Anti-Fascist Attitudes in Britain Between the Wars', unpublished D.Phil thesis, University of Oxford, 1988, p.213.
44. Oswald Mosley, *The Greater Britain* (London: Greater Britain Publications, 1932).
45. *Blackshirt*, 16 November 1934, p.10.
46. *Blackshirt*, 15 November 1935, p.8.
47. *Action*, 15 May 1937, pp.8–9.
48. For an example of the BUF's almost schoolboy infatuation with British imperial adventurers, see E.D. Hart, 'Men Who Built The British Empire', *Action*, 15 May 1937, pp.8–9.
49. Simonetta Falasca-Zamponi, *Fascist Spectacle: The Aesthetics of Power in Mussolini's Italy* (Berkeley, CA: University of California Press, 1997), p.2.
50. *Blackshirt*, 16 August 1935, p.6.
51. *Blackshirt*, 23–29 December 1933, p.2.
52. *Blackshirt*, 11–17 May 1934, p.3.
53. Ibid.
54. Emilio Gentile, *The Sacralization of Politics in Fascist Italy* (Cambridge, MA: Harvard University Press, 1996), pp.26–8.
55. See Tony Kushner and Nadia Valman (eds.), *Remembering Cable Street: Fascism and Anti-Fascism in British Society* (London: Vallentine Mitchell, 2000).
56. For a detailed discussion, see Michael Spurr, 'Living the Blackshirt Life: Culture, Community and the British Union of Fascists, 1932–1940', *Contemporary European History* 12/3 (2003), p.312.
57. Reverend H.E.B. Nye, 'Fascism Versus Democracy', in Erminio Turcotti (ed.), *Fascist Europe: Europa Fascista*, Vol.1 (Milan: National Institute of Fascist Culture of Pavia, 1939), pp.76–9. This collection of essays, written by some of the leading British and Italian Fascists, arose out of an Anglo-Italian Symposium held in Italy in around February 1939. The theme of the Symposium was 'Fascist Europe'.
58. Ibid.
59. Ibid., p.79.
60. *Action*, 20 August 1936, p.7.
61. *Action*, 9 April 1938, p.9.
62. Ibid.

63. *Blackshirt*, 4 July 1936, p.5.
64. *Action*, 2 April 1936, p.11.
65. Jenks (note 28), p.60.
66. Martin Durham, *Women and Fascism* (London: Routledge, 1998), pp.38–40.
67. *Blackshirt*, 19 September 1936, p.1.
68. *Action*, 9 April 1938, p.3.
69. See the essays in Richard J. Wolff and Jörg K. Hoensch (eds.), *Catholics, the State, and the European Radical Right, 1919–1945* (New York: Columbia University Press, 1987).
70. *Action*, 23 January 1937, p.3.
71. *Blackshirt*, 26 April 1935, p.2.
72. Nye (note 57), pp.53–7.
73. Ibid.
74. Ibid.
75. Gordon-Canning (note 18), p.2.
76. John Frederick Charles Fuller, *The Dragon's Teeth: A Study of War and Peace* (London: Constable, 1932), p.14–17. During his time with the BUF, Fuller was one of Mosley's senior lieutenants. For more on Fuller's eugenicist thinking, see Linehan (note 1), pp.28–9.
77. *Blackshirt*, 2 November 1934, p.8.
78. Ibid.
79. Ibid.
80. Mosley (note 14), p.76.
81. Ibid.
82. Ibid.
83. *Blackshirt*, 13 November 1937, p.1.

The Sacralised Politics of the Romanian Iron Guard

RADU IOANID

The main characteristic features of Romanian fascism are: national-ism, antisemitism and racism, the cult of the supreme leader and of its own élite, mysticism, the social diversion, and finally anti-communism. These features define the Romanian fascist movement and its political parties and determine both its originality as well as its resemblance to other fascist movements. Although the most powerful and best known, the Iron Guard was not the only Roma-nian fascist organisation. The League of National Christian Defence (LANC; later the National Christian Party, PNC) as well as other smaller organisations fit into this category too. For the sake of econ-omy of space we will refer in this analysis mostly to the Iron Guard, considered as the most powerful and representative Romanian fascist movement. The Romanian Orthodox Church was closely associated with totalitarian regimes, which controlled Romania from 1938 to 1989. During a short period of time (1938–46) the leadership of the

Romanian Orthodox Church switched allegiance from King Carol II to the Iron Guard, then to General Antonescu and finally to the communist regime. However, long before the Iron Guard entered government in September 1940, links between the Romanian Orthodox Church and the Legionary movement were strong at the grassroots level. The relationship between secular politics and established religion in the context of Romanian fascism is thus particularly intense and complex. What follows is an attempt to disentangle it, and to show that although Legionary mysticism took on an Orthodox shading, not a pagan one, as in the case of Nazism, it nevertheless manifests an attempt to sacralise politics rather than to politicise religion.

The Nationalism of the Iron Guard

Fascist nationalism finds its source in the most traditional and conservative currents that preceded it, but that never reached the degree of vulgarity, intolerance and aggressiveness peculiar to fascism. Fascism proves to be simplistic even as measured against those currents. Many pre-fascist ideologies aimed at human emancipation. By comparison, fascism represents a break with the ideologies preceding it, because even if it proclaims the need for equal opportunity, it supports the doctrine of political inequality. Consequently, the nationalistic side of fascist ideology is not at all accidental. Fascist nationalism has an ethnocentric character, whence its opinion that the ethnic group thought to be superior is the only source of truth, of wisdom, of all human virtues joined together. The fascist does not want the equality of one's nation with other nations, but rather the prosperity of one's own people at the expense of the others, usually achieved via openly aggressive means:

> Fascism or the fascist state is not the first bourgeois form of power that has led to wars of conquest, to the detriment of other peoples. However, it is the first bourgeois form of power in which there is an open predominance of aggressive goals with regard to other peoples that have a similar standard of economic life and culture, and that live in identical social systems.[1]

In the eyes of the Romanian fascists, the specific national ethos of Romania was identified with everything that was least inclined to evolve. That is why, in their thinking, while respecting tradition,

currents such as the 1848 Revolution, which had an important moder-
nising role in recent Romanian history, were denuded of all value.
Furthermore, Romanian fascists envisaged Orthodox religion as an
element of first importance in defining and affirming Romanian spirituality. Romanian fascists were regressive and, to a very large extent,
given to archaic visions. They separated ethnicity from social reality
and thus denied its historical character. In their conceptual thinking as
well as on the level of practical politics, chauvinism was advanced to
the rank of supreme criterion in approaching reality.

The first leader of the Iron Guard (also called the Legionary Movement), Corneliu Zelea Codreanu argued that the nation is the 'patri-
mony both physical and biological in nature, namely flesh and blood'.[2]
According to him, the nation was composed of Romanians who were
alive and those who will be born, as well as the souls of the dead and
the ancestral tombs. Continuing Codreanu's idea, P.P. Panaitescu, one
of the main Iron Guard ideologists, affirmed that the nation means
'the social survival of the living and the dead in their common struggle
to accomplish the mission that has fallen to them'.[3] In the national-
Legionary conception, 'the Nation, the Legionary Movement, the
State, and the King together *form* the country where the earth and its
fruits, man and his deeds, God and his secret will are organically fused
into the same destiny'.[4] In the eyes of the Legion, this entity had to be
protected against outside influences, even if they were cultural in
nature: 'It [foreign civilisation] is generally destructive. The same
posture must be maintained toward foreign culture. Thus we cannot
in any way assimilate its values. From this point of view, they do not
interest us'.[5] Such 'theoretical' attitudes were embodied in violent
attacks against foreigners such as Jews, Hungarians, Greeks, Turks,
Ukrainians and so on.[6] The Legionnaires also wanted to protect 'the
national entity against the process of general modernisation and of
large-scale urbanisation, in order to keep a balance between the world
of the village and the world of the city, for psychological and biological reasons'.[7]

From the perspective of Nicolae Rosu, a Legionary theoretician,

> culture ought to develop organically, taking as its point of depar-
> ture the customs, behaviour, superstitions and legends of the
> past. Every creation that distances itself from this direction is
> sterile, unproductive, isolated from the world and life, an artifi-
> cial construction, deprived of viability. Only works that draw

upon tradition, with roots that run deep into the race and the past can aspire to permanence. Tradition in culture always raises issues of race.[8]

Rosu, who theorised about the 'biology of culture', introduced as his supreme argument a definition of Legionary nationalism articulated in the following way: 'first of all, an essential point must be made: nationalism does not aim to discover, to build up, or to propagate ideas. Nationalism is a fluid that takes its source from the very substance of natural things and is realised in concrete facts'.[9] For his part Alexandru Cantacuzino, an Iron Guard ideologist, proposed a similar characterisation of Legionary nationalism, but he placed an accent on the necessity of separating Legionary spirituality and matter: 'We are forging a superior species of humanity in accordance with Christian concepts, and a new philosophy of life, conceived as a permanent effort, an irrational and persistent impulse, to free ourselves from material needs in order to serve God and the Legionary nation'.[10] While evincing some hesitation with regard to the atheism of Hitler and Mussolini, Cantacuzino advocated the desire to bind Legionary ideology with Orthodox theology: 'Christianity is specific to us because, once its seeds have been sown in the Legionary soil, it bears specific fruits'.[11]

The Legionnaires created a veritable cult of ancestors of the Romanian people, proclaiming themselves the descendants of the Dacians and Romans (in 102 Emperor Trajan occupied Dacia with two Roman divisions). Thus the Legionary song 'Înainte' contains the lines 'In us all the ancestors awaken / Roman Legionnaires, the Dacian people / And demigods, bearers of the glory / That the Thracian people had'.[12] The Legionnaires strove to link this cult with other elements of their ideology, such as the cult of the dead and the pagan belief in the immortality of the soul: 'We are from here, we are the sons of this earth and the descendants of the Dacians. The Legionary movement has revived and brought up to date these ancestral virtues',[13] noted P.P. Panaitescu, while Alexandru Cantacuzino emphatically proclaimed, 'the Legion's concept of death is bound up – after 20 centuries – with the precepts of Zalmoxis, who preached to the Geto-Thracians the cult of the immortality of the soul'.[14]

If, in 1938, the right-wing Romanian extremists still granted a certain authority to the Latin element – 'which will predominate, the Dacian style or the Latin style? Both. But the Dacian will shine still more majestically: it is at home'[15] – a few years later the same Latin element was flatly discredited: 'The mass of the (Roman) colonisers were not of Italic origin ... we must not forget that the Dacian element has a superior range as compared with the Latin element in the racial structure of the Romanian people'.[16] It was along these lines that Romanian fascist nationalism began to include terms like 'racial regeneration' and 'racist theories'. This is how Romanian fascist nationalism strove to propagate the theories of Nazism: 'Thracian space represents the most important racial reservoir in the Aryan world'.[17] For the extreme right-wing Romanian ideologists, racism was not only a theory but also was supposed to be 'an efficient weapon in the struggle against ... [their] neighbours'.[18]

So what were the expectations of Iron Guard ideologists for a future Romania? On this subject, Mircea Eliade wrote: 'we are waiting for a nationalist Romania, frenzied and chauvinistic, armed and vigorous, pitiless and vengeful'.[19] Along the same lines Emile Cioran proposed 'a Romania with the population of China and the destiny of France',[20] 'a Romania in delirium'.[21] 'We don't want a logical, ordered, dutiful, and well-behaved Romania, but a Romania that is agitated, contradictory, furious, and menacing'.[22] Alexandru Cantacuzino also supported a similar notion, when he affirmed that 'our nationalism will accept nothing but the superman and the super-nation elected by the grace of God'.[23]

Antisemitism and Racism

From 1648 to 1658 Poland, the Ukraine and Russia were the scene of bloody events (the revolt of Bogdan Hmielnitki, the Russo-Polish war and invasion by Swedish troops) that prompted Jewish communities to emigrate: 'Simple people emigrate by the thousands into Hungary and Romania, rapidly overwhelming with their numbers the little local Jewish colonies'.[24] Moreover, Polish antisemitism continued to fuel the emigration of Jews to neighbouring countries. Between the years 1775 – when Bukovina became subject to the Habsburgs – and 1812 – when Bessarabia fell to the Tsar – many Jews from these two provinces decided to settle in Moldavia, where they ran no danger of massive violent persecution. At the time of the reign of Alexandru Ioan Cuza, who, during the mid-nineteenth century, unified Moldavia and Valachia, the number of Jews rose to 130,000 (or 3 per cent of the total population). Moldavian antisemitism, which was stronger than that of Valachia, also resulted from the influence of Tsarist antisemit-ism. The Organic Regulations (a sort of constitution imposed by the Russians at the beginning of the nineteenth century) defined 'the legal position of the Jews in a manner similar to that of Russia where, during the reign of Nicholas I, the government's anti-Semitic policies intensified considerably'.[25]

An antisemitic reaction from the Romanian state declared itself at the moment when, in 1878, the signatories of the Treaty of Berlin, Bismarck, Disraeli and Andrassy, intervened to make Romania apply Article 7 of its Constitution, which called for the suppression of anti-semitic discrimination and the granting of civil rights to Jews. The Romanian Jews paid taxes and were obliged to do military service, but did not have the right to vote. As a result of Western pressures, Roma-nia decided to grant citizenship to its Jews through a vote of the parlia-ment on an individual basis only. As a result of this action only 2,000 Jews became naturalised in Romania; 888 of these Jews were veterans of the 1877 Independence War against the Turks.

This situation lasted until the end of the First World War, when the Western powers threatened to not recognise the new and enlarged Romania, which was not eager to give Romanian citi-zenship to the minorities from the newly acquired provinces of Bessarabia, Bukovina and Transylvania. Again, due to heavy Western pressures, Article 8 of the 1923 Constitution granted civil rights to the Jewish minority, which in 1930 amounted to almost 756,000 people. After the First World War, the circumstances of the 'Jewish problem' changed. Romanian antisemitism gradually acquired a populist character, based on the cycle of economic crises and diversions kept up by the mainstream political parties and fascist organisations.

Antisemitism was not the monopoly of fascist organisations in Romania. The Liberal Party flaunted its antisemitism well before the appearance of the Legionary movement. Especially during election times, the National Peasant Party did not forget the Jewish question either: 'In place of "the struggle for respect for civil rights", "for liberty", in a sincerely democratic regime, evidence appeared of anti-semitic and xenophobic slogans. The declarations published, particu-larly by the National-Peasant organisations of Oltenia, could scarcely be distinguished from those put out by the Guard or Cuza'.[26] However, the antisemitism of Romanian mainstream political parties was not systematic like the fascist version.

When it came to antisemitism, there is no essential difference between A.C. Cuza's LANC variety and Iron Guard anti Semitism. As a splinter from LANC, the Iron Guard was identical to its mother organisation when it came to hatred of the Jews and propaganda expressing this. The Iron Guard was less inclined to follow parliamentary rules than the LANC (and later the PNC), and was closer to the Nazi Party than its rival organisation. A.C. Cuza was the true father of Romanian fascist antisemitism. His antisemitism was insistent, violent and racist, and was clearly influenced by H.S. Chamberlain and Edouard Drumont. Cuza's book, *Nationalitatea in arta* (*Nationality in Art*), first published in 1908, contained many references to such notions as 'racial inferiority' and 'race mixing'. In Cuza's eyes, the Jews represented a foreign body, a source of the country's economic difficulties and of the 'alteration' of Romanian culture; an 'inferior race' because of 'their crossbreeding'.[27] As opposed to the 'degeneration' of the Jews, Cuza exalted a 'vigorous Romanian race', which he avoided defining. He affirmed that the introduction of a quota on the number of Jews was a historical necessity for the defence of Romania, maintaining that the *'numerus clausus* is the measure that will decide the fate of the Romanian nation'.[28] Cuza's antisemitic 'theories' had direct and major political implications in Romania after the First World War. The League of National Christian Defence (and later the National Christian Party) and its schismatic offspring, the Legion of the Archangel, systematically picked up the racist and antisemitic arguments of Cuza, who remained faithful to antisemitism into his old age. In this context, mention must also be made of Octavian Goga, who described the Jews as 'impure secretions of Galicia (that) have invaded ... Romania', supposedly endangering the existence of the Romanian state.[29] Once he became Prime Minister in 1937, Goga, in alliance with Cuza, extolled the steady introduction of antisemitic legislation, concretised in the denial of citizenship of up to 200,000 Jews, expulsions of Jews, in measures aimed at regulating their admission to education based on their ethnicity, and in dismissals from public offices by virtue of the same criteria.

In the mid-1930s the Romanian fascist press began to be dominated by ideas holding that 'antisemitism is an extremely serious problem, it constitutes a radical style of life, different from the others',[30] and by xenophobic notions advocating 'a categorical *numerus clausus* for all those who have gotten rich in these areas'. Significant evidence of the *Der Stürmer* type of antisemitic violence by Romanian fascists can be seen in the poetry of Radu Barda:

> To make God happy / Here is what you will do, Romanian / In place of the beasts of burden / Harness the Kike to the plough / To make your country prosper / If you do not harness him to the plough, as you should / It will be he who makes you bow beneath his yoke.[31]

Obsessed by the so-called 'denationalisation of the cities' of Romania, the Iron Guard ideologist Mircea Eliade wrote in 1935 that 'Bucharest, bloodied and intoxicated, must realise the destinies of our race'.[32] Becoming more and more chauvinistic, Eliade described the Hungarians in 1936 as 'the most imbecilic people that ever existed in history, after the Bulgarians'.[33] In 1938 he regretted that 'the Bulgarian element in Dobrogea [had not been] cruelly destroyed', and that in 'Maramures, Bukovina and Bessarabia Yiddish is spoken', that the 'Jews have invaded the villages of Maramures, Bukovina and Bessarabia', affirming that:

> I do not get angry when I hear the Jews cry: 'antisemitism', 'fascism', 'Hitlerism' … It would be absurd to expect the Jews to resign themselves to being a minority with certain rights and many obligations, after having tasted the honey of power and having won the positions of command to such an extent.[34]

Hitler's rise to power determined the appearance in the Romanian fascist press of apologists for German racism as well as partisans for methods of total extermination of the Jewish population in Romania. In 1935 Nicolae Bogdan published an article in which one can clearly see the influence of Nazi ideologists and of Arthur de Gobineau: 'The crude but pure truth is this; all those Yellow, Blacks, Reds, or other colours see in us, the Whites, mortal enemies, whose submission and defeat they desire with unanimous ardour and with common wish'.[35]

In his book *Conceptia eroica asupra rasei* (*The Heroic Conception of Race*), the Legionnaire Ion Foti claims as his sources of inspiration Adolf Hitler, Alfred Rosenberg and Benito Mussolini. He accepts the definition that Rosenberg gives of the race ('Seen from within, the soul means race, and conversely, race is the external clothing of the soul'), while affirming that the Aryan principle constitutes the foundation of the state. Furthermore, according to Foti 'the Legionary state has in its structure, as its backbone, the steel block of the Romanian race and all the privileges that flow from it'.[36] Foti promoted the idea of the blood unity of the Romanian people, arguing that the Romanian race is characterised by 'clarity and precision of expression, seriousness, devotion to God and to the nation, nostalgia for life to the point of enjoying the pleasure of death, the pride of an imperial people whose race has been kept pure, the safeguard of the light of Christ, the pious preservation of tradition'.[37]

In the eyes of Iron Guards ideologists, the solution of all social problems entailed the elimination of the Jews and, in general, of all 'foreign elements'. For example, Traian Braileanu wrote that 'for every nation that wishes to live free in its own country, the foreigner, whether superior or inferior, is a pagan and polluted'.[38] According to another Iron Guard ideologist, Mihail Polohroniade, the practical solution for this problem consisted in 'state antisemitism, a phenomenon that marks a new era in history'.[39]

More exactly, the Iron Guards advocated concentration camps for Jews and racial engineering in order to solve the 'ethnic' problems of Romania. In 1938 Alexandru Razmerita, while criticising the position of a priest who wanted to drown the Jews in the Black Sea (Razmerita rejected this on technical grounds, stating that Romania did not have enough ships to carry out such an operation), described with great abundance of details 'a plan for the total elimination of the Jews', who were to be deported from cities to the countryside for forced labour. According to Razmerita, the Jews ought to be deprived of the right to have recourse to the justice system. Attempts to escape the work camps ought to be punished by execution. He proposed installing the Jews in little village camps containing 24 to 40 men, with forced labour applying also to children over 10. These children were to be separated from their parents and their identity papers were to contain only the name of the owner of the company to whom they were assigned. Practically speaking, this was organised slavery of the Nazi type, quite close to the future reality of the Nazi concentration camps.[40]

Traian Herseni was one of the Legionnaires who pressed a belief in racism to its ultimate theoretical consequences. He maintained that:

> The reality of racism is based on solid scientific foundations, and represents one of the most stable political ideals ... Science proves that men are not equal, that their characters vary as a function of the race to which they belong. There are races ill-suited for culture, there are also races that barely manage to

profit from the culture of others. Only very few races are endowed with the gift of creating culture. The results of studies done up to the present moment seem to prove that of all the races on earth, the Nordic race is the most gifted, and that it is to them that the most noble Romanian cultural productions are due. Once the race lost its purity, and the bloodlines were crossed, the culture fell off little by little until it completely disappeared from history ... The doctrine of inequality is completed by the doctrine of the betterment of the human races.[41]

Along with other Legionnaires, Herseni became an ideological follower of National Socialism through his convictions on the superiority of the Aryan race and the alleged Nordic origin of Romanian values of culture, as well as through his justifications regarding Nazi expansionism. Thus he conceived the perfecting of human society as an operation akin to improving livestock. Declaring his agreement with the slogan of the Legionnaire C. Papanace, who aimed at 'purification from Judaic, Phanariot [Greek], and Gypsy influences', which appeared in the journal *Cuvintul* (*The Voice*), Herseni wrote:

> We are in complete agreement with these conclusions. The racial purification of the Romanian people is a question of life and death. There are a number of ways to solve this problem. To begin with, it must be precisely determined as to the racial characteristics to which the Romanian people owe their present-day creations and their periods of historical flowering, as well as their moral and political defeats, their periods of decadence and of historical shame ... We must struggle against everything that is foreign to our nation and against everything that constitutes a baneful influence, and encourage, in exchange, everything that is authentically Romanian ...[42]

Accordingly, Herseni demanded 'a rigorous social selection based on particular racial qualities', to favour the supremacy of Legionnaires made up of 'the purest, most gifted examples of our race'.[43] This selection was based on the application of eugenics, one of the most essential components of Nazi racial politics. Herseni maintained that 'through the intermediary of eugenics every nation becomes master of its destiny. It can systematically improve its characteristics and attain the highest stages of betterment and of human creation: and the genius of

Adolf Hitler lies in his clear vision of this possibility'.[44] The master was acknowledged, declared and assumed in detail:

> We need eugenic laws and a eugenic practice. Reproduction can no longer be left to chance. Dysgenic people must be eliminated from reproduction, the inferior races completely separated from the ethnic group. The sterilisation of certain categories of men is to be envisaged, not in a stupid manner, as a violation of human dignity, but as a tribute to beauty, to morality, and in general to perfection.[45]

Another Romanian fascist and a supporter of eugenics was P. Tiparescu, who spoke of 'racial maladies' as well as of 'the necessity of a rapid and intense eugenic activity'.[46] Tiparescu maintained that the Jews 'are the most dangerous bearers of infectious diseases because of their dirtiness', without being, for all that, too infested themselves.[47]

The Iron Guard Cult of the Supreme Leader and of its Own Élite

Vasile Marin, one of the top Legionary ideologies, insisted on the role of the Guard's élite, on its obligation not to leave the initiative in politics to the masses:

> The initiative of the foundation of the new state, which the nation demands of us these days, cannot and must not be left to the care of the street. The masses are not in a position to participate in the movements to inaugurate a new order on their own initiative, but only by their conscious adherence. The masses have a role that is anything but dynamic in the currents of fundamental transformation. In what concerns us, the initiative must belong to the élite of our generation, to those few men who have been chosen on the strength of their bold character and their spirit of solidarity. The minority that has been selected and disciplined becomes the instrument for the concrete realisation of all the aspirations that the masses, in their vague and confused way, have nourished.[48]

In refusing the masses 'any dynamic role', Marin was giving free sway to the Legionnaires' desire to reduce them to mere tools to be manipulated. By accepting the supposed distance separating the masses from the élite, the Legionnaires went so far as to affirm the necessity of the existence of two cultures, one destined for the masses, the other for the élite.[49] Another prominent Iron Guard ideologist, Nicolae Rosu, showed his contempt for the role of the masses and his championing of the élite when he wrote in praise of the sum of the 'hereditary and military virtues' of the old aristocracy:

> The lower classes are by definition amorphous and diffuse ... [they] are incapable of leading first of all because by their essence they do not have the virtues necessary to become a ruling force of good quality, and then because they are inclined, by the very laws of their nature, to amputate their biological substance by mixing with the upper classes. Blood circulates from the bottom up. The skeletal structure of societies depends upon the circulation of the élite.[50]

Traian Braileanu followed the same track in recognising still more explicitly the real role played by Iron Guard social selection:

> And so universal and individual suffrage does not solve the problem of selecting the political élite. The Legionary movement, like Fascism and National Socialism, has solved that problem by virtue of an education corresponding to this goal ... By this system, we avoid the emergence of revolutionary currents, of groups of malcontents.[51]

Three years later, Braileanu presented the result of the Iron Guard 'selection' as follows: 'By their deeds and by their example, they have proved that they are destined forever to the role of rulers whom the people obey and follow, and whose right to rule is acknowledged without a murmur'.[52] In Braileanu's eyes this Legionary 'élite' has been called to replace the old Romanian élite that had been 'in decline, was no longer capable of governing and leading the Romanian community toward its historical destinies, an élite separated from the masses, corrupted and spiritually deformed by internationalist ideas, and serving the Jewish community. This élite then, was corrupted and sold to Freemasonry and Judaism'.[53] Nicolae Patrascu, later Secretary General of the Iron Guard, provided explanations as to the methods of selection used within the Legionary movement: 'The selection of the Legionary movement has taken place in combat, during the 15 years of persecution. It has developed naturally because the only ones engaged in this combat are those who had something to give. The *virtuosi* of the different professions do not belong to the élite'.[54]

As a Legionary theoretician of élites, Constantin Noica argued that 'since within the Legion education has taken place through the élite, it follows that the Romanian world too will be transformed by the influence of the Legionary élite that is already in existence or in the course of being born within its ranks'.[55] Noica also provided statistics on the Legionary élite, which 'will have to be so powerful that the Captain [Codreanu] has forbidden their number to exceed 10,000'.[56] Noica likewise insisted on the supposed asceticism of the Legionary élite, while, in a misogynistic way, excluded women from their ranks:

> The Captain has always dreamed of an ascetic élite in his entou-rage. Every spiritual movement perfects itself along the lines of an ascetic élite. Is that a pitiless concept with regard to women? Possibly. But that is how the mind shows itself when it reaches the highest summit: without pity.[57]

According to its supreme leader, C.Z. Codreanu, the Legionary élite would have to show the following qualities: 'purity of soul, capac-ity for work and creation, courage, ability to lead a hard life and engage in permanent combat against the shackles binding the nation, poverty, that is, voluntary renunciation of the accumulation of riches, belief in God, love'.[58] The theme of the ascetic élite with monkish and warlike qualities occurs in an obsessive fashion in the texts of the Legionnaires. Constantin Noica, another prominent Iron Guard ideol-ogist wrote:

> The political leaders of an authentic right-wing regime will not be parasites and will not live on lies, on shameful complicity and Jewish publicity. On the contrary, they will be models of wisdom, of character, of abnegation and voluntary renunciation of earthly things for the moral transfiguration of their fellows and of their brothers who are less gifted than they in this aspect.[59]

In the same spirit, a fascist journalist who exalted absolute submission toward the supreme leader expressed himself this way: 'Obedience is a law of the Captain ... the Legionnaires – monks of love for the fatherland – will not violate this law. The country needs submission, a monastic submission'.[60]

As for Mircea Eliade, he defined in the clearest possible fashion the Legion's 'new élite':

> We are the fortunate contemporaries of the most significant transformation in the thousands of years of Romanian history, that is, the appearance of a new aristocracy ... our old aristocracy, so attached to the soil and to peasant civilisation ... has been thrown into confusion by a whole series of hapless regimes ... the new Legionary aristocracy resurrects the Romanian Middle Ages.[61]

The Legionary 'élite' thus described itself as a new political class with totally different characteristics as compared with the 'classic' political élite. The Legionary theory of élites did not limit itself to singing the praises of its own organisation. It also proceeded to an unbounded adulation of its own leadership, trying to identify it with the aspirations of the Romanian nation. According to C.Z. Codreanu, the leader of the Legion had to have all the following qualities:

> He must be wise, gentle, joyful, just, courageous, and firm, he must take part in joys and pains, he must be skilful, he must give clear orders, he must not use calumny against his comrades, he must maintain harmony, he must be polite, measured, he must keep his word, he must be honest, intrepid (the chief of the Legionnaires is an intrepid man).[62]

A person embodying all these qualities looks more like a Renaissance ideal than the head of a terrorist organisation.

What was to be the relationship between the Iron Guard leader and its élite? The philosopher Nae Ionescu, *the maître à penser* of the Iron Guard, described the relationship between the leader and the masses within the fascist system in the following way:

> In addition there must be a creative element in history that is neither the man against the masses (dictatorship) nor the masses against the man (the degenerate democracy of our times), but the man whom the masses have found. It is evident that a geometrical way of judging has a hard time getting used to such forms within the framework of which mystical (that is, hidden) relations make and unmake the hazards. What sort of man is this? On this topic there is no room for guessing games. The man of the masses is the man who is. He whom the masses recognise as such. By what method do they recognise him? By their faith in him. There are also votes, of course ... But beyond the votes, there is the act of faith, of faith and not of confidence.[63]

Ion Mota emphasised that since the appearance of the Legion, there was an indissoluble bond between the principle of the leader with an incontestable authority and the very existence of the Legion:

> The organisation cannot be born and develop in a healthy way without discipline, without a hierarchy, and above all without a leader. Thus our organisation has a leader whom no one elected but who has the consent of all those who, drawn by a mysterious force, have come to set up, under the leader's direction, the ordered and disciplined cells of the organisation. Our leader is Corneliu Zelea Codreanu.[64]

Later on, Traian Herseni also insisted on this same idea when he wrote that:

> the Legionary movement has a commandant who guarantees its unity and who leads it to victory. Deprived of its commandant the Movement would become an amorphous mass and would be lost in the immense mass of the country. It follows that the commandant represents the very principle of existence and action in the Movement. Without a commandant, the Movement would not be possible.[65]

The mystical obedience, the non-elective status of the Legionary chief, like the obligation to submit absolutely to him, were argued for by Herseni in the following manner:

> The ruler is not the one nominated or elected but the one naturally recognised as such, by the position that he adopts all by himself with regard to the necessities of life and of the victory of the Movement. The rulers who have been selected in this way: must be followed with unbounded devotion.[66]

During the selection of the supreme chief it was not an issue, practically speaking, of any selection, but of the brutal intimidation not only of political adversaries, but also of one's own partisans. The latter were called upon to contribute to the cult of the supreme chief. Many publications presented the Legionary leaders as demigods. Indeed, Mihai Manoilescu compared Ion Mota to the poet Lord Byron.[67] Other texts praised Zizi Cantacuzino-Granicerul or Horia Sima, but most of them dealt with the cult of C.Z. Codreanu. P.P. Panaitescu described him as 'the greatest prophet of our nation. Those who looked him at least once in the eye have felt, without knowing him, that he saw beyond the age',[68] like a 'founder of the country'.[69] Traian Herseni effused about Codreanu that:

> hundreds and thousands of years have prepared his birth, other hundreds and thousands of years will be necessary for the accomplishment of his commandments, but the presence of the Captain in history constitutes, from now on, an unshakable guarantee that at the end of the path he is traversing will be found the eternal city of the redemption of the Romanians.[70]

Dozens of the Legionary press presented immense photographs of Codreanu taken in different poses (giving speeches, visiting work camps, skiing with General Antonescu and so on). In the eyes of his disciples he passed for:

> a hero, in both the legendary and the historical sense of the term. Wisdom and courage, dream and empiricism, power and corporal beauty of a demigod, evangelical simplicity and clarity, and above all, a serene radiation from his marble forehead and his burning look in those moments that were dangerous to the soul, the past, and the land of Romania.[71]

Nicolae Crevedia likewise associated himself with this excessive praise:

> Nevertheless, it is still true that everything that is newest in the ideas and organisation of this mission is due to the Captain of the Legion, Corneliu Zelea Codreanu, to that man of fire who, by the example of his very life, which is made up of virility, faith, and sacrifice, has managed to make us believe that this Nation has not disappeared.[72]

The cult offered to Codreanu was maintained even after his death, taking on a powerful mystical colouring.

As an associate of the Iron Guard and as someone who, even after he split with them, continued to claim to belong to the same cultural roots, General Antonescu should not be forgotten in this respect either. He was not overly afflicted by modesty, and contributed to his own cult of personality. In the eyes of his adulators, the general was identified 'with the ideals of the Romanian people to the point of total fusion ... truly [representing] the soul of the Romanian Nation'.[73]

The same sources that presented the man who was leading Romania into disaster described him as a 'genius, an eminent man with noble principles, just, honest, a remarkable creator, capable of a penetrating comprehension of history'.[74] They also portrayed him as the founder of a new epoch: 'a man with an energetic character, an iron will, animated by the most ardent nationalism and patriotism, a noble mind, dominated by the sense of justice, the fundamental law of his life, correct, honest, and magnanimous, the Leader lays the foundations of a new epoch of our history'.[75]

The Legionary Movement and Religion

'God is a fascist!'[76] This cry of the Legionary journalist, I.P. Prundeni, succinctly captures the place of religion as a distinctive quality of Romanian fascism. Like all fascist movements, the Legion addressed faith rather than reason, employing an intentionally vague and grandiloquent mystique as a bond between the most different sorts of people. However, Legionary mysticism took on an Orthodox shading, not a pagan one, as in the case of Nazism. The Legionary movement willingly inserted strong elements of the Orthodox Christianity into its political doctrine. Thus the Legionary movement is one of the rare modern European political movements with a religious structure. Legionary mysticism did not set itself up as an Orthodox mysticism. On the contrary, the latter underwent alterations owing to the attempts to canonise certain saints chosen from among the 'Legionary martyrs', to the intense cult of death, of instinct, of the providential leader, along the lines established by the myth of youth and of old warriors. Of all these cults, that of death especially served the psychological formation of the executors in the policy of physical liquidation for the Legion's adversaries.

With an eye toward winning over the rural population, which made up the majority in Romania and within which religious beliefs were the strongest, the Legionnaires made use of the 'core of primitivism, the lack of culture and the superstitions with which the Romanian peasantry was imbued'.[77] The Legionnaires had recourse to fanatical forms of religious propaganda. They went around villages, organised special masses, kissed the soil, filled little bags with earth and hung them around their necks, asked the peasants to swear fidelity to them and tried to benefit from 'miracles', such as the one in Maglavit. There, in 1935, Petrache Lupu, 'syphilitic ... tongue-tied and a cretin ... weak in the head' saw God. As a result, 'tens of thousands of peasants from the most remote corners of the country and thousands of people from the city took the road to Maglavit to see and hear Petrache Lupu ... A wave of religious exaltation swept over the whole country, from one end to the other'.[78]

That same year a fascist newspaper spoke of a visionary from the shores of Lake Herastrau: 'Maria Rusu spoke five times to the Holy Virgin. The first sick persons to be cured sleep by the side of the lake and pray every day ... The crowd drinks the water ... the women were with blessed water from the lake'.[79] Nichifor Crainic said of Petrache Lupu: 'This shepherd, gentle as a child ... his solution was simple and practical ... His good sense is faultless'.[80] Dan Botta, an Iron Guard journalist, 'explained' that 'what happens in Maglavit sheds light on the irresistible desire for the ideal, for abnegation, for self-renunciation, the belief in the value of the human soul, the infinite fear of losing it in the vicissitudes that all the Romanian people confront at this moment'.[81]

For its propaganda, the Legionary movement used a part of the Orthodox clergy that was devoted to it. This became obvious when the Legionaries and their ally, General Antonescu, took power:

> During the first days of his ascent to power, the General made extensive use of the Church in order to impose upon public opinion and especially on the lower strata of the population. Some of his appeals and convocations were ostentatiously broadcast through the churches, publicly read by the priests.[82]

The fact that part of the Orthodox clergy lent its support to the Legionary movement also emerges from a book by Ilie Imbrescu, entitled *Biserica si miscarea legionara* (*The Church and the Legionary Movement*), where the author states: 'A true priest will therefore be a Legionnaire by the nature of things, just as a Legionnaire will be in his turn, and again by the nature of things, a Legionnaire, the best son of the Church'.[83] At the same, time the amount of support given the Legionary movement by some of the Orthodox clergy must not be overestimated: 'For Codreanu himself, who was closer to the Church than the other founders of the fascist movements, and whose ideas were greatly valued by the Orthodox Romanian traditionalists, bitterly complained that the immense majority of the priests had been hostile to the Iron Guard'.[84] Yet one should recall that during the elections of 1937, of 103 candidates from the 'All For the Country' Party (a label under which the Iron Guard participated in those elections), 33 were priests.

The Legionary movement was at first called 'The Legion of the Archangel Michael' precisely to justify its religious legitimacy. According to Nae Ionescu, the Legion never made mistakes because it was allegedly 'under the sign of the archangel'.[85] Ion Foti wrote about the role played by mystique in the actions of the Legionnaires:

> By its benevolent mystique, by the triumph of the supreme faith of the Cross, by the rebirth of piety in souls, of the desire, for sacrifice, of the will to illuminate the spirit beneath the heavenly banner of the Archangel Michael, God's envoy to earth, the Iron Guard leads our race toward new destinies. It leads it not only to redemption but it makes it rediscover the great path of magnificent national and cultural achievements.[86]

Mircea Eliade described 'the Legionary ideal [as] a harsh Christian spirituality',[87] while according to P.P. Panaitescu, 'the Legionary movement signifies in itself a religious resurrection of the nation both by the moral purification of man and by putting faith back in the place that it merits'.[88] From Mota's perspective, the Legion was not a political, but a religious organisation: 'we don't do politics and at no time have we done politics ... We have a religion, we are the slaves of faith. Its flame consumes us'.[89] More lucidly, Mihail Polihroniade explained the essence of the relationship between the Christian Orthodoxy and the Legionary movement:

> let us point out that it [the Legionary movement] is capable of manipulating, with a formidable master hand, the elements that touch the masses, the skilfully composed and broadcast popular songs, the impressive marches, the theatrical but impressive cavalcades, a whole cortège of means that induce a quasi-religious impression in the masses, and are not limited to repeating the borrowed tactical clichés, but are adapted to Romanian conditions.[90]

The cult of the dead, common to several fascist movements, occupied a privileged position in the Legionary mystique. The main goal of this mystique was to raise to the rank of 'martyrs' the dead leaders of the movement. Horatiu Comaniciu, one of the Iron Guard leaders, wrote about Codreanu: 'And above our heads, from the Dniester to the Tisza, our Captain [that is, Codreanu] passes in flight. Tears of joy gleam in his steely eyes, while his holy lips murmur: the Fatherland! the Fatherland! the Fatherland!'[91] The Legionnaires' cult of the dead occupied a privileged place in Constantin Noica's writings too. According to him, Codreanu was a reincarnation of Joan of Arc,[92] and Nae Ionescu was 'the man who had paid so that God and Life might descend upon our nation'.[93] Even the insignificant intriguer, Horia Sima, successor of Codreanu as supreme leader of the Iron Guard, took on special virtues in Noica's eyes: 'at this moment when the divine breath is upon us, Horia Sima does not demand taxes on income, he gets the souls moving'.[94] For Noica, the future was to be found in the rule of the Iron Guard ghosts: 'the day of the terrifying domination of the ghosts approaches'.[95] Mircea Eliade also believed that the 'ghosts of Ion Mota and Vasile Marin are going to reign for a time', until Romanians 'make a country like the saintly sun of the sky',[96] the latter formula being a common slogan of the Legion. The theme of the 'holy Iron Guard spirit' similarly recurs in the writings of Traian Herseni, who argued: 'The spirit of the Captain leads the nation to victory'.[97] In this vein, there was a significant attempt made to complete the Orthodox calendar by adding new Legionary 'saints' or 'prophets'. As if to contradict Emile Cioran, who affirmed that 'Romania is a country without prophets',[98] P.P. Panaitescu wrote: 'The greatest prophet of the nation, however, has been the Captain'.[99]

With regard to the arguments for raising Mota and Marin (Iron Guard leaders killed in the Spanish civil war while fighting alongside Franco's troops) to the rank of 'martyrs' and 'saints' of the nation, Mircea Eliade came straight out, calling the death of the two Legionnaires the birth of a Christian revolution:

> Those who had dedicated their youth to the Legion, that is, to prisons and persecution, did not hesitate to sacrifice their life in order to hasten the redemption of the whole nation. This death has borne fruit. It has set the seal on the meaning of life and of creation for our generation. The climate of the spirit against the climate of the temporal, in which the preceding generations have believed. And they have indicated to us what remained to be made of this ephemeral human life. A Christian revolution.[100]

Mircea Eliade was one of the Iron Guard ideologists who tried hard to accredit the spiritual nature of the fascist movement to which he belonged. He denied the political nature of the Legionary movement, while claiming that:

the Legionary movement has a spiritual and Christian meaning. If all the contemporary revolutions have as their goal the conquest of power by a social class or by a man, the Legionary revolution aims, on the contrary, at the supreme redemption of the nation, the reconciliation of the Romanian nation with God, as the Captain said. That is why the Legionary movement has a different meaning with regard to everything that has been done up till now in history; and the victory of the Legion will lead not only to the restoration of the virtues of our nation, of a hard-working Romania, worthy and powerful, but also to the birth of a man who is in harmony with the new kind of European life.[101]

While emphasising the 'spiritual force' of the Legion, Eliade wrote: 'The tide of love that the Legionnaires pour out is so strong that it would suffice to make us hope for the triumph of the Legionary movement'.[102] Praising the 'Legionary spirituality', which he claimed was separate from the terrestrial world of politics, Eliade believed in Codreanu's ideas on the mediation between Romania and God: 'A political leader of youth said that the goal of his movement was "to reconcile Romania with God". Here was a messianic formula that did not appeal to the class struggle, nor to political interests, nor to economic interest, nor the bestial instinct in man'.[103] This interview with Eliade did not go unnoticed by the top leadership of the Legion. During his trial in 1938, Codreanu mentioned it as eloquent proof of the specific nature of the Legionary movement, stressing the exemplary fashion in which Eliade had distinguished between the Legionary movement – founded on 'the Grace of God' – Italian fascism and National Socialism.[104]

Despite its pronounced Orthodox character, Legionary mysticism did not simply mean the total assimilation of Orthodox theology by a fascist political movement, but on the contrary, an attempt at subordinating and transforming that theology into a political instrument. Through an abusive extrapolation all the Legion's adversaries became in the writings of its followers adversaries of the Church, Christ and God.[105]

The Iron Guard Vision of the Future Society

The Iron Guard and Capitalism

The Iron Guard sought to realise, at the national scale, the idea of national unity, of harmony, as the only possible reality. All social groups, and organisations representing different or contradictory interests, were dissolved. If the Romanian fascists condemned capitalism in their writings, they did so almost always by identifying it with Judaism. Mihail Manoilescu wrote there were no social problems in Romania only ethnic ones. Therefore he stated that 'the national revolution (that is, the Legionary movement) aims at the massive elimination of the Jews and their replacement in the leading economic posts'.[106] For Leon Topa, another Iron Guard ideologist, 'the Legionary revolution means ... the primacy of the political over the economic: the suppression of free competition and generous help given to Romanians'.[107] Traian Braileanu insisted on the 'social harmony' that was supposed to wipe out the divergent or fundamentally opposed interests of the various social groups:

> the upper classes must become aware of the duty incumbent upon them *vis-à-vis* the lower classes, and share their surplus with the poor. The latter must not look at the rich with an eye full of hatred, with the idea of dispossessing and exterminating them. They must, on the contrary, offer them an example of patience and disciplined work. Only if both do their duty to the fatherland will it be possible to arrive at that unity of views, that unity of souls that is the only guarantee of the future of this country.[108]

Along the same lines, Mihai Polihroniade affirmed that the bankers, the businessmen and capitalism in general all had to disappear; he maintained at the same time that there was 'a hard-working, modest, limited bourgeoisie; an active, orderly, decorous bourgeoisie, which in all societies assures the stability necessary to the collectivity, as well as the impulse to progress without which history would fall back into the animal state'.[109]

In a blunter fashion, P.P. Panaitescu defined the relations between the Romanian bourgeoisie and the Legionary movement in the following terms:

> What is the situation of the Romanian bourgeoisie in the face of the Legionary revolution? ... The bourgeoisie will acquire from it a stable economic position, and it will have prospects for the future in Legionary Romania, but at the price of great sacrifices, to which it consents. In the totalitarian state the bourgeoisie can no longer preserve mentalities and activities that are liberal in the

theoretical sense of that word ... In the totalitarian state the situation changes. The bourgeoisie is no more than one organ, and perhaps not the most important one, alongside the peasants, the workers in the cities and the intellectuals ... The so-called democratic states are based in fact on a terrible dictatorship of the plutocrats, or a rich stratum of the bourgeoisie living at the expense of the other classes. This dictatorship must come to an end, while in exchange assuring the bourgeoisie a development in conformity with its development within the framework of the nation ... In our days the nations have the choice between totalitarian nationalism, which limits but assures an existence for the bourgeoisie, and communism, which completely annihilates the bourgeoisie.[110]

Yet the Legionary movement was not willing to give any guarantees to the political élite of Romania, which was criticised for its acceptance of democratic rules, for liberalism and, above all, for tolerance toward ethnic minorities. In his article, 'Pilotii orbi' ('The Blind Pilots'), Mircea Eliade offers an eloquent example of this. After enumerating the dangers posed by Hungarians, Ukrainians, Bulgarians and, to be sure, Jews, Eliade wrote: 'After the [First World] War democracy succeeded in preventing all the attempts at a national awakening. Through the intermediary of blind pilots at the helm, democracy has led us to the point where we are. Democracy has definitively crushed the *state instinct* of our leaders'.[111] According to Eliade, the Romanian political élite was made of 'unthinking people, brigands, or lunatics',[112] and in particular the political élite of Transylvania was made of 'traitors who believe in democracy and who have learned French',[113] for whom Eliade anticipated a tragic end: 'They are going to pay and everything that has been built upon their turpitude and brigandage from 1918 to 1921 will be necessarily burned to the root'.[114] More concretely, 'What military court will be able to judge so many thousands of traitors – how many forests will have to be transformed into gibbets for all the miscreants and imbeciles from these 20 years of Romanian politics?'[115]

The Iron Guard and the Middle Class

Following the path of his mentor, A.C. Cuza, on the issue of the role and significance of the middle class, C.Z. Codreanu wrote: 'it is the only class in touch both below, with the peasantry, on which it is superimposed, exercising its powerful authority there by means of its economic and cultural well-being, and above, with the ruling class which it carries on its shoulders'.[116] For his part, Traian Braileanu thought that one of the essential problems of Romania derived from the non-Romanian origin of the middle class: 'between the élite and the mob, a foreign middle class slips in, a middle class tending to seize first of all the Romanian élite and then the Romanian state'.[117] Furthermore, one of the principal points of the programme of the Legionary movement aimed at the necessity of supporting and encouraging the middle class: 'the creation of the middle class of tradesmen and manufacturers, thanks to the legal support of the state, and the encouragement of active Romanian energies'.[118] Along the same lines, P.P. Panaitescu wrote: 'The Legionary doctrine foresees the constituting of a petty bourgeoisie on the basis of workers made wealthy, of artisans and tradesmen with workshops and stores, rather than the protecting of large industry based on capitalism'.[119] The economic situation of the Romanian middle class depended, however, on its ethnic origins, as Nicolae Rosu explained. According to him, the precarious position of the Romanian middle class was due 'to the large number of foreigners' in the country. Rosu wrote: 'the petit bourgeoisie, which has been anathematised for failing to understand the dynamism of the modern world, when it is accused of cowardice and lack of energy, at least in our country, ought to be encouraged and supported'.[120]

The Iron Guard and the Peasantry

The rural source of Romanian fascism's ideological inspiration is explained by a massive recruitment of members from the countryside. This was clear from Codreanu's *Carticica sefului de cuib*: conceived as an élitist organisation with rather strict rules of recruitment, the Iron Guard was ready to become a mass organisation when it came to the rural areas: 'so that a chief may be sure that no bad elements are entering the organisation, the number of the Legionnaires in any village will not exceed half its inhabitants'.[121] The rural origin of a large part of the Romanian middle class, as well as the Legion's intention of capturing the peasantry *en masse*, generated 'the birth between 1935 and 1939 of a whole Iron Guard literature, designed to praise the obscurity that Romanian peasants lived in and to recommend warmly his way of life'.[122] The Legionnaires argued that the Romanian village represented not only 'ethnicity in the pure state as opposed to the cosmopolitan city, but also an ideal system of production'.[123]

Legionary ideologues therefore recommended that the social and governmental organisation, which they wanted to put into practice at the level of the nation, find its inspiration – or even its replication – in the Romanian village. Alongside other Legionary theoreticians, Mihail Manoilescu praised the traditional mode of rural life, while taking a stand against the penetration of capitalism into the villages. Manoilescu went so far as to claim that 'the peasant is above all an anti-economic creature ... the lure of gain and economic calculations is the most foreign thing to the soul of our peasantry'.[124] It follows from this that capitalist economic relations had altered the soul of the Romanian peasant. Therefore, from the Iron Guard's viewpoint, it was necessary to restructure Romanian economic life in conformity with the norms of the patriarchal village. Thus, as early as 1932, Nae Ionescu wrote of the need to establish 'the foundations of a Romanian state with a peasant structure, the only framework within which we can really live, following the tendencies of our nature, and which permits a true and total flowering of the forces of our race'.[125] With the exception of Emil Cioran, the champion of industrialisation, who thought that 'our misery comes from the condition of the agrarian peoples',[126] all the Legionnaires, practically speaking, sided with Nae Ionescu.

In the eyes of most Legionnaires, the Romanian peasant supposedly refused all the progress of civilisation. The peasant did not want to be 'erudite', but wanted to retain his 'purity'. Books did not interest him. Through this exaggerated portrait of the inhabitants of the rural milieu, the Legionnaires intended to pass over in silence the Romanian peasantry's lack of real possibilities to access education and culture, as well new agrarian technologies. Along these lines of thought, Ion Ververca concluded that:

> in order to affirm the vigour of his race and his cardinal virtues, the Romanian man will seek out the friendship and warmth of the ancestral soil, his reconciliation with the spirit of the earth and the hill. He wishes to be a peasant bent over the shepherd's crook or the effort of the spade and the plough, refusing everything that comes from the filth-encrusted cosmopolitan city. He does not wish to know the life of books nor does he formulate a learned universe. He wants direct judgement, issuing from real psychic experience, tortured, revealing.[127]

Such an individual – deprived of education, superstitious and often even illiterate – suited the Legion, for he would be easier to manipulate.

The Legionnaires promised the peasantry the family vote and, above all, land, in keeping with the slogan, 'To every man his own half-hectare'. The utopian and profoundly demagogic character of this slogan led even some Legionnaires to consider it a calumny against the Legion: 'The stupidest of calumnies was "To every man his own half-hectare", Codreanu's alleged promise, made to the peasantry concerning a new agrarian reform. This slogan was, on the other hand, in complete contradiction to the doctrine of the Captain and the movement', wrote Mihai Sturdza, the Iron Guard Foreign Minister of the Antonescu-Sima government.[128] The Legion's demagoguery took on grotesque forms during the electoral campaigns, as witnessed by debates in the Assembly of Deputies, or the stories of certain Legionnaires who took part in the events:

> You don't know Monsieur C.Z. Codreanu going the propaganda rounds … when he arrives with his 200 Legionnaires wearing their plumed fur hats, their sword belts, with their pistols and so on. Tall, thickset, a commanding presence, he would begin in this way: 'Little mother, why do you eat nothing but polenta with onion? Don't you have a cow? –No. –Secretary, put her down for a cow!' Almost all the villagers whom he visited were put down on a list by Mr Codreanu's 'secretary' for a cow, for a shop, for a patch of land. 'After the elections', he would tell the peasants, 'Go into the stores and you'll be given merchandise for free.[129]

Often Legionary propaganda addressed to the peasants used antisemitism as a means to explain the problems of the Romanian rural world:

> In the countryside, in the most remote hamlets, the Yids placed their inns a step away from the church, and making their way around the houses, one after the other, they seized and they bought everything possible so that the poor peasant would remain as poor as Job (often the land itself no longer belonged to him). After corrupting him with money, flattery and everything that his satanic existence could promise, he forced him to leave for the city, where he hired him as a domestic … Over time the peasant was obliged, given the temptations of Jewish money, to leave his land, to renounce his tombs and to flee to the city, where the arms of the Yids were open wide, waiting to destroy him.[130]

The Iron Guard and the Working Class

Unlike Germany and Italy, the fascist parties in Romania did not initially benefit from a large following among the working class. In 1930, workers represented 17 per cent of the Italian Fascist Party members and 28 per cent for Nazis. In Romania at this time, the Iron Guard was not preoccupied with the problem of working-class support. It was only several years later that the dissidents in the Legion joined together in the *Cruciada Romanismului* (Crusade of Romanism) in an attempt to make themselves popular among the workers. Among the ranks of the workers, Romanian fascist propaganda was late in coming, and its results were far from spectacular. The second half of the 1930s was marked by a major effort on the part of Iron Guard propaganda to woo the working class. Thus the first Legionary Workers Corps was created in Azuga in 1937, and in 1938 – the Legion's 'peak year' – the Legionary Workers Unit counted 8,000 members in Bucharest.[131] Like their former mentor A.C. Cuza, the Iron Guard hastened to call for 'the harmonising of the interests of capitalists and workers',[132] to aid 'the unhappy, deceived working class',[133] which was guilty of 'transforming the administrative and professional problem into a terrible political weapon'.[134] While claiming that 'the evil does not arise from the fact that some are owners and others are workers',[135] the Iron Guard longed to strike a deal with 'authentic workers, diligent and resigned to their poverty, proud of their people and trusting the country and its real leaders, who wish them well'.[136]

The sociologists of the Iron Guard baptised the factory, calling it 'a family', within which the boss and the worker were 'comrades'.[137] The leaders of the Legion promised to replace 'the exploitation of man by man' with 'brotherhood and love'. Sacrifice and obedience to the Legionary movement were also demanded:

> I see today as in a beautiful dream what will be achieved tomorrow: all the workers, all those who embellish the world by their labour, like an army blessed by God, fraternising in love, under one command, advancing firmly on the soil of our Romanian land, eyes raised to heaven, serene and happy to have work and someone to work for.[138]

C.Z. Codreanu, 'the Messiah of the Romanian worker',[139] as Dumitru Groza, head of the Legion's Workers Corps, described him, promised that:

the Legionary movement would give the working class more than an unfeasible programme, more than whiter bread, more than a better bed in a healthy house. It will give the workers the right to feel that they are masters in their own country, just as all the other Romanians do. They will be able to mark their way down the *Calea Victoriei* [the central boulevard of Bucharest], walking like masters and not like slaves. For the first time the worker will taste the sensation, the joy, the pride of being a master. Of being the master of his own country. Compared with that, all the other questions count for little. For the worker-master will have his laws, his organisation in the state, and the lot that he will build for himself all by himself, with his own hands, with the thought and the awareness of the master.[140]

Horia Sima, vice-president of the Iron Guard government between 6 September 1940 and 21 January 1941, wrote: 'the worker must be integrated into the state and society, not as the member of a class, but as the member of a nation'.[141] This new status allegedly signified the transformation of the workers into factory owners. Along these lines, Vasile Iasinschi, the Legionary Minister of Labour and Social Assistance in the same government, stated that 'among the workers today will be recruited tomorrow's factory owners, if not in the first generation, at least in the second'.[142]

The Iron Guard and Anti-Communism

Anti-communism represented one of the most important *raisons d'être* of all fascist movements, and this is true for the Iron Guard too. In fact, communism in Romania was extremely weak, almost non-existent. All historians and political scientists agree that the Romanian Communist Party never had a membership higher than 1,000, and most of these party members belonged to various ethnic minorities. Indeed, concerning 'the ethnic origin of the RCP membership the following situation emerges in 1933: Romanians 375, Hungarians 444, Jews 330, Bulgarians 140, Russians 100, Ukrainians 70'.[143] In reality, fear of communism (fascist or non-fascist) in Romania, was more related to the USSR – a giant and often aggressive neighbour – which never recognised the loss of Bessarabia in 1919.

Nevertheless, the necessity of struggling against communism was a priority for certain Romanian fascist leaders or ideologues, such as C.Z. Codreanu and Traian Braileanu, who both emphasised the incompatibility of communism and 'the psychic structure' of the Romanian people. Similarly, after calling for the crushing, and casting into the fire, of communist functionaries, Mircea Strainul argued:

> the communist hydra does not belong in this country where Stephen the Great still lives in the monastery of Putna bathed in the sun. The sinister hyenas are mistaken in imagining that they can make the pyre of their crimes come crashing down on our country of wheat, of ewe lambs and of fairies.[144]

In the same vein, Mihail Polihroniade wrote that 'the Legion and its creator have won great merit before God and before men for having given a concrete and definitive expression to the Romanians' manifest anti-Marxism'.[145]

Basically, the Legionary movement denied the legitimacy of all ideologies except its own, as Traian Herseni wrote: 'In Romania today no one, except for the Legion, represents a political position that is valid and capable of electrifying the people. Beyond the Legion there is only the return to darkness and chaos'.[146] One of the notions that the Legion insistently attacked was that of the class struggle. Thus Traian Braileanu, in affirming the strictly anti-communist character of the Legion, emphasised the necessity of taking a firm position on class struggle.[147] Similarly, Vasile Marin declared sententiously: 'We condemn and we reject with disdain the doctrine that incites lucrative and productive categories against other lucrative and productive categories'.[148] Rallying to Marin's assault, Nicolae Bogdan wrote that the followers of Marxism 'adopt an infernal principle of life–class struggle, which issued from base envy, from sadistic calculations, from manifest perversion'.[149] In an article significantly entitled 'Noi, reactionarii' ('We, the reactionaries'), Bogdan further maintained that the origins of communism were satanic because it

> offered the most characteristic prototype of the infernal and destructive revolution. This form of life, plainly diabolical in inspiration, making use from the very first of the most seductive lie, in order to push naive souls into succumbing to the temptation of the most bloody terror, and then, in order to dominate and become masters of these souls, just as a drunken peasant dominates his ox or his horse. This form of life thus represents a catastrophic regression in the history of humanity. Bolshevism signifies the return to the state of barbarism, systematic and

scientific brutalisation of all humanity, reduced forever to slavery, condemned to serve forever without appeal a closed caste of terrorists, of sadistic criminals, of maniacal kikes.[150]

Presenting communism in much the same way, the following text was published by the newspaper *Buna Vestire* (*Good News*): 'Present-day communism means, in the economic order, the regime of collective property and the suppression of the family, in the spiritual order the regime of atheism, in the social order the primacy of the proletariat, in the political order internationalism'.[151]

Additionally, Alexandru Cantacuzino wrote that communism is aimed at a systematically pronounced 'annihilation of the human personality', that the 'communists are elements harmful to the essence of Romania and to the national life ... The communist spirit is anti-national'. Other accusations were added to the pile, such as: 'Communist internationalism does not want to recognise the [human] races'.[152]

If the Legion ever expressed itself in a clear, unequivocal, unambiguous fashion, this surely would have been through its anti-communism: 'in the social order there is nothing more anti-communist than the Legionary movement'.[153] The idea of an absolute opposition between the Legion and communism was noted by Alexandru Cantacuzino when he claimed that 'the sensibility and the reflexes of thought provoked by Legionary spirituality stir up in humanity a new force, diametrically opposed to the communist, Marxist world's way of being'.[154] The opposition between the Legionary movement and communism was most often absolute. This was a long-term and short-term conflict of interest, a contradiction in form and substance. That is why the annihilation of communism was the dream of all Legionary ideologues: that was one of the main goals of the Legionary movement. Iron Guard writings on communism in Romania mix hostility to class struggle, chauvinism, antisemitism and even death threats. Romanian fascists presented communism as a Jewish product and Romanian communists as 'strangers to their nation'. The Legionnaires often mixed together communists, Jews and freemasons, while attributing the most satanic qualities to this combination.

Fascist journalists, such as Toma Vladescu, used the trials of various militant anti-fascists in order to launch violently anti-communist polemics. For example, Vladescu approved the sentence pronounced at the trial of Petre Constantinescu-Iasi, a communist fellow-traveller, while emphasising 'the imperious need to protect the public consciousness of this country from so many intellectual blackguards, who get their most criminal slogans from the latest dictionary of mystification fabricated in Moscow during the sessions of the Comintern'.[155] In cases where communist militants and sympathisers were still free, the Romanian fascists called for their immediate arrest.

Quite often, Iron Guard anti-communist propaganda conflated communists with personalities who had nothing in common with this movement. Thus Nicolae Rosu attacked not only Lenin, Zinoviev, Trotsky and Liebknecht, but also Baudelaire, Dostoyevsky, Stefan Zweig, Gide, Tristan Tzara, Romain Rolland, Eugene Ionesco, Victor Brauner, Heinrich Mann, Freud, Proust, Durkheim and Bergson.[156] In the same spirit, Nae Ionescu, in a collection of texts edited by Mircea Eliade, expressed his contempt for Brancusi, Bergson and Kokoschka. For his part, Toma Vladescu, in an editorial in *Porunca Vremii* (*Master of the Times*), violently attacked Gide, Malraux and Tzara.[157] By means of this deliberately chosen amalgam of politicians and writers of the most varied political and literary stripe – not to mention scholars, painters and sculptors – the Iron Guard tried to inculcate fear in the face of diversity and novelty, wherever it appeared. This supposed state of disorder was due, they claimed, to democracy, which 'had created this microcosm of ideas, while ignoring, through excessive liberty, all the possibilities of being, opening the way to invasion by the rebel, by the free and equal individual, the critical, anarchist spirit'.[158] As Vasile Marin stated, the 'parasitic democracy' that allowed creations by the above-mentioned intellectuals had to be opposed by a state with totalitarian functions – obviously the Iron Guard state.[159] According to Marin, the ultimate goal was the creation of a *new man*, the Iron Guard man: 'Democracy produces the universal, abstract, ideal man, always identical to himself, whereas we need men who are solidly rooted in our soil, in our history, in the national consciousness, adapted to the national necessities'.[160]

NOTES

The assertions, arguments and conclusions contained herein are those of the author. They reflect solely his opinions and not those of any organisation or agency with which the author is affiliated.

1. Mihaly Vajda, *Fascism as Mass Movement* (London: Alison and Busby, 1976), p.26.
2. C.Z. Codreanu, *Pentru legionari* (Sibiu: Totul pentru Tara, 1936), Vol.I, p.426.
3. P.P. Panaitescu, 'Ce este 0 natiune', *Cuvintul*, 18 December 1940.
4. Traian Herseni, 'Noua rinduiala a tarii', *Cuvintul*, 20 December 1940.

5. Ion Veverca, *Suflet si gind legionar* (Bucharest: Serviciul propagandei legionare, 1937–40), p.10.
6. See *Porunca Vremii*, 3 April 1936.
7. Ion Veverca, *Nationalism economic* (Bucharest: Editura Cartea Romaneasca, 1941), p.177.
8. Nicolae Rosu, 'Biologia culturii', *Cuvintul*, 10 January 1941.
9. Nicolae Rosu, *Dialectica nationalismului* (Bucharest: Editura Cugetarea, 1937), pp.341–2.
10. Alexandru Cantacuzino, *Romanismul nostru* (Bucharest: 1936), p.8.
11. Ibid., p.5.
12. Viorica Lazarescu, 'Înainte', *Cântece Legionare* (Bucharest: 1937; reprinted Salzburg: Colectia 'Omul Nou', 1951), p.10.
13. P.P. Panaitescu, 'Noi sintem de aici', *Cuvintul*, 20 November 1940.
14. Cantacuzino (note 10), p.204.
15. S. Dimancea, 'Elogiul dacismului', *Sfarma Piatra*, 3 March 1938.
16. Alexandru Randa, *Rasism romanesc* (Bucharest: Editura Bucovina, L E. Toroutiu, 1941), p.7.
17. Ibid., p.17.
18. Ibid.
19. Mircea Eliade, 'Elogiu Transilvaniei', *Vremea*, 29 November 1936.
20. Emil Cioran, *Schimbarea la fata a Romaniei* (Bucharest: Vremea, 1934), p.115.
21. George Calinescu, *Istoria literaturii romane* (Bucharest: Fundatia Regala pentru Literatura si Arta, 1941), p.368.
22. Cioran (note 20), p.281.
23. Cantacuzino (note 10), p.10.
24. Leon Poliakov, *Histoire de l'antisemitisme*, Vol.1, *Du Christ aux Juifs de Cour* (Paris: Calmann-Lévy, 1955), p.282.
25. Emanuel Turczynski, 'The Background of Romanian Fascism', in Peter F. Sugar (ed.), *Native Fascism in the Successor States* (Santa Barbara, CA: ABC-Clio, 1971), p.104.
26. Lucretiu Patrascanu, *Sub trei dictaturi* (Bucharest: Humanitas, 1996), p.106.
27. Erno Gall, *Sociologia burgheza in Romania* (Bucharest: Editura Stiintifica si Enciclopedica, 1963), pp.222–3.
28. A.C. Cuza, *Numerus Clausus* (Bucharest: Editura Ligii Apararii Nationale Crestine, 1924), pp.6–7.
29. Octavian Goga, 'Primejdia strainilor', *Porunca Vremii*, 5 June 1934.
30. Septimiu Bucur, *Sfarma Piatra* 1/2 (1935).
31. Radu Barda, 'Romane iata-ce-ai sa faci', *Porunca Vremii*, 20 September 1935.
32. Mircea Eliade, 'Bucuresti centru viril', *Vremea*, 12 May 1937.
33. Eliade (note 19).
34. Mircea Eliade, 'Pilotii orbi', *Vremea*, 19 September 1937.
35. Nicolae Bogdan, 'Problemele demografice ale rasei albe', *Porunca Vremii*, 12 May 1935.
36. Ion Foti, *Conceptia eroica asupra rasei* (Bucharest: Biblioteca Eroica Generatia Noua, 1936), pp.17, 133.
37. Ibid., pp.153–5.
38. Traian Braileanu, *Sociologia si arta guvernarii politice* (Cernauti: Editura Insemnari Sociologice, 1937), p.67.
39. Mihail Polihroniade, 'National-socialismul si problema jidoveasca', *Buna Vestire*, 11 February 1938.
40. Alexandru Razmerita, *Cum sa ne aparam de evrei – Un plan de eliminare totala* (Turnu Severin: Tipografia Minerva, 1938), pp.65–9.
41. Traian Herseni, 'Mitul singelui', *Cuvintul*, 23 November 1940.
42. Traian Herseni, 'Rasa si destin national', *Cuvintul*, 16 January 1941.
43. Ibid.

44. Herseni (note 41).
45. Herseni (note 42).
46. P. Tiparescu, *Rasa si degenerare* (Bucharest: Tipografia Bucovina, I.R. Toroutiu, 1941), p.8.
47. Ibid.
48. Vasile Marin, *Crez de generatie* (Bucharest: Cartea Romaneasca, 1940), p.21.
49. P.P. Panaitescu, 'Profetii neamului', *Cuvintul*, 1 December 1940.
50. Rosu (note 10), pp.318, 322.
51. Traian Braileanu, 'Legiunea si Parlamentul', *Buna Vestire*, 31 December 1937.
52. Traian Braileanu, 'Problema elitelor in statul national-legionar', *Universul*, 11 January 1941.
53. Ibid.
54. Nicolae Patrascu, 'Pozitia nelegionarilor fata de miscarea legionara', *Universul*, 16 January 1941.
55. Constantin Noica, '10.001', *Buna Vestire*, 20 September 1940.
56. Ibid.
57. Constantin Noica, 'Electra sau femeia legionara', *Buna Vestire*, 9 October 1940.
58. Codreanu (note 2), Vol.I, p.420.
59. Anonymous, 'Doctrina stingei', *Porunca Vremii*, 14 September 1935.
60. G. Racoveanu, 'Ascultarea, lege a Capitanului', *Cuvintul*, 4 December 1940.
61. Mircea Eliade, 'Noua aristocratie legionara', *Vremea*, 23 January 1938.
62. C.Z. Codreanu, *Carticica sefului de cuib* (Bucharest: 1937; reprinted Munich: Omul Nou, 1971), p.28.
63. Nae Ionescu, *Cuvintul*, 27 January 1938.
64. Ion I. Mota, *Pamintul stramosesc* 1 (Jassy: August 1927).
65. Traian Herseni, 'Noua rinduiala a tarii', *Cuvintul*, 20 December 20, 1940.
66. Traian Herseni, 'Tilcul disciplinei legionare', *Cuvintul*, 30 December 1940.
67. Mihail Manoilescu, 'De la Lord Byron la Ion Mota', *Buna Vestire*, 24 February 1937.
68. P.P. Panaitescu, 'Profetti neamului', *Cuvintul*, 1 December 1940.
69. P.P. Panaitescu, 'Descalecator de tara', *Buna Vestire*, 14 September 1940.
70. Traian Herseni, 'Duhul Capitanului', *Cuvintul*, 5 December 1940.
71. Mihai Sturdza, *România si sfârsitul Europei. Amintiri din tara pierduta* (Rio de Janeiro, Madrid: Editura Carpati, 1959; reprinted Paris/Alba Iulia: Editura Fronde, 1994), p.99.
72. Nicolae Crevedia, 'Zece ani de legionarism', *Porunca Vremii*, 9 June 1937.
73. I. Popa, *Geniul si personalitatea Maresalului Antonescu, conducatorul Statului roman* (Bucharest: 1943), p.13.
74. Ibid., pp.93–5.
75. Ibid., p.14.
76. I.P. Prundeni, 'Dumnezu e fascist', *Porunca Vremii*, 20 July 1937.
77. Lucretiu Patrascanu, *Problemele de baza ale Romaniei* (Bucharest: Editura Socec, 1945), p.242.
78. Patrascanu (note 26), p.50.
79. 'Sfinta de la Herastrau', *Porunca Vremii*, 27 September and 1 October 1935.
80. Nichifor Crainic, 'Vizita la Maglavit', *Sfarma Piatra* 1/8 (1936).
81. Dan Botta, *Sfarma Piatra* 2/8 (1936).
82. A. Simion, *Regimul politic din România în perioada sept. 1940–ian. 1942* (Cluj Napoca: Editura Dacia, 1976), p.48.
83. Ilie Imbrescu, *Biserica si miscrea legionara* (Bucharest: Editura Cartea Romaneasca, 1939), p.201.
84. Ernst Nolte, *Le Fascisme dans son époque* (Paris: Julliard, 1970), p.60.
85. Nae Ionescu, 'Sub semnul Arhanghelului', *Buna Vestire*, 27 June 1937.
86. Foti (note 36), p.163.
87. Mircea Eliade, 'Provincia si legionarismul', *Vremea*, 13 February 1938.

88. P.P. Panaitescu, 'Nae Ionescu si Universitatea din Bucuresti', *Cuvintul*, 7 December 1940.
89. Ion Mota, *Cranii de lemn, 1922–1926* (Sibiu: Editura Totul pentru Tara, 1936), p.57.
90. Mihail Polihroniade, 'Garda de Fier', *Calendarul*, 17 November 1932, reproduced in *Pamintul stramosesc*, 1 January 1933.
91. Horatiu Comaniciu, 'Se reface sufletul tarii', *Buna Vestire*, 18 September 1940.
92. Constantin Noica, 'Procesul Ioanei d'Arc, *Buna Vestire*, 26 September 1940.
93. Constantin Noica, *Buna Vestire*, 21 September 1940.
94. Constantin Noica, 'Sinteti sub har', *Buna Vestire*, 4 October 1940.
95. Constantin Noica, 'Cumplita lor calatorie', *Buna Vestire*, 12 September 1940.
96. Mircea Eliade, 'Strigoii', *Cuvintul*, 21 January 1938.
97. Traian Herseni, 'Duhul Capitanului', *Cuvintul*, September 1940.
98. Cioran (note 20), p.8.
99. Panaitescu (note 49).
100. Mircea Eliade, *Buna Vestire*, 14 January 1938.
101. Ibid.
102. Mircea Eliade, 'De ce cred in biruinta miscarii legionare', *Buna Vestire*, 17 December 1937.
103. Mircea Eliade, 'Un popor tara misiune', *Vremea*, 1 December 1935. See also 'Cele doua Romanii', *Vremea*, 4 October 1936.
104. Horia Cosmovici, *Adevarul în procesul lui Corneliu Zelea Codreanu* (Bucharest: May 1938), p.73.
105. See Nichifor Crainic, *Ortodoxia, conceptia noastra de viata* (Sibiu: Editura TTS, 1937); and Alexandru Cantacuzino, *Intre lumea legionara si lumea comunista* (Bucharest: Serviciul de propaganda legionara, 1940).
106. Mihail Manoilescu, 'Sensul antiburghez al revolutiei nationale', *Lumea Noua* (October–November 1937), p.321.
107. Leon Topa, 'Intre economic si politic', *Cuvintul*, 28 December 1940.
108. Traian Braileanu, 'Socialism National', *Cuvintul*, 22 December 1940; lecture given by Braileanu, Minister of National Education, Religion, and Art in Ploiesti, 19 December 1940.
109. Mihail Polihroniade, 'Foamca si setea de dreptate', *Buna Vestire*, 8 August 1937.
110. P.P. Panaitescu, 'Burghezia romaneasca', *Cuvintul*, 11 January 1941.
111. Eliade (note 34), original emphasis.
112. Mircea Eliade, 'Roumain, Rumenien, Rumme, Romeno', *Vremea*, 3 March 1936.
113. Eliade, (note 19).
114. Mircea Eliade, '1918–1921', *Vremea*, 27 October 1935.
115. Mircea Eliade, 'Sa veniti odata in Maramures', *Vremea*, 5 December 1937.
116. Codreanu (note 2), Vol.I, p.87.
117. Braileanu (note 52).
118. Traian Braileanu, *Legiunea Arhanghelului Mihail-Garda de Fier-Programul si caracterul general* (Cluj: 1931), p.5.
119. P.P. Panaitescu, 'Orasele noastre', *Cuvintul*, 14 December 1940.
120. Nicolae Rosu, 'Soarta marii burghezii', *Cuvintul*, 12 January 1941.
121. Codreanu (note 62), p.11.
122. Patrascanu (note 77), p.242.
123. Ibid., p.244.
124. Mircea Vulcanescu and Mihail Manoilescu, *Tendintele tinerei generati: Doua conferinte* (Bucharest: Tipografia ziarului Universul, 1934), p.27.
125. Ionescu (note 85), p.287.
126. Cioran (note 20), p.134.
127. Veverca (note 5), p.17.
128. Sturdza (note 71), p.114.

129. Stelian Neagoe, 'Garda de Fier in Parlamentul Romaniei – Din dezbaterile Adunarii deputatilor', 3 December 1931, p.304, in *Impotriva fascismului* (Bucharest: 1971), p.57.
130. Gabriel Balanescu, 'Taranul din nou stapin', *Buna Vestire*, 22 January 1941.
131. Eugen Weber, 'The Men of the Archangel', *Journal of Contemporary History*, 1/1 (1996), p.118 Eugen Weber mentions the same figure of 8,000 for the Bucharest legionary workers corps in 1938. He adds that in October 1940 it reached 13,000 members; see also *Buna Vestire*, 10 November 1940; and C.Z. *Codreanu, 20 de ani de la moarte* (Madrid: Carpatii, 1955).
132. A.C. Cuza, *Programul L.A.N.C.* (Cluj: Tipografia Nationala SA, 1934), p.2.
133. Nicolae Bogdan, 'Biata muncitorime inselata', *Porunca Vremii*, 25 June 1935.
134. Nicolae Bogdan, 'Nemultumirile ceferistilor exploatati de iudeo-bolsevici', *Porunca Vremii*, 28 August 1935.
135. George Macrin, 'Discursul Fuhrerului pentru muncitori', *Cuvintul*, 14 December 1940.
136. Anonymous, 'Comentariu la rechizitoriu in procesul a 19 comunisti', *Porunca Vremii*, 3 July 1936.
137. Gall (note 27), p.245.
138. Gheorghe Clime, *Buna Vestire*, 26 October 1940.
139. Dumitru Groza, 'Capitanul, mesia muncitorului roman', *Cuvintul*, 22 December 1940.
140. C.Z. Codreanu, *Buna Vestire*, 8 August 1937.
141. Interview with Horia Sima, in Jacques de Launay, *Les derniers jours du fascisme en Europe* (Paris: Editions Albatros, 1977).
142. Vasile Iasinschi, 'Discurs', *Cuvintul*, 1 December 1940.
143. M.C. Stanescu, *Moscova. Cominternul, filiera comunista balcanica in Romania (1919–1944)* (Bucharest: 1941), quoted in Florian Banu, 'Foametea din '46 si cresterea anti-semitismului in Moldova', in Kurt Treptow, *Romania: A Crossroads of Europe* (Iasi: Centre for Romanian Studies, 2002), p.246.
144. Mircea Streinul, 'Hidra rosie', *Buna Vestire*, 10 March 1938.
145. M. Polihroniade, 'Legiunea in Viata Romaniei', *Buna Vestire*, 22 February 1937.
146. Traian Herseni, 'N-aveti nici un ideal', *Cuvintul*, 15 December 1930.
147. Braileanu (note 38), p.143.
148. Marin (note 48), p.40.
149. Nicolae Bogdan, 'Pomind de la criteriul antimarxist', *Buna Vestire*, 22 February 1937.
150. Nicolae Bogdan, 'Noi reactionarii', *Porunca Vremii*, 7 July 1939.
151. Anonymous, 'Ultima calomnie: comunismul legionarilor', *Buna Vestire*, 27 January 1938.
152. Cantacuziono (note 105), p.29.
153. Anonymous (note 151).
154. Cantacuziono (note 105), p.29.
155. Toma Vladescu, 'Sentinta de la Chisinau', *Porunca Vremii*, 3 April 1936.
156. Nicolae Rosu, *Orientari în veac* (Bucharest: Editura Cugetarea, 1937).
157. Toma Vladescu, 'Elitele si comunismul', *Porunca Vremii*, 16 July 1935.
158. Ibid.
159. Marin (note 48), p.16.
160. Ibid., p.8.

The Upward Path: Palingenesis, Political Religion and the National Alliance

MARTIN DURHAM

On 23 July 2002, William Pierce died of kidney failure and cancer. First an associate professor of physics, then a senior research scientist, he was initially a member of the anti-communist John Birch Society. However, he complained, the Society was 'against the civil rights revolution, but they wouldn't deal with it on a racial basis'. In 1964, he arranged a meeting with George Lincoln Rockwell, the Commander of the American Nazi Party. While he never joined Rockwell's party, Pierce had found the politics that would shape his life. Pierce proposed to Rockwell the creation of a journal that would elaborate the party's beliefs, and in 1966 he launched *National Socialist World*. It was not an association that would last. In 1967, Rockwell was assassinated by a former party member, John Patler. Pierce finally decided to join what was now the National Socialist White People's Party, but following a conflict with Rockwell's successor, Pierce broke away to become a leading official in a recently formed racist group, the National Youth Alliance. In 1974, the organisation became the National Alliance, an organisation that Pierce was to lead until his death.[1] Committed to a total revolution and the rebirth of the white race, the National Alliance is a particularly good exemplar of Roger Griffin's definition of fascism. As we will see, however, whether it can also be understood as a political religion is a more complex question.

In recent years, the National Alliance has been the subject of considerable media attention. In large part, this is a result of Pierce's (pseudonymous) authoring of a futuristic novel, *The Turner Diaries*, in which the protagonist, Earl Turner, plays a central part in a guerrilla war against what is seen as a Jewish-controlled American government. The book opens with gun confiscation raids, and it was at gun shows that copies of the book were sold by Timothy McVeigh, who, in 1995, achieved notoriety for the bombing of the Oklahoma City federal building and the resulting deaths of 168 people. That the biggest terrorist attack on American soil before *al-Qaeda*'s 2001 attacks on the World Trade Center and the Pentagon had been partly inspired by Pierce's novel made him the most publicised American right-wing extremist of recent decades.[2]

The Turner Diaries is a work of fiction. But as the National Alliance's own book service observes, it is 'a vehicle' for his 'ideas about race and society', and we can gain important insights into his thinking by an examination of some of its contents. The book portrays a protracted war between 'the Organisation' and 'the System'. The Organisation's campaign escalates from bombing the FBI's headquarters to a mortar attack on the Capital. But the campaign does not generate mass support, and abandoning its earlier hopes in the effect of 'propaganda of the deed', the attacks are turned towards economic targets. Most whites, the Organisation had concluded, had fallen 'under the Jewish spell' and no longer cared for their race. 'What the Organization began doing ... is treating Americans realistically, for the first time – namely, like a herd of cattle ... And, when they begin getting hungry, we will make them fear us more than they fear the System'.[3]

The Organisation grows, in part, through clandestine recruitment within the armed forces. After numerous attacks, it is finally strong enough to seize control of much of California, and in 'the Day of the Rope', thousands of white women who are married to, or living with, non-whites are hung, with placards around their necks bearing the legend, 'I defiled my race'. Ultimately, missiles are launched against Israel, the Soviet Union and New York. Turner himself dies in a suicide air attack on the Pentagon, but the 'dream of a White world' triumphs. The Organisation spreads across Europe, 'race traitors' and guest workers perish as 'the New Era' dawns, and chemical, biological and radiological warfare is unleashed to depopulate millions of square miles from the Urals to the Pacific.[4]

Pierce's novel has long played an important part in the National Alliance's propaganda, and it has reportedly sold over 350,000 copies. In his second, lesser known, novel, entitled *Hunter*, Pierce returned to the subject of political violence, but in a way that might at first sight seem less than conducive to the Alliance's purposes. Dedicated to Joseph Paul Franklin, a former member of the National Socialist White People's Party who had committed a number of racial murders during the 1970s, Oscar Yeager, *Hunter*'s leading character, kills inter-racial couples. As Pierce was later to describe, he had decided that where in his first novel, the main character had sprung 'full-blown into the world', it would be more effective to show a character that developed from merely being anti-black to understanding 'the Jewish angle'. But what of the strategy advanced in the novel? Was Pierce advocating that readers should emulate Franklin? More broadly, was he espousing the view, increasingly popular among sections of the American extreme Right, that the only way that racists can avoid government infiltration and incarceration was by abandoning centralised organisation and turning instead to individual or, at most, small group terror? The answer is no. The leading protagonist is persuaded by another of the characters that a greater service to the race would be to join an organisation, which can actually destroy 'the System'. As with *The Turner Diaries*, Pierce's hero joins a group that may be seen as a fictional equivalent of the National Alliance.[5]

Much of what Pierce wrote in these works is echoed in the organisation's more programmatic writings, two of which deserve particular study. The first is a publication which is described in its introduction as 'a chronicle' of white awakening to 'the reality of their race's degradation, and to their responsibility for their future'. The chronicle consists of articles selected from the National Alliance's paper, initially known as *Attack!*, then retitled *National Vanguard*. The articles, originally published between 1970 and 1982, range widely, but at their core is race. Thus, one article described blacks as less intelligent, more likely to commit violent crimes and culturally inferior, while in an 'Open Letter to the U.S. Congress', elected officials were denounced for passing civil rights legislation, supporting the bussing of black school children to aid their integration into society, and introducing '"reverse discrimination" which takes jobs away from Whites and gives them to Blacks'. The time would come, it proclaimed, when they would pay for their lives for their treason.[6]

America was threatened too, the Alliance contended, by immigration. There was 'a massive invasion of racially and culturally foreign elements', and the race that had built the nation's institutions and forged its culture was facing disaster. In part, Pierce's organisation believed America was in danger because of machinations by big business. Not only did it benefit from cheap labour, its interests were 'distinct from those of the people, of the nation, of the race'. But beyond its hostility to the black presence in America, its abhorrence of immigration and its conviction that 'Capital' had become a 'power unto itself' rested the central feature of the National Alliance's politics. There was a plan to 'undo God's greatest piece of handiwork, a piece of handiwork which has required millions of years for its slow evolution and which, once undone by wide-scale miscegenation, will be gone forever'. The plan to destroy the white race was part of the Jews' 'age-old dream of world domination'. Thus the Bolshevik Revolution had been the work of Jews, and America itself was now in a 'Jewish stranglehold'. Jews, it claimed in one particularly vitriolic article, could not 'live without their Gentile prey to feed on'. And again, they had been 'specially adapted by Nature to their parasite role ... they scribble lies for the newspaper ... they sicken our children's minds in the schools ... they incite riots ... they own; they rent; they lend; they undermine; they subvert; they destroy'.[7]

In confronting enemies of the race, the Alliance believed only its politics would suffice. Conservatives, it complained, failed to understand what was at stake. What was needed was 'a race-based fighting creed', but all they had to offer were 'defensive, race-denying clichés'. Libertarianism too, with its belief that individual freedom stood higher than the collective, had to be rejected. But if both conservatism and libertarianism were antithetical to the 'race soul' and 'service to the whole', was there an alternative?[8]

As National Alliance readings of European history showed, there was. Thus one article celebrated the Hungarian Arrow Cross. In elections in 1939, it recalled, the movement had gained nearly 40 per cent of the vote in elections, and towards the end of the Second World War had seized power. The 1956 Hungarian revolt, it remarked, was rightly remembered today. But the Arrow Cross's battle to save Hungary from Soviet invasion stood even higher. If this contribution defended one nation's fascist organisation, it also linked its struggle to the force that had fought alongside it, 'that unique pan-European fighting force, the Waffen S.S.'. Another article made this argument even more strongly, heroising Leon Degrelle, the Belgian fascist who led a brigade of his fellow-countrymen on the Russian front. As a result of their valour, it declared, they had been made part of the Waffen SS: 'Nor did they fight alone. There fought beside them half-a-million other volunteers, from thirty different European peoples'.[9]

The articles, as the introduction to the collection recognises, map a developing view. The earliest articles culminate with a call to 'Smash the System!' and another the following year declared that if revolution meant 'blood and chaos and battling the alien enemy from house to house in burning cities throughout our land – then, by God, it is better that we get on with it now'. Nearly a decade later, however, in 'The Task of the National Alliance', Pierce set out a more long-term perspective. At the present time, any strategy based on 'mass support for revolutionary action', he argued, was doomed. The masses were mindlessly opposed to change, while 'the more illuminated strata of the White population' were unable to grasp the values necessary for a new order. Where the National Alliance had once sought to mobilise the masses, now it sought to recruit an élite and create 'a fixed pole of the spirit ... a citadel of the ageless values of our race'. Eventually, when conditions were ripe, the National Alliance could finally achieve the leadership it had long sought. But only by forging an organisation that restricted its recruitment to the 'elite minority capable of responding to our message' could it finally triumph.[10]

What would that triumph entail? As we have seen, *The Turner Diaries* gives one answer. Another can be found in the text given by the organisation to new recruits. The National Alliance's *Membership Handbook* calls for an end to multi-racial 'sickness', and the reversal of the 'long-term demographic trend toward a darker world'. In 'spiritually healthier times', it states, all of Europe, Australia and parts of the Americas and of Africa had been 'our living area and our breeding area, and it must be so again ... We will do whatever is necessary to achieve this White living space and to keep it White'.[11]

The *Handbook* argues that this will involve much preparatory work. Only by 'first building a solid revolutionary infrastructure' could power eventually be gained. Thus work would have to be carried out inside the armed forces. A mass media would need to be set up to bring the organisation's message to those who would listen.

But only in the final stages would it be possible to win the attention of those who cared more for 'spectator sports or *Star Trek*'. The result would be the creation of a government 'wholly committed to the service of our race and subject to no non-Aryan influences'. It would be structured to avoid 'corruption' and 'subversion', and in order to do so could not be democratic. It should be made up of men and women 'whose attitude toward its mission is essentially *religious*; a government more like a holy order than like any existing secular government today'. It would span 'several continents' and would be responsible for the co-ordination of crucial tasks 'during the first few decades of a White world: the racial cleansing of the land, the rooting out of racially destructive institutions, and the reorganization of society on a new basis'. Of these, the most important task would be 'to reverse the racially devolutionary course of the last few millennia and keep it reversed: a long-term eugenics program involving at least the entire populations of Europe and America'.[12]

Living space, racial cleansing, eugenics: even without knowing Pierce's background in the American Nazi Party, such language inevitably evokes National Socialism of the 1930s. Unlike a number of American groupings, such as the SS Action Group or the National Socialist Movement, the National Alliance has sought to avoid being identified with what it terms 'made-in Hollywood "Nazis"'. The *Handbook* argues that it is vital not to become identified with the symbolism of Hitler's movement, an imagery that is alien to America. But it would also be wrong 'to shut our minds to the eternal truths enshrined in the National Socialist idea: they are the truths on which our own creed is based'.[13]

We need not only draw upon its *Membership Handbook* to understand the relationship between the National Alliance's world view and National Socialism. Its enthusiasm for Hitler is evident in other publications, from Pierce's description of him as 'the Great One' in *The Turner Diaries* to the Alliance book service's promotion of *Mein Kampf*. It has also been strikingly present in issues of *National Vanguard*. Indeed, in one article it expresses anxiety over the popularity of Holocaust revisionism on the extreme Right. While it was a lie to claim that the Third Reich had pursued a policy of the mass gassing of Jews, Pierce claims he had 'spoken with SS men who told me that they shot Jews, and I believed them'. The revisionist who could not 'face the Holocaust squarely and judge it on the basis of a higher morality, according to which it is only the upward course of Life which is sacred' would be unable to face the new problems of non-white immigration and a high non-white birth rate.[14]

As with *The Turner Diaries*, the article defended both National Socialism and a race war that would culminate in a fight to the death between ethnic groups. The Alliance's admiration for the Third Reich is also graphically illustrated in the magazine's choice of covers. One reproduced a NSDAP poster of a joyful family, on which was superimposed the words 'What We Killed: Germany Under Hitler'. A second showed a family sitting beneath a poster of Hitler, this time captioned 'A People Redeemed: The German Revolution of 1933'. A third simply showed a photo of Hitler, and the dates 1889–1989. Marking the centenary of Hitler's birth, the latter issue's editorial acclaimed his economic policies, his restoration of German morale and his inspiration of 'idealistic young men' across Europe and beyond. Hitler had been 'the greatest man of our era ... more closely attuned to the Life Force which permeates our cosmos and gives it meaning and purpose ... than any other man of our times'.[15]

This reference to 'the Life Force' should draw our attention to one of the most important characteristics of the National Alliance, that is its relationship to Pierce's distinct religious conceptions. Its *Membership Handbook* explicitly rejects what it describes as 'the Semitic view, which separates man from the rest of the world'. There is no man-like divine being ruling the world by supernatural law, it contends. Instead what the race needed was a religion that would be 'conducive to our mission of racial progress'.[16]

The *Handbook* holds that it is vital to strive for 'the advancement of our race in the service of Life'. In forging such a view, the National Alliance drew on a variety of earlier sources. In an article that appeared in the early 1980s, those authors cited include D.H. Lawrence, George Bernard Shaw and Friedrich Nietzsche. Lawrence, it observed, had understood that humans and the cosmos were one. Shaw, 'the greatest British playwright since William Shakespeare', had argued that the 'exceptional few' consciously serve 'the Life Force', the 'primordial Essence' that 'eternally strives towards its own self-realization through the attainment of higher and higher forms of life'. But the most important writer, the article contended, was Nietzsche. 'Man is a rope', he had declared, 'fastened between animal and Superman – a rope over the abyss ... What is great in man is that he is a bridge and not a goal'. Centuries might be needed for the crossing of the abyss, the article held, but 'the best men and women of our race' could take part in it now. A 'finite life ... can acquire true meaning only when it partakes in the Infinite', and for those few who understood, 'it is their consciousness and their purpose which will determine the form and the spirit of the new order which will one day rise on this earth, and it is their descendents who will take the next step within that new order toward the Superman'.[17]

In another article shortly after, Nietzsche's view was contrasted with the belief that man 'exists in order to amuse a supposed divine archetype in the sky'. Instead, just as 'sub-man existed to prepare the way for man', so man would prepare the way for higher man, and 'higher man will exist to prepare the way for an even higher manifestation of life'. Nietzsche had declared that he loved those who sought to 'build a house for the Superman'. Neither pleasure nor religious piety was the purpose of existence: 'We know that our deepest and most consistent motivation is ... to climb toward the Light ... Knowledge of this sort ... is essentially religious in nature'. It could not be proved, 'but it is nonetheless certain'.[18]

Such a view is evident in *The Turner Diaries* too. At the heart of the Organisation, Turner discovers, is a secret grouping, the Order, through whose teachings he comes to see the struggle he is engaged in from a wider context. After reading its book, he 'could see the ages spread out before me ... from the steaming, primordial swamps ... to the unlimited possibilities ... ahead'. He is initiated into the Order, and told that members 'are to be the bearers of the Faith'. We are 'truly', he has come to believe, 'the instruments of God in the fulfilment of His Grand Design'.[19]

But how had this belief-system come about? Two authors have discussed its relationship to the National Alliance's politics. In the earlier discussion, Brad Whitsel explores the amalgam of ideas that were combined to produce what Pierce has described as Cosmotheism. Pierce's doctrine rejects traditional religion, Whitsel argues, and appears at first glance to be a secular philosophy, rooted in a crude biologism. But in a speech delivered in 1977, 'Cosmotheism: Wave of the Future', Pierce had portrayed man's 'mission as an agent of the universal will', and in a later interview, he had discussed its 'emphasis on eternity'. Cosmotheism, Whitsel concludes, is clearly religious.[20]

In a later discussion, Robert Griffin notes how Pierce had cited Lawrence's quote on humans and the cosmos during his 1977 speech. As for Shaw, he had been a crucial influence on Pierce as an undergraduate. Griffin discusses three pamphlets produced by Pierce on the subject in the late 1970s and early 1980s. The first, *The Path*, is particularly crucial:

> Man and the world and the Creator are not separate things, but man is part of the world, which is part of the Whole, which is the Creator. The tangible Universe is the material manifestation of the Creator ... Those who attain Divine Consciousness will ascend the Path of Life ... which ... leads upward through a never ending succession of states, the next of which is that of higher man, and the ultimate that of the Self-Realized Creator.[21]

As with the National Alliance's strategy, Cosmotheism has evolved over time, and Pierce's focus on the Life Force seems to have displaced his belief in a Creator. But, as Whitsel argues, he had forged a syncretic religion. Although Cosmotheism is distinct to him and the National Alliance, there are parallels with some of the religious manifestations entangled with the National Socialism shaping Pierce's early beliefs. In the early 1980s, an article appeared in *National Vanguard* written by a National Alliance member, who had been born in Germany and had lived there during the Second World War, editing a National Socialist women's publication. She had, she wrote, directly experienced 'the National Socialist revolution'. The changes the new regime had brought about had been inspired by the ancient sagas, by mystics and by prophets, and a 'new inner cosmology of being' had been created.

> It was as if every fiber of life, impelled by some organic force within, strained toward a higher level of existence, in order to become absorbed into that dimension of high consciousness that is the domain of godliness ... To one who was witness to the phenomenon, this self-realization was like a celebration of the God within, risen to consciousness after almost 2,000 years of kneeling to an alien god.

National Socialism had released 'a flood of creative energies into all areas of thought and action ... And the new sense of religiosity moved like an undercurrent through everything'.[22]

Pierce espoused the importance of both the National Alliance and Cosmotheism. What is the relationship between the two? Certainly members of the first do not have to adhere to the second. But this religious toleration was not unlimited. Its *Membership Handbook* makes it clear that it did not see Christianity as 'an Aryan religion'. Regardless of the problems such views might cause, it declared, the Alliance needed to take a stance on Christianity. Its other-worldliness was fundamentally incompatible with 'the Aryan quest for knowledge and for progress; its universalism conflicts directly with Aryan striving for beauty and strength; its delineation of the roles of man and god offends the Aryan sense of honor and self-sufficiency'.[23]

In this, the Alliance was significantly different from National Socialism. We have noted the similarity of Pierce's religious views to some of the religious manifestations of the Third Reich. But as Richard Steigmann-Gall has recently shown, contrary to what is frequently assumed, Hitler's party was closer to a racialised Protestantism than it was to the paganism that certainly motivated some of its members. Indeed, Hitler himself had declared in the 1920s that Christ was 'our greatest Aryan leader'. National Socialism, he told his followers, sought to exhume Christ's teachings. 'Through us alone, and not until now, do these teachings celebrate their resurrection!' Where the Alliance explicitly rejected Christianity, National Socialism did not.[24]

The National Alliance differs in other ways from its German predecessor, of which one is particularly important. This concerns its understanding of the scope of racial revolution. It uses the term American coterminously with white, eliminating others from America both symbolically and actually, yet its identification with America is literally skin-deep. It envisages a co-ordinated onslaught across the globe, and while different nations, its *Membership Handbook* states, will have their own societies, 'with their own roots, traditions, and language', over them all will stand one government spanning the race as a whole. For some on the American extreme Right, the only way forward is to divide the United States into racial enclaves. For Pierce's organisation, not even a racially homogeneous America would be enough. Instead, it sees the world as dominated by a '*Jew* World Order', and advocates an 'Aryan World Order' in its place.[25]

Distinct from National Socialism, the National Alliance also sees itself as distinct within the American extreme Right. Soon after its creation, it explicitly argued that those who urged that 'pro-White organisations' should unite were mistaken. Some groups were led by hucksters, out for what they could get. Some leaders were 'intoxicated with the feeling of being the biggest frog in his particular pond', or simply could not get along with others. Combining together would not change the situation for the better. Instead Nature showed the way, a ruthless weeding out through which one group would finally emerge as 'most fit to lead our people'. A quarter-century later, in the last speech he would make, Pierce made a similar point in a more brutal way:

> To sum up, the Alliance has no interest at all in the so-called 'movement'. We're not interested in uniting with the movement, and we're not interested in competing with the movement for members. If anything, we should be grateful that the movement is out there to soak up a lot of the freaks and weaklings who otherwise might find their way into the Alliance.[26]

The organisation that Pierce built over decades saw itself as the only force that could lead an American and ultimately pan-Aryan revolution. In comparison with rival organisations in America today, or those it admired in inter-war Europe, it has distinctive characteristics. But it also has crucial features in common. It is an example of fascism, and here it would be useful to turn our attention to attempts to understand that broader phenomenon. Are there particular theoretical approaches that shed light on the National Alliance? And, conversely, what light does the National Alliance shed on such approaches?

The most important development in this area has been the contribution of Roger Griffin, and here we need to recognise it involves a definition that has importantly changed since it was first formulated. In its early form, he characterised fascism as 'a genus of political ideology whose mythic core in its various permutations is a palingenetic form of populist ultra-nationalism'. Palingenesis, he proposes, should be understood as a new birth after *'a period of perceived decadence'*. Conservatism, liberalism and socialism are all host to this decadence, and in its place populist ultra-nationalism seeks a totalitarian order, drawing on the traditions of the past but brought together by new institutions and a new ethos. In a more recent formulation, the notion of ultra-nationalism is replaced by the suggestion that fascism can diverge on the 'type of ... homeland' it seeks. Yet while it might differ in what 'national or ethnic community' it sought to revive, what it shared was the belief that the path to a post-liberal new order lay in 'a total revolution'.[27]

The National Alliance does indeed believe in a total revolution. American society, and the West in general, it claims, is decadent and only a new order can offer a way out. Its commitment to a palingenetic vision is evident not only by its use of notions of decay and a new order, but in the very symbol it has adopted as its own. Originating in the alphabets of 'the ancient Germanic peoples', the Life Rune is described in its *Membership Handbook* as standing for 'birth, rebirth and renewal'. If Griffin's early definition is highly apposite, his subsequent shift away from seeing fascism as necessarily ultra-nationalist is similarly appropriate. The National Alliance, as we have seen, does not believe in an American palingenesis, but one spanning whole continents.[28]

In other ways too, Pierce's organisation is an exemplar of Griffin's definition. In his argument, the new ethos fascism seeks to introduce is not one that is populist in the sense arising from the people itself. Instead, it believes it speaks for the people, contaminated as they are by the decadence that has threatened to destroy the homeland. Only an élite, it holds, can lead the awakened land, a belief that the Alliance maintains in a particularly forthright way.[29]

But if the National Alliance accords with Griffin's definition of fascism, particularly in its later form, its entanglement with religion should take us in a different (but supplementary) direction. Can the NA be understood not only through the concept of palingenesis, but as a political religion? This concept has been applied to fascism in its classical form. Emilio Gentile has applied it to Italian Fascism, which, he declares, in pursuit of its totalitarian concept of politics, constructed its own system of beliefs, 'centred on the sacralization of the state'. When fascism finally emerged, it was on a terrain that had long been prepared for a political religion. Enrico Corradini, the leading Italian nationalist at the beginning of the century, had called for a 'religion of nature and heroes'. During the First World War and its aftermath, the 'soldier poet' Gabriele D'Annunzio invented 'religious metaphors' which fascism took over for its own symbolic purposes. The movement that Mussolini was ultimately to build represented a fully-fledged political religion. In 1922, Mussolini described his movement as a 'belief that has reached the level of religion', while ten years later he had characterised it as 'a religious concept of life'. Michael Burleigh has likewise applied the concept to National Socialism, which, he argues, was a faith with its own eschatology, where the believers were convinced that they would eventually progress 'from perdition to redemption' and from 'tiny sect to mass movement'. Hitler's movement, he contends, was 'the intellectual legatee of those who had reconciled racial science with the consolations of religion, by ascribing a redemptive mission to the racially-defined elective people'. Each of these discussions is evocative of the later grouping that we are examining. When the Italian movement referred to its local branches as 'churches of our faith' or 'altars of the Fatherland's religion', it was drawing on the Catholicism that saturated the country's political culture, just as the National Alliance's allusions to God or 'the Creator', while embedded in a non-Christian outlook, also resonates with the Christianity that has shaped America. Similarly, when Burleigh cites a writer in the 1930s arguing that National Socialism takes different religious forms, entailing an Aryanised Christianity, neo-paganism and the quasi-religious stance of the movement as a whole, we cannot but think of the German-born National Alliance member writing of the religious ferment that marked the Third Reich of her youth. But if we see religious elements within Italian Fascism, National Socialism and the National Alliance, can we see all three as examples of a political religion?[30]

Here we should turn to the elaboration of this conception by Emilio Gentile. He argues that the sacralisation of politics consecrates 'the primacy of a *collective secular entity*, placing it at the centre of a system of beliefs and myths that define the meaning and ultimate goals of social existence'. He distinguishes between democratic civil religion and totalitarian political religion, the former existing alongside traditional religions and different political ideologies, the latter rejecting ideological competition and adopting either a hostile stance to traditional religion or attempting to incorporate it into its own system of beliefs and myths.[31]

Because of the emphasis on the interface between totalitarianism and religion, and his detailed discussion of this in the context of Mussolini's Italy, it might at first sight appear that Gentile's conception is exactly what we might be looking for in understanding the distinctiveness of Pierce's organisation. However, the concept of totalitarianism has been the subject of some criticism. A particularly important part of this critique is the argument that the concept of totalitarianism liquidates the fundamental distinctions between fascism and communism, both with regard to ideology and economy.[32] There are, indeed, important distinctions between the two movements, but to conceptualise both as totalitarian need not deny this. Just as defining conservatism and fascism as parts of the Right, or communism and social democracy as parts of the Left, runs the risk of obscuring differences, so too with the concept of totalitarianism. But, as with the related concept of total revolution, totalitarianism can be deployed well to gain a better understanding of the National Alliance. But the exact way in which Gentile formulates the religious attributes of fascism poses a problem for our understanding of the grouping we have been discussing. The sacralisation of politics, Gentile suggests, involves the consecration of a secular entity. But neither in the classical period nor today does that adequately characterise all forms of fascism. In the early twentieth century, Romania's Iron Guard propounded an antisemitic politics shaped by an interpretation of the teachings of the Romanian Orthodox Church. The Guard was also known as the Legion of the Archangel Michael. According to its leader, Corneliu Codreanu, 'The archangel leads us, he defends us ... But in order for him to stand by us, we must believe in God and in the power of his archangel'. Rather than sacralising the secular state, the Iron Guard believed it was promoting 'the Resurrection of nations in the name of Jesus Christ'.[33] Such a relationship between religion and politics is importantly different from the specific way in which Gentile defines political religion. The National Alliance represents yet another relationship. Instead of seeking to subordinate traditional religion to its political project, the NA argues that it is incompatible with its politics. Instead, it is a religion tailored to the Alliance's purposes that must motivate the most advanced elements of the race.

How then shall we ultimately understand the National Alliance? It is firstly a palingenetic movement, committed to a monopoly of power and the conquest of society within an ethnic community that reaches far beyond America. With some reworking of the definition, it can also be understood as a political religion. But it is one in which the secular is not consecrated, but transcended. As we see in the National Alliance *Membership Handbook*, *The Turner Diaries* and other of its publications, the fascism that it seeks would be importantly different from that which came to power in the 1920s and 1930s. In the Aryan New Order William Pierce dreamed of creating, the state will be infused with a syncretic religion, and ruled by adepts of its teachings.

NOTES

1. R.S. Griffin, *The Fame of a Dead Man's Deeds: An Up-Close Portrait of White Nationalist William Pierce* (1st Books, 2001), pp.38, 83–119; and *Intelligence Report* (Fall 2002).
2. A. Macdonald, *The Turner Diaries* (Hillsboro, WV: National Vanguard Books, 1980), pp.1–5; S. Jones and P. Israel, *Others Unknown: The Oklahoma City Bombing Case and Conspiracy* (New York: Public Affairs, 1998), p.61; and *Rolling Stone*, 8 June 2000.
3. *Resistance* (Fall 1999); and Macdonald (note 2), pp.38, 60–1, 100–2.
4. Macdonald (note 2), pp.138–43, 160–1, 190, 201–5, 209–11.

5. A. Macdonald, *Hunter* (Hillsboro, WV: National Vanguard Books, 1989) pp.ii, 1–21, 153; J. Kaplan (ed.), *Encyclopedia of White Power* (Walnut Creek, CA: Rowman and Littlefield, 2000), pp.112–14; and G. Michael, *Confronting Right-wing Extremism and Terrorism in the USA* (London: Routledge, 2003), pp.115–19.
6. *Washington Post*, 12 January 2000; *The Best of Attack! and National Vanguard Tabloid* (Arlington, VA: National Vanguard Books, 1984), pp.iii, 53, 157.
7. *The Best of Attack!* (note 6), pp.14, 47, 52–3, 64–5, 81, 120–1.
8. Ibid., pp.7, 110–11.
9. Ibid., pp.153–5, 184–5.
10. Ibid., pp.iii, 1, 10, 160–2.
11. *Membership Handbook For Members of the National Alliance* (Hillsboro, WV: National Vanguard Books, 1993), pp.28–9.
12. Ibid., pp.30–1, 55–6.
13. Ibid., pp.120–2.
14. Macdonald (note 2), p.210; *Resistance* (Winter 2000); *The Best of Attack!* (note 6), pp.212–13.
15. *National Vanguard*, August 1983, May 1984, March–April 1989.
16. *Membership Handbook* (note 11), pp.22, 50.
17. Ibid., p.27; *National Vanguard*, June 1982.
18. *National Vanguard*, August 1982.
19. Macdonald (note 2), pp.70–3.
20. B. Whitsel, 'Aryan Visions for the Future in the West Virginia Mountains', *Terrorism and Political Violence* 7/4 (1995), pp.122–3, 128–9, 136, 138.
21. Griffin (note 1), pp.193–4, 197–8.
22. Ibid., p.195; Whitsel (note 20), p.129; *National Vanguard*, May 1984.
23. *Membership Handbook* (note 11), pp.46–50.
24. R. Steigmann-Gall, *The Holy Reich: Nazi Conceptions of Christianity, 1919–1945* (Cambridge: Cambridge University Press, 2003), pp.10–11, 27.
25. *Membership Handbook* (note 11), p.29; B.A. Dobratz and S.L. Shanks-Meile, *The White Separatist Movement in the United States: 'White Power, White Pride!'* (Baltimore, MD: Johns Hopkins University Press, 2000), pp.97–106; *National Vanguard*, March–April 1994.
26. *The Best of Attack!* (note 6), p.59; *Intelligence Report* (Fall 2002).
27. R. Griffin, *The Nature of Fascism* (London: Routledge 1993), pp.32–6, 44–5; R. Griffin, 'The Primacy of Culture: The Current Growth (or Manufacture) of Consensus within Fascist Studies', *Journal of Contemporary History* 37/1 (2002), p.24.
28. *Membership Handbook* (note 11), pp.19–21.
29. Griffin, *Nature of Fascism* (note 27), p.41.
30. E. Gentile, 'Fascism as Political Religion', *Journal of Contemporary History* 25 (1990), pp.230–5, 240; M. Burleigh, 'National Socialism as a Political Religion', *Totalitarian Movements and Political Religion* 1/2 (Autumn 2000), pp.1–26.
31. E. Gentile, 'The Sacralisation of Politics: Definitions, Interpretations and Reflections on the Question of Secular Religion and Totalitarianism', *Totalitarian Movements and Political Religion* 1/1 (2000), pp.22, 24–5.
32. M. Kitchen, *Fascism* (London: Macmillan, 1976), pp.28, 31–2. See also I. Kershaw, *The Nazi Dictatorship* (London: Edward Arnold, 1989), pp.32–5.
33. S.P. Ramet (ed.), *The Radical Right in Central and Eastern Europe* (Pennsylvania: Pennsylvania State University Press, 1999), p.12; Griffin, *Nature of Fascism* (note 27), pp.126, 139.

Christian Identity: The Apocalyptic Style, Political Religion, Palingenesis and Neo-Fascism

CHIP BERLET

Christian Identity as a Litmus Test of 'Political Religion' Theory

This article uses Christian Identity as a case study in the relationship between fascism, political religion and totalitarian movements that is the subject of this special issue. Since Emilio Gentile is the main theorist who has sought to clarify this relationship in analytical terms, it is appropriate to take his analysis as the starting point. Gentile has studied totalitarian movements of inter-war Europe, and argues that the sacralisation of politics takes place when:

> more or less elaborately and dogmatically, a political movement confers a sacred status on an earthly entity (the nation, the country, the state, humanity, society, race, proletariat, history, liberty, or revolution) and renders it an absolute principle of collective existence, considers it the main source of values for individual and mass behaviour, and exalts it as the supreme ethical precept of public life.[1]

Gentile sees political religion as only one element found in totalitarianism, but it is a crucial element. Totalitarianism is a term that is much abused. Gentile, however, carefully defines it in his article.[2] The term retains validity and usefulness in describing ideologies and systems that attempt to enforce total control over every aspect of a person's life – political, economic, social and cultural – in order to reshape the individual and unify society.[3] A totalitarian state is a central goal of fascist movements, including Nazism.[4] Arendt argued that Nazism (and Stalinism) were examples of totalitarian movements that gained state power.[5] Fascist movements, however, seldom succeed in seizing state power, and Gentile points out that even when they do, their totalitarian systems are flawed and often fail to achieve established goals.[6] What matters for this analysis is that fascist movements envision a future totalitarian society, rather than how successful a particular historic fascist group was in actually achieving totalitarian control.

According to Griffin, at the core of fascism is

> a revolutionary form of nationalism, one that sets out to be a political, social and ethical revolution, welding the 'people' into a dynamic national community under new elites infused with heroic values. The core myth that inspires this project is that only a populist, trans-class movement of purifying, cathartic national rebirth (palingenesis) can stem the tide of decadence.[7]

One way to unpack the concept of palingenesis is to see it as a version of apocalyptic belief common to all millenarian movements. I will revisit this idea at length later in this study.

To prove my thesis, I must:

- Demonstrate that the version of Christian Identity promulgated by Aryan Nations is totalitarian, sacralises politics and fits Griffin's definition of fascism.
- Illustrate how the sacralisation of politics and palingenesis are related to apocalypticism and millenarianism.

Christian Identity, Aryan Nations and Neo-Fascism

Christian Identity is an idiosyncratic form of Protestant religious belief that considers white Christians in the United States to be descended from the 12 tribes of Israel, and thus God's 'Chosen People'.[8] Christian Identity evolved from a pre-existing theology called Anglo-Israelism or British Israelism, which grew as a movement in the late nineteenth century and made similar claims about white Christians living in the British Isles.[9] The core claim is of an historic covenant with God expressed through the nation, defined as a biological 'racial' entity.

Christian Identity is inherently a racialised religious philosophy, but the degree of white supremacy and antisemitism can vary depending on the views of each relatively autonomous local group. Support for segregation of the races, for example, was championed by leading Christian Identity writers in the 1960s.[10] To an 'Identity' believer, those people who call themselves 'Jews', or who consider 'Israel' to be a state in the Middle East, are mistaken, mendacious or malignant. The most virulently bigoted forms of Christian Identity claim the 'so-called' Jews are a race of people who serve as agents of Satan to steal the birthright of white Christians by controlling the economy, manipulating the media and placing subhuman people of colour into positions of power.[11]

Wesley Swift was a Christian Identity minister who nurtured the bigoted, racist and antisemitic form of the theology that developed in the 1930s. Swift founded an Identity church in the late 1940s and promoted Identity through the 1960s. He was a prolific writer of sermons, scores of which are still available in pamphlet form as well as online. Swift converted and ordained William Potter Gale as an Identity minister in the mid-1950s.[12] According to Levitas, 'Gale saw all of history as a Manichaean struggle between white, divine, Anglo-Saxon Christians, and Satanic Jews'.[13] Richard G. Butler, a Californian engineer, was influenced by the teachings of Swift and Gale, but set up his own version of the Identity religion, under the name Church of Jesus Christ–Christian. In 1973, Butler moved to Idaho, where he eventually built a survivalist compound and training facility in Hayden Lake to promote the idea of creating a racially pure country composed solely of people from the various historic and genetic 'Aryan Nations'.[14] In 2000, Butler lost the Aryan Nations compound in a civil lawsuit (filed by the Southern Poverty Law Center), stemming from the thuggish aggression of Butler's security squad toward local residents. The compound was converted into a peace park. As of this writing, Butler has been in failing health and died in September 2004 and the organisation Aryan Nations is in disarray.[15] Nonetheless, Christian Identity continues to survive as a series of autonomous churches and local adherents.

In a statement of 'What We Believe', Aryan Nations lays out its version of Christian Identity as a belief in God's demand for the 'preservation of our Race, individually and collectively, as a people'.[16] It continues:

> WE BELIEVE the bible is the true word of God (Yahweh) written for and about a specific people. The bible is the family history of the White Race, the children of Yahweh placed on earth through the seedline of Adam.
>
> WE BELIEVE that Adam, man of Genesis, is the placing of the White Race upon this earth. Not all races descend from Adam. Adam is the father of the White Race only. (Adam in the original Hebrew is translated: 'to show blood in the face; turn rosy'.) Genesis 5:1.[17]

This claim of racial ancestry is linked to God's covenant with Israel traceable to Adam, who must be white, because only white people (it is claimed) have the ability to blush ('show blood in the face') with shame for disobeying God's laws. Accordingly, the Aryan Nations version of Christian Identity claims that the 'true, literal children of the Bible are the twelve tribes of Israel, now scattered throughout the world and now known as the Anglo-Saxon, Germanic, Teutonic, Scandinavian, Celtic peoples of the earth'.[18] Aryan Nations – plural – wants to establish many racially pure 'Aryan' nations around the world. It is nationalist in desire and yet internationalist in scope.

Aryan Nations believes that those who today call themselves Jews 'are the descendants of Cain, who was a result of Eve's original sin, her physical seduction by Satan'. Jews are thus the 'literal children of Satan in the world today' and the 'natural enemy of our Aryan (White) Race'. In addition, the 'Jew is like a destroying virus that attacks our racial body to destroy our Aryan culture and the purity of our Race. Those of our Race who resist these attacks are called "chosen and faithful." John 8:44; 1 Thessalonians 2:15; Revelations [sic] 17:14'.[19]

Integralism, Totalitarianism and Fascist Revolution

The Aryan nations 'Platform For The Aryan National State' lays out the plan for an integralist totalitarian society. The platform states that 'only Aryans (White Race) are allowed citizenship of the nation', and only Aryan citizens can 'vote and own property within the nation's borders' or conduct business, or hold any office in 'government,

industry or society'. Only Aryan citizens can possess firearms, serve in
the military, or be law enforcement personnel. Only Aryan citizens 'have
equal rights and duties', and are 'free men to perform mental or physical
work as they chose'.[20] In addition, 'A ruthless war must be waged against
any whose activities are injurious to the common interest', and there
must be 'an immediate cessation of dishonouring the nation'.[21]

This totalitarian programme demonises and scapegoats Jews as a
primary source of societal problems:

> All hybrids called Jews are to be repatriated from the Republic's
> territory, all their wealth be redistributed to restore our people,
> and it shall be a capital offence to advocate or promote Jew
> Talmudic anti-Christ Communism in any manner or any other
> crimes against nature.
>
> All Talmudism (Judaism), devil and heathen religions and
> practices end immediately, and there be an encouragement of the
> expansion of True Positive Christianity.
>
> Abolish the current materialistic Jew–'Law Merchant' judicial
> system and all the 'Laws of men' and establish return to our own
> God-ordained, racially inherent Anglo-Saxon, Germanic
> Common Law Order.[22]

How will this be accomplished? The nation will be 'cleared of the
parasites which fatten in the wallow of the present political parties; for
a Race or nation divided against itself can neither prosper nor survive'.
One step is to 'nationalise all monopolies and multi-national trusts',
and begin 'land reform and completely prohibit land speculation or
ownership of the nation's land and industries by aliens'. This invokes
a common theme in early National Socialism. The economy will be
redesigned by abolishing 'the present fraudulent money system with its
privately Jew-owned Federal Reserve', and in its place there will be 'an
interest-free monetary system based upon a just set of weights and
measures'.[23] This last point reinforces the antisemitic stereotype of
Jews as parasitic usurers and cheaters, which is common in the produc-
tivist narrative of right-wing populism.[24]

Throughout the Aryan Nations literature are populist appeals for
white people to recognise their heritage, rise up against the corrupt
élites and transform decadent society. Although carefully worded,
there are obvious calls for armed revolution followed by a murderous
purge of parasitic and subversive elements to purify the society and to
establish a transcendent utopia.

Other palingenetic aspects of the Aryan Nations version of Christian Identity are found in the statement calling for 'a thorough reconstruction' of the local citizenry. There will be an emphasis on 'parental responsibility and control of the educational process in order that the curriculum will be brought into line with the requirements of practical life'. There also will be a mandatory 'renaissance of White Aryan Heritage, Arts, Sciences and Humanities'. Finally, in order to implement the grand plan, there will be a 'renewal of Racial self-respect' based on the 'knowledge of our God's Eternal Natural Law Order', and that to accomplish this, the 'will to return to it with heart, soul and mind is imperative'.

Christian Identity's white supremacy and antisemitism are rooted in much the same pseudo-science of racial eugenics utilised by the German Nazi movement. The founding texts include de Gobineau's *The Inequality of Human Races* (1853–55); Galton's *Hereditary Genius: An Inquiry into Its Laws and Consequences* (1870); and Grant's *The Passing of the Great Race* (1916). Eugenicists in the United States and Germany worked together prior to the Second World War, and some in the US worked directly with the 'Nazi scientists whose work provided the conceptual template for Hitler's aspiration toward "racial hygiene" in Germany', according to Lombardo.[25]

Aryan Nations certainly sees itself as part of a neo-Nazi tradition. The 2003 website of Aryan Nations opened with an animated scene with the following sequence: the title 'Aryan Nations World Headquarters'; a rotating Aryan Nations logo; the slogan 'Fighting Jewish Takeover for Over 26 Years'; and a flying swastika twirling off into a black void. On the main page, SS thunderbolts slice into a red dragon, while a Nazi medallion, bearing an eagle and a swastika, sails over a sylvan new dawn.[26]

On the website, the swastika is described as derived from the sacred 'gam-ma'di'on ... [a] cross formed of four capital gammas ... [especially] in the figure of a swastika. Gamma among early Christians symbolised Christ as a cornerstone of the church'. This is cited on the website for Webster's Dictionary. If all this symbolism is deemed insufficient to establish neo-Nazi pedigree, consider that two main subsections on the website are 'Adolf Hitler' and 'Der Stürmer'. Under 'Hitler' one finds '25 Points of the NSDAP', 'Hitler on the Jewish Question', 'My Political Testament' and 'The Oath To Adolf Hitler'.

Eschatology, Exegesis and Intellectualism

Some scholars argue that, despite the open embrace of Nazi lore and ideology, it is not appropriate to call Aryan Nations neo-fascist, much less neo-Nazi, because it lacks a body of serious intellectual literature, and is little more than a crude amalgam of white supremacy and anti-semitism.[27] Aryan Nations *is* crude and bigoted, but it is far more. It is unlikely that many of the Nazi thugs who attacked synagogues and Jewish businesses on *Kristallnacht* in 1938 had read Nietzsche – yet the Nazi intellectuals who bent Nietzsche to their will influenced the acts of those thugs.

It is not uncommon to find scholars who dismiss religious belief as superstitious nonsense, but there is both sense and interior logic to religious belief. Furthermore, it is a core contention of sociology that situations that are defined as real are real in their consequences.[28] It does not matter if *you* believe, it matters that *they* believe. We could call Christian Identity a pseudo-religion based on racialist pseudo-science, producing texts that are pseudo-intellectual, but how does this explain why otherwise 'normal' people join Aryan Nations?[29]

Christian eschatology and exegesis has content and meaning, even in a tiny and marginalised sect such as Christian Identity.[30] Wesley Swift may not be in the same league as St Thomas Aquinas, but Swift's numerous sermons are detailed, internally logical (if one accepts a contorted seminal premise), and constructed in the longstanding fundamentalist tradition of searching for and citing biblical sources for guiding current analysis and action.[31] Furthermore, Butler of the Aryan Nations Identity Church of Jesus Christ–Christian is not just relying on the work of Swift, Gale and other Identity 'intellectuals', but on a centuries-old tradition of apocalypticism within Christianity.

Christian Identity shares with Hitler's Nazis not just a crude racism and antisemitism, but also a vision of a racialised apocalypse that will usher in a thousand year Reich – or reign of the white man's God: a millennium. The idea that inter-war Fascism and Nazism involved elements of apocalyptic millenarianism is not new.[32] Eatwell writes of how neo-fascists and other denizens of the extreme Right have to be 'seen within the context of Western political thought', with roots in Christianity and monotheism, 'which simplifies world conflict into a struggle between God and Satan, a tendency which encourages a belief in the existence of a hidden, evil, hand'.[33] Rhodes, in an extensive and focused study, states, 'the Hitler movement was a millenarian-gnostic revolution', full of apocalyptic metaphors and anticipating a 'modern battle of Armageddon for a worldly New Jerusalem'.[34]

The same analytical lens can be used to view totalitarian movements of the Right and Left. Coogan writes that 'Nazism and communism may perhaps one day be seen as twentieth century examples of a long line of European-centred millenarian movements'.[35] Kovel observes that:

> Whatever its claims to be a scientific understanding of society, Marxist Communism showed unmistakable influences of [the biblical book of] Revelation in its central texts, indeed, in its whole sense of mission, in the rising of the underclass to over-throw the 'beast' of capital (corrupt as the Whore of Babylon) and redeem history.[36]

After all, when communists sing the 'International', they salute the apocalyptic 'final conflict'.

Gentile sees in the sacralisation of politics 'revolutionary, democratic and nationalist origins' that drew from 'traditional Christianity tinged with millenarian culture'. He observes that both the American and French Revolutions involved elements of 'messianic and millenarian lay religion', which were in part 'based on secularised biblical archetypes'.[37] Gentile writes that many victims of inter-war totalitarianism were 'terrorised at the prospect of an apocalyptic catastrophe that would result in the triumph of the Antichrist', and that, in a general sense, this idea of totalitarianism's 'diabolical astuteness' was shared by persons who were not 'followers of religious beliefs'.[38]

It is clear that apocalyptic belief spread from religious into secular belief systems, but does it pose a problem when I claim the sacralisation of secular civil politics can take place in a religious apocalyptic group? In Gentile's formulation, there does not appear to be any prohibition of a group being religious and *also* being totalitarian, or fascistic, or engaging in the sacralisation of secular civil politics. Indeed, Gentile makes this point in several ways; specifically observing 'The relationship between the sacralisation of politics and traditional religion' is complicated and varies according to the specific political movement that adopts 'the characteristics of a secular religion, and according to the part played by traditional religion'.[39]

Ellwood suggests that 'Nazism was a peculiarly modern blend of the political and religious' that involved aspects of 'modern millenarianism' in which 'the miraculous or supernatural element was present only to the extent, though this was to a significant degree, that Nazi belief in the superior qualities and destiny of the Aryans took on the nature of non-rational, transcendentally sanctioned, self-validating faith'.[40] In the Aryan Nations version of Christian Identity, the supernatural element is nested inside a hyperbolic and racist version of an otherwise common Christian apocalyptic tradition. Understanding the power of the apocalyptic style when it is used as a technique to mobilise social and political movements is central to understanding Christian Identity. And it helps us see how apocalypticism, palingenesis and the sacralisation of politics are related phenomena in building the envisioned fascist society, even in secular fascist movements.[41]

The Apocalyptic Style

In its more generic usage, the word 'apocalypse' has come to mean the belief in an approaching confrontation, cataclysmic event, or transformation of epochal proportion, about which a select few have forewarning so they can make appropriate preparations.[42] Those who believe in a coming apocalypse might be optimistic about the outcome of the apocalyptic moment, anticipating a chance for positive transformational change; or they might be pessimistic, anticipating a doomsday; they may even anticipate a period of violence or chaos with an uncertain outcome. Responses range from passive withdrawal from society to await the outcome, to aggressive intervention in society.[43]

The apocalyptic tradition pre-dates Christianity and ancient versions can be found in Zoroastrianism, Judaism, Islam and other religions.[44] In Christianity, the Apocalypse refers to a worldwide battle with Satanic forces in what are called the 'End Times'. The exact order of the events in the End Times is hotly contested, especially among fundamentalist Christians.

Apocalyptic themes influence many diverse Christian groups, including those who do not think the End Times are close at hand. In fact, apocalypticism has escaped its religious wellsprings to flood across secular, political and cultural discursive landscapes in Western societies, especially in the United States.[45] For example, apocalypticism can be found in the text of some New Age and environmental activists.[46] Secular and religious apocalyptic narratives intersect and cross-fertilise each other and spread across the political spectrum in what Barkun has called an 'improvisational style' of apocalypticism.[47]

Revelation

Prophesies about the apocalyptic End Times appear throughout the Christian Bible. The Old Testament books of Daniel and Ezekiel, and the New Testament Gospels of Matthew and Mark and the Book of Revelation all provide examples.[48] Goldberg points out that 'biblical prophecy was history before its time. Scriptural passages that foretold the end of days, though, were difficult to decipher. Prophets had repeatedly shared their visions, but they spoke allegorically'.[49]

Revelation is the allegorical chronicle of a series of prophetic visions about the End Times written about 95 AD. The identity of John of Patmos, the author of Revelation, is disputed, and most experts now believe it was not the same John who authored the Gospel and Epistles.[50] 'The New Testament's Book of Revelation was particularly rich in imagery and thus invited vigorous interpretation', explains Goldberg.[51]

In Revelation the world is described as sinking into a sea of sin, awash in wanton sexuality, rapacious greed and grotesque materialism. God punishes the sinful by sending waves of tribulations, including disease, natural disasters and wars. A popular world figure emerges during these tribulations to call for world unity, and the establishment of a world government that will ensure peace among nations. Some suspect he is the returning Jesus Christ. They are wrong. It is actually part of a secret plan by Satan, who has created this false leader, the 'Antichrist', to fool devout Christians into renouncing their faith and betraying their God. One way in which Christians are deceived is by tricking them into accepting the 'Mark of the Beast', a symbol of allegiance to Satan sometimes represented by the number 666.

The Tribulations lead to a cataclysmic confrontation between the armies of good and evil on the plains of Armageddon in the Middle East. When good triumphs over evil, the world is transformed and there follows one thousand years – a millennium – of peace and tranquillity under Christian leadership. Protestant evangelicals, especially fundamentalists, continuously inspect Revelation's symbolic language to serve as a guide for their actions in the contemporary world.[52] Official Roman Catholic doctrine tries to suppress eschatological expectation and debate, but there is a subculture of apocalyptic Catholicism that flourishes with both overt and covert support from some in the Catholic hierarchy.[53] The situation is similar in the Orthodox Christian churches.

Millennialism and Millenarianism

One objection to seeing fascism as a millenarian movement is based on the notion that all millennialist or millenarian groups are awaiting divine intervention and have no need aggressively to pursue earthly activism. This is an oversimplified view of millenarianism based on a specific version of millennialism found in Protestantism.[54]

The word 'millennium' specifically refers to a span of one thousand years. It has also come to mean the point at which one period of one thousand years ends and the next begins. The millennium can be seen as beginning at any calendar date, often based on obtuse and complex numerological divinations. So the turn of the calendar to the year 2000 did not *necessarily* have theological significance (although it caused a flurry of activity). Any date in any calendar system (Judaic or Islamic for example) can be understood as significant given the creativity of those looking to find justification for their apocalyptic beliefs.[55] Cohn chronicles how Christian apocalyptic fervour appears at seemingly random dates throughout Western history.[56] A major American episode of Christian millennialism occurred among the Millerites in the 1840s.[57]

The terms millennialism and millenarianism are sometimes used interchangeably to describe apocalyptic social and political movements.[58] I find it more useful to use the term millenarian in a broad generic sense, and reserve millennialism to describe movements that are millenarian, but which also have some apocalyptic vision of the beginning or end of a one thousand year cycle – a millennium. And while the phrase 'apocalyptic millenarianism' is somewhat redundant, I think it is useful to keep the concept clear for those new to the ideas involved.

Those who believe Jesus Christ returns at the end of a thousand years of Christian rule are called post-millennialists because they believe they have to intervene in earthly affairs and seize society and hold it for one thousand years – a millennium – before Christ returns. Post-millennialism is therefore an inherently interventionist theology. Most Christians in the United States believe that when Jesus Christ returns, He starts the clock ticking on a Christian millennium. This version of eschatology is called pre-millennialism. The pre-millennial apocalypticism of Christian Identity is certainly vivid and aggressive, but it evolves from this longstanding and widespread Protestant pre-millennialist world view. The basic theme of pre-millennialism is explained by a commentary in the popular Protestant NIV translation:

the final showdown between God and Satan is imminent. Satan will increase his persecution of believers, but they must stand fast, even to death. They are sealed against any spiritual harm and will soon be vindicated when Christ returns, when the wicked are forever destroyed, and when God's people enter an eternity of glory and blessedness.[59]

For many decades, the primary Protestant eschatology has been a form of pre-millennialism called Dispensationalism (an interpretation developed in the nineteenth century by English theologian John Nelson Darby), which outlined specific epochs of history or 'dispensations' pre-ordained by God.[60] Based on this timeline, at a specific point early in the End Times, Christians will be swept up safely away from Earth in a process called the 'Rapture'. In this way, devout Christians are protected from some or all of the Tribulations. After the sinful are punished and purged, Christ returns for a millennium of rule over his loyal flock, which has been restored to an earthly paradise. This combination of pre–tribulationist and pre-millennialist theology has sometimes encouraged a large sector of the Christian faithful to await salvation passively while remaining aloof from sinful secular society. At other times, however, pre-millennialists can become activists seeking to intervene in public affairs. Pre-millennialist religious leaders who urge political activism argue that Christians are required to save souls and search out sin even if they expect to be Raptured.[61]

Millennial prophetic belief is still widespread in the US. The mainstreaming of pre-millennial apocalypticism received a major boost when, in 1983, Ronald Reagan cited scriptural authority to demonise the Soviet Union as an 'evil empire'. Halsell noted that some evangelists, including Jerry Falwell, Hal Lindsey and Pat Robertson, hinted that use of atomic weapons might be part of the inevitable final battle of Armageddon.[62] As FitzGerald explains:

> Elements of premillennialist thinking seem to exist in vague and diffuse form quite generally in the United States. Fundamentalist theology, for example, dictates that God and the Devil are everywhere immanent; thus, politics is not simply the collision of differing self-interests but the expression of a transcendent power struggle between the forces of good and the forces of evil … If the United States is the 'Christian nation', then the Soviet Union must be the 'evil empire'.[63]

Lamy reports that during the first Gulf War, 14 per cent of one CNN national poll thought it was the beginning of Armageddon, and 'American bookstores were experiencing a run on books about prophecy and the end of the world'.[64] In 1993 a *Times*/CNN national survey found that 20 per cent of those polled thought the second coming of Christ would occur near the year 2000.[65] As the year 2000 approached, Christians with a conspiracist interpretation of the Book of Revelation were especially alert to betrayal by political leaders whom they suspected of promoting collectivism and a tyrannical one-world government.[66]

A significant number of Christian Right activists in the United States are mobilised into action by apocalyptic and millennialist themes.[67] A secular version of this narrative appears in conspiracy theories about liberal collectivists building a global new world order through the United Nations or multinational corporations – a version popular in the Patriot and armed militia movements.[68]

Apocalyptic Demonisation and Conspiracism

Those that believe the apocalypse is at hand can choose to act out those theological beliefs in secular arenas. Apocalyptic millenarian movements often anticipate the betrayal of an idealised community by secret malevolent forces conspiring against the common good. Those persons sounding the warning urge immediate and drastic measures to stop the secret conspiracy from achieving its sinister goals.

One interpretation of Revelation's narrative is that in the End Times, righteous Christians are tricked and betrayed by trusted political and religious leaders, who are secretly agents of Satan and working with the Antichrist. This literal conspiracist reading of Revelation can create a timetable in which devout Christians look for their place in the prophetic script detailing the battle between good and evil. Episodes of this type of dualistic apocalyptic conspiracism appear periodically throughout US history.

In colonial times, witch hunts in Salem in the seventeenth century burst into the public square. The young nation had barely agreed on a Constitution when there were fears of 'alien' sedition in the late eighteenth century. In the nineteenth century, there were scares over alleged plots involving Freemasons or Catholics. Allegations of a Jewish banking cabal behind the Federal Reserve circulated in the early twentieth century. This set the stage for a series of red scares in the United States, from the anti-immigrant Palmer Raids of 1919–20 to the Cold War McCarthy period in the 1950s.[69] Donner explains that after the revolution in Russia:

> Bolshevism came to be identified over wide areas of the country by God-fearing Americans as the Antichrist come to do eschatological battle with the children of light. A slightly secularised version, widely shared in rural and small-town America, postulated a doomsday conflict between decent upright folk and radicalism – alien, satanic, immorality incarnate.[70]

Hofstadter wrote of the 'apocalyptic and absolutist framework' that buttresses right-wing conspiracy theories in the United States.[71] He argued 'the central preconception of the paranoid style [is the belief in the] existence of a vast, insidious, preternaturally effective international conspiratorial network designed to perpetrate acts of the most fiendish character'.[72] Hofstadter saw grandiose conspiracy theories being concocted when a sense of persecution and hostility were aggressively channelled through overheated apocalyptic suspicions.

According to Thompson, Hofstadter was right to articulate the 'startling affinities between the paranoid style and apocalyptic belief', especially the demonisation of opponents and 'the sense of time running out'. Thompson, however, argues Hofstadter should have made a more direct connection by considering 'the possibility that the paranoia he identified actually derived from apocalyptic belief; that the people who spread scare stories about Catholics, masons, Illuminati and Communists' were extrapolating from widespread Protestant End Times beliefs. The 'persistence of such belief in the United States rather than Europe surely explains why the paranoid style seems so quintessentially American', writes Thompson.[73]

Christian Identity and Apocalypse

Considering the way Christianity influences apocalyticism and millennialism in American culture makes christian identity less mysterious and easier to decipher. It also places it in a well-developed theological and intellectual tradition. In many ways, the Aryan Nations version of Identity is a hyperbolic exaggeration of tendencies found in more mainstream religious, social and political movements.

Barkun traces the influence of apocalypticism on major racist and antisemitic ideologues within Christian Identity, including Wesley

Swift, William Potter Gale, Sheldon Emry, Pete Peters and Richard Butler of Aryan Nations.[74] As Minges explains, a 'critical element in the "Christian Identity" movement is a militant apocalypticism rooted in the dispensational pre-millennialism of the Christian right and its fundamentalist counterparts'. Identity theology sees the current period as the final dispensation in which there is 'particular depravity, reaching its climax in a seven year tribulation'.[75]

The Aryan Nations statement of 'What We Believe' lays this out by referencing biblical prophecy, while inserting the Jews as Satanic agents:

> WE BELIEVE that there is a battle being fought this day between the children of darkness (today known as Jews) and the children of light (Yahweh, The Ever living God), the Aryan Race, the true Israel of the bible. Revelations 12:10–11.
>
> WE BELIEVE that there is a day of reckoning. The usurper will be thrown out by the terrible might of Yahweh's people, as they return to their roots and their special destiny. We know there is soon to be a day of judgement and a day when Christ's Kingdom (government) will be established on earth, as it is in heaven. 'And in the days of these kings shall the God of heaven set up a kingdom which shall never be destroyed; and the kingdom shall not be left to other people, but it shall break in pieces and consume all these kingdoms and it shall stand forever. The saints of the Most High, whose kingdom is an everlasting kingdom, and all dominions shall serve and obey Him'. Daniel 2:44; 7:18; 7:27.[76]

This is the classic scenario of an apocalyptic battle followed by the transformation of society sought by all millenarian movements. Identity theology is pre-millennialist, but rejects the notion of the Rapture.[77] God will not save devout Christians from the tribulations; they must fight for the survival of the true Israelite Aryan Race as agents of God against the fake Jews, who are literally demonised as the 'children of darkness'.

Dualism and Demonisation

In reviewing the literature of the Aryan Nations' version of Christian Identity, it is clear that there is a particular type of apocalyptic millenarianism at work. As Minges puts it:

'Identity' theorists begin to weave a web of ideology that traces the hidden hand of evil throughout history from the crucifixion of Christ to the Trilateral Commission of the postmodern era. Their ideology developed as nativist impulses combined with a racist and anti-Semitic 'Identity' philosophy of history to create a panoply of conspiracy theories in which the common denominator is this face of evil.[78]

The ideology begins with a premise of dualism or Manichaeism, and then constructs a framework using demonisation, scapegoating and conspiracism to divide the world into a good 'us' and a bad 'them'. Scapegoating is built on top of this dualistic dichotomy.[79]

Scapegoating

Arendt argues 'an ideology which has to persuade and mobilise people cannot choose its victim arbitrarily'.[80] Something is happening in a society where scapegoating is promoted by demagogues and adopted by a large mass of people, even when there are only a tiny number of persons in the scapegoated group.[81] Scapegoated groups sometimes play some objective role in a real conflict, even when they are innocent of the irrational and fabricated charges used to demonise them.

Lyons and I arrived at the following formula:

> We use the term *scapegoating* to describe the social process whereby the hostility and grievances of an angry, frustrated group are directed away from the real causes of a social problem onto a target group demonised as malevolent wrongdoers. The scapegoat bears the blame, while the scapegoaters feel a sense of righteousness and increased unity. The social problem may be real or imaginary, the grievances legitimate or illegitimate, and members of the targeted group may be wholly innocent or partly culpable. What matters is that the scapegoats are wrongfully stereotyped as all sharing the same negative trait, or are singled out for blame while other major culprits are let off the hook.[82]

Landes explains: 'Psychologically, the tendency to find scapegoats is a result of the common defence mechanism of denial through projection'.[83] This is a powerful mechanism and fills a deep psychological need, even though the outcome for some in the society can be disastrous and grotesque.[84] Scapegoating serves a social purpose, and as

Landes suggests, 'In some cases the first steps toward social cohesion may be built' on demonising rituals of scapegoating the 'other'.[85]

The scapegoat thus serves a dual purpose by representing the evil 'them' and simultaneously illuminating, solidifying and sanctifying the good 'us'.[86] According to Aho, even when it is unconscious, the objectification of evil through scapegoating has this wondrous outcome: 'The casting out of evil onto you not only renders you my enemy; it also accomplishes my own innocence. To paraphrase [Nietzsche] ... In manufacturing an evil one against whom to battle heroically, I fabricate a good one, myself'.[87]

In addition, Girard argues, 'the effect of the scapegoat is to reverse the relationship between persecutors and their victims'.[88] When persons in scapegoated groups are attacked, they are often described as having brought on the attack themselves because of the wretched behaviour ascribed to them as part of the enemy group.[89] They deserved what they got. Scapegoating evokes hatred rather than anger. The 'hater is sure the fault lies in the object of hate', notes Allport.[90]

Fuller links scapegoating to Christian apocalyptic millennialism by noting how frequently throughout US history scapegoated groups have been named as harbouring agents of the Antichrist. Fuller also sees a psychological dimension:

> Many efforts to name the Antichrist appear to be rooted in the psychological need to project one's 'unacceptable' tendencies onto a demonic enemy. It is the Antichrist, not oneself, who must be held responsible for wayward desires. And with so many aspects of modern American life potentially luring individuals into nonbiblical thoughts or desires, it is no wonder that many people believe that the Antichrist has camouflaged himself to better work his conspiracies against the faithful.[91]

Conspiracism

In his study of apocalyptic strategies, O'Leary claims the process of demonisation is central to all forms of conspiracist thinking.[92] And the US extreme Right, writes Zeskind, needs to be understood as envisioning an 'all-powerful cosmology of diabolical evil', seen through 'essentially theologically constructed views' of world events. 'Conspiracy theories are renderings of a metaphysical devil which is trans-historical, omnipotent, and destructive of God's will on earth', writes

Zeskind, and this 'is true even for conspiracy theories in which there is not an explicit religious target'.[93]

Gardner points out that many current 'conspiracy theories directed against the government are part of a *rhetorical strategy* genuinely intended to undermine state power and government authority', but this occurs in a 'metaphysical context' in which 'those in control are implicated in a Manichean struggle of absolute good against absolute evil. That they are the agents of the devil is proved by the very fact that they control a corrupt system'.[94]

According to O'Leary, while conspiracism 'strives to provide a spatial self-definition of the true community as set apart from the evils' spread by the scapegoated 'other', apocalypticism 'locates the problem of evil in time and looks forward to its imminent resolution' while warning that 'evil must grow in power until the appointed time'.[95] Minges cites O' Leary's discussion and then extends it to show the interrelatedness:

> [The] discourses of conspiracy and apocalypse are linked by a common function: each develops symbolic resources that enable societies to define and address the problem of evil. In fact, conspiracy arguments are often enveloped into the larger theoretical framework of apocalyptic mythologies in order to find expression within given communities.[96]

Blee observes, 'Conspiracy theories not only teach that the world is divided into an empowered "them" and a less powerful "us" but also suggest a strategy by which the "us" (ordinary people, the non-conspirators) can challenge and even usurp the authority of the currently-powerful'.[97] If the conspirators are unmasked, the argument goes, societal problems can be solved, thus conspiracism offers a possibility of transformative change – the goal of apocalyptic millenarianism. Conspiracy theories are a narrative form of scapegoating based on dualistic apocalypticism and demonisation.[98]

Fundamentalism

Both religious and secular groups can carry out this process of apocalyptic demonisation. In the secular setting, the scapegoats are not linked to religiously defined evil or satanic plots, but to corrupt, subversive or traitorous plans. In the religious setting, the call for revival is not just a call for revitalisation, but for a transcendental campaign against evil to restore the godly community. This type of palingenetic call to arms can be heard around the world in militant sectors of several religious traditions, where there are calls for a fundamentalist revival to combat the decadence and decay of what is sometimes called contemporary Westernised 'Coca-Cola culture'.[99] Christian Identity is a particular version of Christian fundamentalism, in the broad sense of the term, but it developed at the same time as, and in opposition to, the original Christian Fundamentalist movement of the early twentieth century.

There is much confusion and disagreement surrounding use of the term fundamentalism, to the point of even questioning its use to describe movements exclusive of Christianity.[100] The term fundamentalism at first referred exclusively to a dissident populist movement arising within Protestantism in the early twentieth century. It was a reaction against mainstream Protestant denominations in the United States such as the Presbyterians and Baptists, and to a lesser extent Methodists, Episcopalians and others.[101] Leaders of these major denominations were accused of selling out the Protestant faith by forging a compromise with the ideas of the Enlightenment and modernism. In the early twentieth century, conservative critics of this leadership developed voluminous lists of what they considered the fundamental beliefs required for people to consider themselves Christian – thus the term fundamentalism. Wallace says similar revitalisation movements exist across many spiritual and religious traditions.[102] But not all revitalisation movements, even within Christianity, are fundamentalist.[103]

Fundamentalism can also adopt dualistic apocalypticism as a mode. Wessinger offers a short definition of this form of fundamentalism:

> 'Fundamentalism' is the belief that one has access to an infallible source of authority. That source of authority may be a text, a tradition, a leader, or a combination of these. The fundamentalist, whether Jewish, Christian, Muslim, Hindu, or Buddhist is certain that he or she knows the 'Truth', and that truth resides in an idealised earlier way of religious life. There is no openness to alternative points of view. Fundamentalism involves the belief that pure Good is battling pure Evil. This dualistic perspective pits believers against unbelievers, us versus them.[104]

This is an accurate definition of dualistic fundamentalism, but some theologians and scholars of religion note that other versions of fundamentalism exist that do not necessarily demonise groups of people.[105] In this study, we are examining the dualistic and demonising versions of fundamentalism and apocalypticism. Armstrong argues that with 'most extreme types of fundamentalists, members see conspiracy everywhere and cultivate a theology of rage and resentment'.[106]

Just as not all forms of fundamentalism necessarily demonise opponents, neither are they necessarily theocratic or violent. Rapoport notes that all religions have peaceful and violent sides, and holds that critics of fundamentalist Islam who claim it is unusually violent compared to other religions have scant historical support for such as view.[107] Methodologies vary. Wessinger explains that religious fundamentalists may use 'prayer and faith as weapons', or engage in political activism, but '[r]evolutionary fundamentalists resort to violence to destroy enemies and establish the righteous kingdom. Those designated the "other" are demonised, and thus it may become acceptable, even praiseworthy, to kill them'.[108] Jurgensmeyer concludes that religious violence and terrorism flow from that aspect of religious imagination having 'the propensity to absolutise and to project images of cosmic war'. People who use it often feel buffeted by social tensions and political shifts, leaving them feeling a 'sense of personal humiliation' and a longing to 'restore an integrity' they feel has been lost.[109]

Fundamentalism is not the same thing as orthodoxy or traditionalism. Fundamentalists claim to be restoring the 'true' religion by returning to 'traditional' beliefs and enforcing 'orthodox' ideas – the set of theological doctrines approved of as sound and correct by an established faith's religious leaders. In fact, while fundamentalist movements claim to be restoring tradition and orthodoxy, they actually create a new, syncretic version of an existing religion based on a mythic and romanticised past. So, while fundamentalism is a reaction against the Enlightenment and modernity, it is at the same time a modern phenomenon.[110] Armstrong observes that fundamentalists frequently 'create an ideology that provides the faithful with a plan of action [and they eventually] fight back and attempt to resacralise an increasingly sceptical world'.[111]

Fundamentalist belief has real consequences in the world today, especially through the political activism of fundamentalist groups within Christianity, Judaism and Islam.[112] This is especially true in the Middle East, and in the United States, where apocalyptic Christian Zionism helps shape American foreign policy in the Middle East.[113]

According to Gorenberg, some fundamentalists in all three religions have apocalyptic stories about heroic battles with evil prior to some expected messianic event – all of which involve mutually exclusive plans for the Temple Mount/Haram Al-Sharif in Jerusalem.[114] Around the world, militant apocalyptic fundamentalist religious movements make plans for palingenetic revolution.[115]

Clerical Fascism and Theocratic Neo-Fascism

Christian Identity, as practiced by Aryan Nations, is a neo-fascist religion. Combining fascism with religion is not a new phenomenon. Between the First and Second World Wars in Europe, there were two major forms of fascism: Italian economic corporatist fascism and German racial nationalist Nazism. There was also a minor form, sometimes dubbed clerical fascism. Several nationalist movements in inter-war Europe have been classified as forms of clerical fascism.[116] Some scholars reject this classification, and some argue against even including Nazism as a form of fascism, especially Sternhell and his allies.[117]

Payne has made a strong case for including a variety of inter-war movements as forms of fascism. Payne first divides movements into three categories of 'Authoritarian nationalism': the conservative Right, the radical Right and the fascists. Under fascism, he lists specific movements not only in Germany and Italy, but also in Austria, Belgium, Estonia, France, Hungary, Latvia, Lithuania, Poland, Portugal, Romania, South Africa, Spain, and Croatia (later incorporated into Yugoslavia).[118] Some of these movements – based in established religious traditions – are called 'clerical fascism' in this paper.

A precursor to clerical fascism was tested in Austria, where dictator Englebert Dollfuss attempted to create 'the Christian corporative state recommended by [Pope] Pius XI in ... *Quadragesimo anno* [as] an appropriate means of overcoming class antagonisms'.[119] A variety of fascistic religious movements flourished in varying ways in inter-war Europe, and many collaborated (at least briefly and sometimes uneasily) with the German Nazis. There were Catholic-based movements, such as the *Ustase* in Croatia, with Archbishop Alojzije Stepinac among the leaders; the Arrow Cross in Hungary; and the Hlinka Guard in Slovakia, led by Monsignor Josef Tiso.

In Romania the Iron Guard, led by Corneliu Codreanu, was influenced by a sectarian version of the Romanian Orthodox Church.[120] The writings of Codreanu have been translated and republished by contemporary neo-Nazis.[121] At the same time, there is renewed critical interest in the role Mircea Eliade played in valorising the Iron Guard and spreading antisemitism, anti-masonry and anti-Marxism in Romania in the 1930s.[122] All clerical fascist movements in inter-war Europe promoted the scapegoating of Jews, especially a conspiracist mode that, in Romania for example, portrayed 'Rabbinical aggression against the Christian world' in 'unexpected "protean forms"': Freemasonry, Freudianism, homosexuality, atheism, Marxism, Bolshevism, the civil war in Spain'.[123] In Poland, after the First World War, Catholic unity was built in part by scapegoating Jews for societal ills ranging from pornography to prostitution, and it was common 'to equate the word "Jew" with "Bolshevik," "Freemason," "liberal," and "international capitalist"'.[124]

In the contemporary United States there are a number of fascistic groups and movements interwoven with religion. They have been described as clerical fascism, theocratic fascism or 'fascistised clericalism'.[125] Lyons and I put Christian Identity into the category of clerical fascism, and we also included a militant theocratic Protestant movement called Christian Reconstructionism.[126] Around the world there are other religious ethno-nationalist movements where a case can be made for categorisation as some form or hybrid of fascism, including the *Taliban* in Afghanistan, *al-Qaeda* network and the Hindu nationalist (*Hindutva*) *Bharatiya Janata Party* (BJP) in India (which grew out of the *Rashtriya Swayamsevak Sangh* Hindu religious movement). Various other religious nationalist movements, such as those in Iran and Israel, contain bits and pieces of fascist ideology merged with theology. Even more diffuse are general religious nationalist movements, such as the Lebanese Christians and the *Afrikaner Broederbond* of South Africa.[127] Sorting out the classification of these movements is unfinished business.

Apocalypse, Palingenesis and the Sacralisation of Politics

The interrelationships among totalitarianism, apocalypticism, palingenesis, millenarianism, the sacralisation of politics and fascism have been written about for years in a variety of different ways. When Gentile denounces totalitarianism, he uses the same language others use to describe dualistic apocalypticism. In an earlier draft of the article that appears in this special issue Gentile wrote:

Whether one judges totalitarianism to be a political religion or not, it remains beyond doubt that the various totalitarianisms were driven by the fanaticism of those who believed themselves to belong to an elite community; who arrogated for themselves the privilege to define the meaning and objectives of existence for millions of people; who believed themselves uniquely qualified to distinguish between good and evil; and who, consequently, acted with implacable and ruthless violence to eliminate from 'good' society those 'evil' elements that threatened and corrupted it, and prevented it from becoming a single and homogenous body politic.

It is this type of totalitarian vision that Quinby is describing, when she points out that apocalypse is compelling because of 'its promise of future perfection, eternal happiness, and godlike understanding of life, but it is that very will to absolute power and knowledge that produces its compulsions of violence, hatred, and oppression'.[128] Wessinger argues a 'radical dualism' that demonises and dehumanises opponents is characteristic of certain types of millennialism.[129] This form of dualistic apocalyptic millenarianism can fuel a sense of persecution and the fear that time is running out in the battle against evil forces. It can lead some to see violence (or even acts of terrorism) as justified, and even when not intended, violent confrontations can result.[130]

When millenarian movements turn to political revolution, the revolution is a form of 'progress speeded up to an apocalyptic rate'.[131] These apocalyptic rituals of purification are a way to mediate social change and transfer power between generations, according to Fenn, and thus to challenge death itself, at least on a metaphoric level. Apocalyptic rhetoric is used by fascist movements to defend imperilled traditional communities based on race or kinship, against the bewildering and intrusive forces of modernity.[132]

This is certainly true with Fascism and Nazism. Steigmann-Gall suggests many in the Nazi movement thought they were locked in an apocalyptic battle, and that this idea of 'defending good by waging war against evil, fighting for God against the Devil, for German against Jew', was 'predicated on a dualistic understanding of human behaviour hegemonic in Western Christian civilisation'.[133] Dualism and apocalypticism, however, existed before the rise of Christianity, and exists outside of Christianity. While Christianity profoundly and directly influences the forms of dualism and apocalypticism in

Western culture, these tendencies have long escaped their roots, and established themselves in both various secular modes and non-Christian religions.[134]

Using a psychological approach, Anthony and Robbins describe how some persons may be able to rebuild a fractured self-image through their participation in a 'totalist movement' such as '[i]deological and religious groups with highly dualistic worldviews' and 'an absolutist apocalyptic outlook', where they engage in the 'projection of negativity and rejected elements of self onto ideologically designated scapegoats'.[135] Anthony and Robbins identify a form of apocalyptic ideology they call 'exemplary dualism', a world view in which 'contemporary sociopolitical or socioreligious forces are transmogrified into absolute contrast categories embodying moral, eschatological, and cosmic polarities upon which hinge the millennial destiny of humankind'.[136]

While exemplary dualism is obvious in totalist groups, it appears in more muted forms in other settings. Niewart points out that rhetoric employing exemplary dualism is not limited to the margins of American society, but is distressingly common in public discourse, especially in certain sections of the Christian Right.[137] Rhetorical demonisation as part of an aggressive campaign is hardly limited to totalitarianism. Rothschild describes the foreign policy of US President George W. Bush as 'messianic militarism'.[138] Sagan says the 'paranoidia' of greed and domination, exemplified by 'fascist and totalitarian regimes of this century', can be detected in less extreme forms in many societies. He adds, 'The normal, expectable expressions – imperialism, racism, sexism, aggressive warfare – are compatible with the democratic societies that have existed so far'.[139]

Dualistic apocalypticism is a common element of many types of movements and governments; however, it would be overly simplistic to leave the impression that this is the only way apocalyptic prophecy is interpreted and millenarian desire for transformation manifested. O'Leary has offered a complex theory of how millennial rhetoric functions in different modes and settings. He sees the 'tragic' version based on literal readings of prophetic texts that are used to construct a timetable and geography of the anticipated physical confrontation. The 'comedic' version accepts the irony that we never know when God chooses to intervene, and thus specific calendar dates and deadlines are irrelevant to God's expectations concerning our behaviour while on Earth.[140] Wessinger also describes several complex forms of millennialism.[141] And Landes conceives apocalypticism and millennialism as differentiated along several dimensions, so there are versions that are active or passive, cataclysmic or transformational, and hierarchical or egalitarian.[142]

In the broadest sense, all dissident social or political movements – Left or Right, religious or secular – contain some element of apocalypticism, at least in the sense of seeking transformative societal change. It is not apocalypticism or millenarianism alone that creates a danger for society. The dangerous formula that concocts an explosive mixture includes textual literalism, scripted timetables, populist demagoguery, authoritarian coercion, dualistic demonisation, conspiracist scapegoating and oppressive prejudices. Each totalitarian movement assembles its arsenal for the coercive palingenetic crusade by choosing from a vast warehouse of weapons.

Gentile spends more time discussing the role of coercion in his book.[143] In his article in this collection, it is easier to see how apocalypticism and millennarianism are complementary to his theory. For a complete picture, we need to consider apocalypticism *and* dualism, palingenesis *and* totalitarianism, coercion *and* scapegoating. The elements of totalitarianism and dualism seem to be likely candidates for addition to the idea of a fascist minimum. As Gentile observes, the totalitarianism need not be accomplished, merely present as a goal. As for dualism, it need not be as overt and deadly as Nazi genocide, but can be as simple as dividing the society into two groups: those that support the palingenetic transformation and those that do not.

We must be careful to not end up condemning all apocalyptic tendencies, fundamentalist religious groups, or millenarian social change movements. This is the great mistake made by early critics of totalitarianism, who ended up smugly celebrating the *status quo* and élite secular intellectualism in a way that was profoundly anti-democratic and tended to trivialise certain religious beliefs. This is where we get the notion of an idealised centre embattled by 'extremists' of the Left and Right. The 'centre' in Nazi Germany was hardly 'ideal'.[144]

We still need to sort out further issues of taxonomy and nomenclature to deepen our understanding of the phenomenon we are observing. Our taxonomic tasks can benefit the use of modifying language such as 'quasi-fascist' to describe movements containing certain elements of fascism, but which do not quite make the grade; 'proto-fascist' to describe groups sliding toward full-blown fascism; and 'crypto-fascist' for those which appear to be right-wing populists, but which have a portrait of Hitler on their living room wall. For example, the Ba'athist parties in Iraq and Syria are certainly quasi-fascist (and perhaps more).[145]

What about the difference between political religion and politicised religion? Protestant evangelicals dominate the Christian Right in the US and have created a form of politicised religion; but unlike Christian Identity, with few exceptions (such as Christian Reconstructionism), the Christian Right is not an example of a political religion. Thus all neo-fascist movements in the US are forms of political religion (the sacralisation of politics), but not all examples of a politicised religion are examples of political religion.

Nazism itself clearly picked up themes and styles historically used by Christianity, but it was not a form of Christianity, even though there were many Christian collaborators, as Steigmann-Gall amply documents.[146] These collaborators fashioned a hybrid Christianity that coexisted with paganism and secularism within the Nazi permutation of fascism. This is not the same, however, as the Romanian Iron Guard, Croatian *Ustase*, or Hungarian Arrow Cross, which were hybridised from one religious tradition to the exclusion of all others. I agree with Griffin when he argues that the German Nazis were a secular political movement that was not a hybrid of an 'established religious or metaphysical tradition' but operated 'entirely within the sphere of historical notions of the immortality of the nation or the race', while they nonetheless extensively used religious language, and liturgical-style 'displays of theatrical politics', as part of their mobilisation of the masses around palingenetic myths.[147]

Griffin wants to reserve the term 'clerical fascism' for factions within a pre-existing orthodox clergy that create a form of fascism based solely on a specific established religion with a recognised institutional presence in a society.[148] This would make the Iron Guard, *Ustase* and Arrow Cross candidates for listing as forms of clerical fascism. Not Christian Identity, however, because Christian Identity is a tiny sect and considered a heresy by the more institutionalised and established Protestant denominations, as well as the Catholic and Orthodox churches in the United States. It would be more accurate to call Christian Identity a form of 'theocratic fascism'. Theocratic fascism would then be the broader category under which clerical fascism would be a subset.

What can we call various syncretic and non-syncretic religious nationalisms not qualifying as fascism? 'Theocratic nationalism' is more accommodating than 'fundamentalist nationalism', although some forms of theocratic nationalism could also be fundamentalist. Authoritarian elements of the Christian Right in the Unites States are a form of theocratic nationalism, but not all participants are fundamentalist. The *Taliban* and *al-Qaeda* are forms of fundamentalist theocratic nationalism, but are they a form of clerical fascism? I say yes, but Griffin has dubbed them 'fascistised clericalism', a term that describes a movement where religious leaders have developed a syncretic hybrid of an institutionalised religion that coexists with fascist ideas, despite vivid internal contradictions.[149] Griffin calls the *Bharatiya Janata* Party (BJP) of India a 'fascistised form of Fundamentalism'.[150]

At some point, however, is it not possible for a politicised religion to take that one last step over the boundary and become a form of political religion? Consider that before the Puritans sought to build their godly theocracy in America, 'Protestant apocalyptic tradition envisioned the ultimate sacralisation of England as God's chosen nation'.[151] Are not the roots of the sacralisation of politics in the septic soil of religious dualism, apocalypticism and totalitarianism?

The matter of syncretism and orthodoxy also needs further debate. Griffin has argued that there is something spurious and secular happening when hybrids of fundamentalism and fascism occur.[152] He claims the incongruous stew of 'syncretism is anathema to orthodox forms of established religion, and especially to Fundamentalism, which is driven by the urge to keep faith pristine and uncontaminated by extraneous elements'.[153] I see fundamentalism, orthodoxy and syncretism from a different perspective. While fundamentalism claims to be restoring orthodoxy and tradition, it is actually creating a hybrid form of the established religion, so fundamentalism is itself in some ways syncretic.[154]

The issue of orthodoxy and syncretism is especially complicated in the United States. As Europe offloaded their religious dissidents to colonial America it created a dynamic where variations on a Protestant theme proliferated into a cacophony of marching bands. Syncretism, at least in the US Protestant context, does not necessarily imply secularisation or a retreat from orthodoxy. The Church of Jesus Christ of Latter-Day Saints (Mormon), The Church Of Christ, Scientist (Christian Science), and Seventh Day Adventist Church are examples of syncretic hybrids of Protestantism that are not secularised and have an orthodox clergy and an institutionalised presence in the society as established religions.

When looking at the BJP or Christian Identity, Griffin argues they are a:

> fundamentalist form of religion [which] has apparently under-gone such an intense process of secularisation in upholding nationalist or racist claims within historical time, and the super-historical realm of eternity has receded so far from the concerns of the believers, that a genuine hybrid seems to have resulted.[155]

At least with Christian Identity, the dualistic form of apocalyptic funda-mentalism is merged with racial nationalism precisely through the invo-cation of sacred text to claim the 'superhistorical realm of eternity' can only be honoured through devotion to white racial consciousness.[156] The Christian Identity reading of the sacred biblical text is unorthodox and syncretic, but how can it be called 'secularised' unless one claims to be able to determine who is showing legitimate religious devotion and reading sacred text 'properly'? Gentile warns against the label 'pseudo-religion', and cites Pettazzoni arguing that a historian 'does not recognise false religions or real religions, but only different religious forms within which religions develops'.[157] So when Griffin describes Codreanu of the Romanian Iron Guard as 'perverting a long-standing Christian apocalyptic tradition', I understand and share his revulsion. In my view, however, I see competing traditions within Christianity (and other religions) in which dualistic apocalypticism, coercion and theocracy, are not a perversion ... but merely an *Ur* version.[158]

There is more to understand about the sacralisation of politics and the concepts of exclusionary political religion opposing pluralist civil religion. What are the characteristics and interactions of palingenesis, apocalypticism, millennialism and millenarianism? When we speak of totalitarianism, are we assuming it includes subsets of authoritarianism and coercion, or do we need to make these elements more explicit? Do all forms of totalitarianism, including fascism, involve to varying degrees the processes of dualism, demonisation, scapegoating and conspiracism? What are the different ways a movement can package its ideology and construct persuasive frames using integralism, organ-icism, *völkish* nationalism and populist demagoguery? Just where is the boundary between right-wing populism and neo-fascism?[159]

This all may seem like quibbling, but by increasing the precision of our taxonomic vocabulary, there can be a more fruitful discus-sion on how properly to categorise (and understand) a variety of ethno-nationalist and religio-nationalist movements. Even if you dispute all my categorisations of groups as varieties of fascism – if you can challenge my claims with new and more useful language, then scholarship will move forward. Sorting this out will take time, but if we maintain a comedic view of the apocalypse, then we have until the end of time, and who knows when that will be, so we might as well get started.

NOTES

Conversations with Roger Griffin on religion and fascism, and with Simon Baalham on Christian Identity and neo-fascism, helped inform and shape my research for this essay. My thesis on fascism and millenarianism is an extension of the work of Norman Cohn, Michael Barkun and James H. Rhodes, among others; but the arguments and conclusions here are my own to defend. Considerable assistance in locating material on clerical fascism and its roots came from Dan Sharon at the Norman and Helen Asher Library of the Spertus Institute of Jewish Studies in Chicago.

1. Emilio Gentile, 'The Sacralisation of Politics: Definitions, Interpretations and Reflections on the Question of Secular Religion and Totalitarianism', trans. Robert Mallett, *Totalitarian Movements and Political Religions* 1/1 (2000), p.18.
2. Ibid.
3. Hannah Arendt, *The Origins of Totalitarianism*, new edn., new prefaces (New York: Harcourt Brace Jovanovich, 1973 [1951]); Robert Jay Lifton, *Thought Reform and the Psychology of Totalism*, reprinted edn. (Chapel Hill, NC: University of North Carolina Press, 1989 [1961]); and Bob Altemeyer, *The Authoritarian Specter* (Cambridge, MA: Harvard University Press, 1996).
4. Paul M. Hayes, *Fascism* (New York: Free Press, 1973); see especially the chapter on 'The Concept of the Totalitarian State', pp.39–50.
5. Arendt (note 3).
6. See Gentile (note 1), p.4: 'By defining totalitarianism as an *experiment*, rather than as a *regime*, it is intended to highlight the interconnections between its fundamental constituent parts and to emphasise that totalitarianism is a *continual process* that cannot be considered complete at any stage in its evolution'.
7. Roger Griffin, *The Nature of Fascism* (New York: St Martin's Press, 1991), p.xi.
8. Leonard Zeskind, *The 'Christian Identity' Movement* (Atlanta, GA: Center for Democratic Renewal/Division of Church and Society, National Council of Churches, 1987); Patrick Minges, 'Apocalypse Now! The Realized Eschatology of the "Christian Identity" Movement', paper presented at the annual conference of the American Academy of Religion, 1994; Kenneth S. Stern, *A Force Upon the Plain: The American Militia Movement and the Politics of Hate* (New York: Simon and Schuster, 1996); Michael Barkun, *Religion and the Racist Right: The Origins of the Christian Identity Movement*, rev. edn. (Chapel Hill, NC: University of North Carolina Press, 1997 [1994]); Jeffrey Kaplan, *Radical Religion in America: Millenarian Movements from the Far Right to the Children of Noah* (Syracuse, NY: Syracuse University Press, 1997), pp.47–68; Susan DeCamp, 'Locking the Doors to the Kingdom: An Examination of Religion in Extremist Organizing and Public Policy', in Eric Ward (ed.), *American Armageddon: Religion, Revolution and the Right* (Seattle, WA: Northwest Coalition Against Malicious Harassment [Peanut Butter Publishing], 1998), pp.13–43; and Daniel Levitas, *The Terrorist Next Door: The Militia Movement and the Radical Right* (New York: Thomas Dunne/St Martin's, 2002).

9. For early examples of how British Israelism came to the Americas, see J.H. Allen, *Judah's Sceptre and Joseph's Birthright*, 15th edn. (Haverhill, MA: Destiny Publishers, 1917 [1902]); and W.G. Mackendrick (The Roadbuilder), *The Destiny of Britain and America*, rev. edn. (Toronto: McClelland and Stewart, 1922).

10. Howard B. Rand, *Segregation: A Divinely-Instituted Precept*, pamphlet, (Merrimac, MA: Destiny Publishers, 1961).

11. Zeskind (note 8); see also Barkun (note 8); and Kaplan (note 8). For detailed explanations of variations within Identity on the 'seedline' theories of Jewish heritage, see Zeskind (note 8); and Burkun (note 8).

12. Levitas (note 8), p.24–37.

13. Ibid., p.81. While I dissent from Levitas when he implies that the right-wing populist armed militia movement is virtually identical to the neo-fascist Christian Identity movement, the Levitas book is nonetheless an exceptionally detailed study of the Christian Identity role in the Posse Comitatus movement, and contains a tremendous amount of original research.

14. Barkun (note 8), pp.68–71.

15. Bill Morlin, 'Verdict Busts Butler: Jury Orders Aryans To Pay $6.3 Million', *Spokesman-Review*, 8 September 2000; 'Aryan Buildings Bite The Dust Symbols Of Racist Past Come Tumbling Down', *Spokesman-Review*, 24 May 2001; and 'Butler Names Ohio Follower As Successor', *Spokesman-Review*, 7 December 2002; online archive.

16. Aryan Nations, 'What We Believe', http://www.aryannations.org/an/goals.html, accessed 3 August 2004. With few exceptions, obvious typos from websites have been corrected.

17. Ibid.

18. Ibid.

19. Ibid.

20. Aryan Nations, 'Platform For The Aryan National State', flyer, no date, c.1990, on file at Political Research Associates. Online version http://www.aryannations.org/an/goals.html, accessed 3 August 2004. These are patterned, in part, on the 'Programme of the NSDAP', issued 24 February 1920, online (with some variation in text) at several sites, including: http://www.hitler.org/writings/programme, accessed 8 August 2004.

21. Ibid.

22. Ibid.

23. Ibid.

24. Moishe Postone, 'Anti-Semitism and National Socialism', in Anson Rabinbach and Jack Zipes (eds.), *Germans and Jews Since the Holocaust: The Changing Situation in West Germany* (New York: Homes and Meier, 1986), pp.302–14; and Chip Berlet and Matthew N. Lyons, *Right-Wing Populism in America: Too Close for Comfort* (New York: Guilford, 2000).

25. Paul A. Lombardo, '"The American Breed": Nazi Eugenics and the Origins of the Pioneer Fund', *Albany Law Review* 65/3 (2002), pp.743–830; see also William Tucker, *The Funding of Scientific Racism: Wickliffe Draper and the Pioneer Fund* (Urbana, IL: University of Illinois Press, 2002). On contemporary manifestations, see Barry Mehler, 'Foundation for Fascism: The New Eugenics Movement in the United States', *Patterns of Prejudice* 23/4 (1989), pp.17–25; Barry Mehler, 'In Genes We Trust: When Science Bows to Racism', *Reform Judaism* 23 (Winter 1994), pp.10–13, 77–9; and Barry Mehler, 'Race and "Reason": Academic Ideas a Pillar of Racist Thought', *Intelligence Report*, Southern Poverty Law Center (Winter 1999), pp.27–32.

26. http://www.twelvearyannations.com, accessed 2 October 2003.

27. Email exchanges with Jeffrey M. Bale and Kevin Coogan, August and December 2003. Both argue that Christian Identity, even in Aryan Nations, is too rooted in homegrown American ideologies such as fundamentalism, xenophobic nativism and generic

notions of white supremacy to be considered neo-fascist. As an avowed Sternhellian, Bale also argues that the 'Aryan Nations version of Christian Identity – or any other form of Christian Identity, for that matter – is not neo-fascist because' he argues 'it lacks both the radical nationalist components and any of the left-leaning (anti-capitalist, syndicalist, and non-Marxian socialist) ideological components characteristic of European proto–fascism, "Fascism of the first hour" in Italy, and most other' fascist and neo-fascist doctrines; quoted from email. See Jeffrey M. Bale, 'Fascism and Neo-Fascism: Ideology and "Groupuscularity", A Response to Roger Griffin', *Erwägen Wissen Ethik* 15/1 (2004), a draft of which was supplied to the author by Bale.

28. This is sometimes called the Thomas Theorem. William I. Thomas and Dorothy Swaine Thomas, 'Situations Defined as Real are Real in their Consequences', in Gregory P. Stone and Harvey A. Farberman (eds.), *Social Psychology Through Symbolic Interaction* (Waltham, MA: Ginn Blaisdell/Xerox, 1970), pp.154–5, quoted p.154.

29. Two studies of members of hard Right groups in the US have found that they are roughly similar in demographics and apparent mental health to others in the surrounding population. James A. Aho, *The Politics of Righteousness: Idaho Christian Patriotism* (Seattle, WA: University of Washington Press, 1990); Kathleen M. Blee, *Inside Organized Racism: Women in the Hate Movement* (Berkeley, CA: University of California Press, 2002).

30. Eschatology is the study of the prophesied End Times. Exegesis in Christianity is primarily the analysis of biblical text to find core meaning.

31. See as examples pamphlets from sermons by Wesley A. Swift, 'Mystery Babylon'; 'The Children of the Beast'; 'Who are the Jews?'; 'Was Jesus Christ a Jew?'; The Bible and the Race of Destiny'; 'Michael, Prince Of Space'; http://churchoftrueisrael.com/swift, accessed 8 August 2004.

32. Norman Cohn, *The Pursuit of the Millennium: Revolutionary Millenarians and Mystical Anarchists of the Middle Ages*, revised and expanded (New York: Oxford University Press, 1970 [1957]; London: Serif, 1996 [1967]); Michael Barkun, *Disaster and the Millennium* (New Haven: Yale University Press, 1974); James M. Rhodes, *The Hitler Movement: A Modern Millenarian Revolution* (Stanford, CA: Hoover Institution Press, Stanford University, 1980); Robert Wistrich, *Hitler's Apocalypse: Jews and the Nazi Legacy* (New York: St Martin's Press, 1985); Robert Ellwood, 'Nazism as a Millennialist Movement', in Catherine Wessinger (ed.), *Millennialism, Persecution, and Violence: Historical Cases* (Syracuse, IL: Syracuse University Press, 2000), pp.241–60; and Richard K. Fenn, *The End of Time: Religion, Ritual, and the Forging of the Soul* (Cleveland: Pilgrim Press, 1997).

33. Roger Eatwell, 'The Nature of the Right, 2: The Right as a Variety of "Styles of Thought"', in Roger Eatwell and Noël O'Sullivan (eds.), *The Nature of the Right: American and European Politics and Political Thought Since 1789* (Boston: Twayne Publishers, 1990 [1989]), pp.62–76, quoted p.72. See also Frederick Wall, 'The Fate that Hate Produced: Religion, Science, and Fiction in New Millennial Racialism', in Martha F. Lee (ed.), *Millennial Visions: Essays on Twentieth-Century Millenarianism* (Westport, CT: Praeger, 2000), pp.71–93.

34. Rhodes (note 32), p.18, citing the work on apocalypticism by Cohn and on gnosticism by Voegelin. For Cohn, see note 32. For Voegelin, see Eric Voegelin, *The New Science of Politics* (Chicago: University of Chicago Press, 1952); idem, *Science, Politics, and Gnosticism* (Chicago: Henry Regnery, 1968); *From Enlightenment to Revolution* (Durham, NC: Duke University Press, 1995).

35. Kevin Coogan, *Dreamer of the Day: Francis Parker Yockey and the Postwar Fascist International* (Brooklyn, NY: Autonomedia, 1999), p.563.

36. Joel Kovel, *Red Hunting in the Promised Land: Anticommunism and the Making of America* (New York, Basic Books, 1994), p.77.

37. Gentile (note 1), p.35.

38. Ibid., p.20.
39. Ibid., p.24.
40. Ellwood (note 32), pp.241–3.
41. This analysis of apocalyptic demonisation and millennialism is drawn primarily from the following sources: Norman Cohn, *Cosmos, Chaos and the World to Come: The Ancient Roots of Apocalyptic Faith*, revised and updated (New Haven, CT: Yale University Press, 2001 [1993]); Cohn (note 32); Paul Boyer, *When Time Shall Be No More: Prophecy Belief in Modern American Culture* (Cambridge, MA: Belknap/Harvard University Press, 1992); Charles B. Strozier, *Apocalypse: On the Psychology of Fundamentalism in America* (Boston: Beacon Press, 1994); Stephen D. O'Leary, *Arguing the Apocalypse: A Theory of Millennial Rhetoric* (New York: Oxford University Press, 1994); Lee Quinby, *Anti-Apocalypse: Exercises in Genealogical Criticism* (Minneapolis: University of Minnesota Press, 1994); Robert C. Fuller, *Naming the Antichrist: The History of an American Obsession* (New York: Oxford University Press, 1995); Damian Thompson *The End of Time: Faith and Fear in the Shadow of the Millennium* (Hanover, NH: University Press of New England, 1998 [1996]); and Elaine Pagels, *The Origin of Satan* (New York: Vintage, 1996).
42. Portions of this section first appeared as papers for the annual meetings of the International Sociological Association and American Sociological Association, which were converted into an article: Chip Berlet, 'Dances with Devils: How Apocalyptic and Millennialist Themes Influence Right Wing Scapegoating and Conspiracism', *Public Eye* 12/2–3 (Autumn 1998); http://www.publiceye.org/apocalyptic/Dances_with_Devils_1.html, parts of which were incorporated into Berlet and Lyons (note 24). For extended discussions from which snippets from this section were also plucked (and in the spirit of full copyright compliance), see Chip Berlet, 'Apocalypse', 'Conspiracism', 'Demonization', 'Demagoguery', 'Totalitarianism' and 'Year 2000', in Richard A. Landes (ed.), *Encyclopedia of Millennialism and Millennial Movements* (New York: Routledge, 2000); idem, 'Apocalypse', 'Nativism', 'Devil and Satan' and 'Illuminati', in Brenda E. Brasher (ed.), *Encyclopedia of Fundamentalism* (New York: Routledge, 2001); and idem, 'Three Models for Analyzing Conspiracist Mass Movements of the Right', in Eric Ward (ed.), *Conspiracies: Real Grievances, Paranoia, and Mass Movements* (Seattle: Northwest Coalition Against Malicious Harassment [Peanut Butter Publishing], 1996), pp.47–75.
43. Cohn (note 32), especially the 'Introduction'; David G. Bromley, 'Constructing Apocalypticism: Social and Cultural Elements of Radical Organization'; and Catherine Wessinger, 'Millennialism With and Without the Mayhem'; both in Thomas Robbins and Susan J. Palmer (eds.), *Millennium, Messiahs, and Mayhem: Contemporary Apocalyptic Movements* (New York: Routledge, 1997), pp.31–45 and 47–59 respectively.
44. Cohn (note 41).
45. Pagels (note 41), p.182. See, for example, Gerry O'Sullivan, 'The Satanism Scare', *Postmodern Culture* 1/2 (January 1991); Susan Harding, 'Imagining the Last Days: The Politics of Apocalyptic Language', in Martin E. Marty and R. Scott Appleby (eds.), *Accounting for Fundamentalisms: The Dynamic Character of Movements*, Fundamentalism Project 4 (Chicago: University of Chicago Press, 1994), pp.57–78; and Ted Daniels (ed.), *A Doomsday Reader: Prophets, Predictors, and Hucksters of Salvation* (New York: New York University Press, 1999).
46. Strozier (note 41), pp.223–48; and John M. Bozeman, 'Technological Millenarianism in the United States', in Robbins and Palmer (note 43), pp.139–58.
47. Michael Barkun, *A Culture of Conspiracy: Apocalyptic Visions in Contemporary America* (Berkeley, CA: University of California Press, 2003).
48. Boyer (note 41), pp.21–36, 189–90; Fuller (note 41), pp.14–30; and Philip Lamy, *Millennium Rage: Survivalists, White Supremacists, and the Doomsday Prophecy* (New York: Plenum, 1996), p.37.

49. Robert Alan Goldberg, *Enemies Within: The Culture of Conspiracy in Modern America* (New Haven, CT: Yale University Press, 2001), p.67.
50. Fuller (note 41), pp.15, 26; and Lamy (note 48), pp.36–7.
51. Goldberg (note 49), p.67.
52. Fuller (note 41), pp.27–30; Lamy (note 48), pp.32–6; and George Johnson, *Fire in the Mind: Science, Faith, and the Search for Order* (New York: Knopf, 1995), pp.308–13.
53. Michael W. Cuneo, *The Smoke of Satan: Conservative and Traditionalist Dissent in Contemporary American Catholicism* (New York: Oxford University Press, 1997); and Victor Balaban, 'The Virgin and the Millennium: Marian Sightings in the United States', paper presented at a conference of the Center for Millennial Studies and Boston University School of Theology, 20 January 1998. For examples, see issues of the magazines *Wanderer* and *Fatima Crusader*, for example, Charles Martel, 'The Antichrist', *Fatima Crusader* (Summer 1994), pp.6–9.
54. Michael Barkun (ed.), *Millennialism and Violence*, Cass Series on Political Violence (London: Frank Cass, 1996); Robbins and Palmer (note 43); David S. Katz and Richard H. Popkin, *Messianic Revolution: Radical Religious Politics to the End of the Second Millennium* (New York: Hill and Wang, 1998); and Catherine Wessinger (ed.), *Millennialism, Persecution, and Violence: Historical Cases* (Syracuse: Syracuse University Press, 2000).
55. Stephen Jay Gould, *Questioning the Millennium: A Rationalist's Guide to a Precisely Arbitrary Countdown* (New York: Harmony Books, 1997). Gould examines the difference between 'millenarian' groups and 'millennial' expectation.
56. Cohn (note 32).
57. Boyer (note 41), pp.80–5.
58. The classic study of millenarianism is Peter Worsley, *The Trumpet Shall Sound: A Study of 'Cargo' Cults in Melanesia*, 2nd rev. edn. (New York: Schocken Books, 1968).
59. Preface to Revelation, *New International Version of the Holy Bible* [Protestant 'NIV' version] (Grand Rapids, MI: Zondervan Bible Publishers, 1984 [1973]), p.1698.
60. Boyer (note 41), pp.80–112.
61. Harding (note 45), see especially her explanation of how fundamentalists who expect to be Raptured can nonetheless justify becoming politically active, pp.69–71; note that this does not make them post-millennialists according to their own theology. See also: Gershom Gorenberg, *The End of Days: Fundamentalism and the Struggle for the Temple Mount* (New York: Free Press, 2000).
62. Grace Halsell, *Prophecy and Politics: Militant Evangelists on the Road to Nuclear War* (Westport, CT: Lawrence Hill, 1986).
63. Frances FitzGerald, 'The American Millennium', *New Yorker*, 11 November 1985, pp.105–96; quoted p.106.
64. Lamy (note 48), p.155. See also Boyer (note 41), pp.327–31.
65. Sara Diamond, 'Political Millennialism within the Evangelical Subculture', in Charles B. Strozier and Michael Flynn (eds.), *The Year 2000: Essays on the End* (New York: New York University Press, 1997), pp.206–16, cited on p.210.
66. Gary H. Kah, *En Route to Global Occupation* (Lafayette, LA: Huntington House Publishers, 1991); Pat Robertson, *The New World Order: It Will Change the Way You Live* (Dallas: Word Publishing, 1991); Donald S. McAlvany, *Toward a New World Order: The Countdown to Armageddon* (Oklahoma City, OK: Hearthstone Publishing/ Southwest Radio Church of the Air, 1990); Dee Zahner, *The Secret Side of History: Mystery Babylon and the New World Order* (Hesperia, CA: LTAA Communications, 1994); Dave Hunt, 'Global Peace and the Rise of the Antichrist', videotape (Dave Hunt, 1990); and *What's Behind the New World Order*, booklet (Jemison, AL: Inspiration Books East, 1991).
67. See, for example, Boyer (note 41), pp.254–339; Strozier (note 41), pp.108–29; O'Leary (note 41), pp.34–193; Fuller (note 41), pp.165–90; Sara Diamond, *Not by Politics Alone: The Enduring Influence of the Christian Right* (New York: Guilford

Press, 1998), pp.197–215; idem, *Spiritual Warfare: The Politics of the Christian Right* (Boston: South End Press, 1989); idem, 'Political Millennialism within the Evangelical Subculture', in Strozier and Flynn (note 65); Frederick Clarkson, *Eternal Hostility: The Struggle Between Theocracy and Democracy* (Monroe, ME: Common Courage, 1997), pp.125–38; Linda Kintz, *Between Jesus and the Market: The Emotions that Matter in Right-Wing America* (Durham, NC: Duke University Press, 1997), pp.8–9, 134–9, 266–7; and Didi Herman, *The Antigay Agenda: Orthodox Vision and the Christian Right* (Chicago: University of Chicago Press, 1997), pp.19–24, 35–44, 125–8, 171–2.

68. Berlet and Lyons (note 24), pp.13, 179, 193, 242, 293, 317.
69. Richard Hofstadter, 'The Paranoid Style in American Politics', in *The Paranoid Style in American Politics and Other Essays* (New York: Alfred A. Knopf, 1965), pp.3–40; David Brion Davis (ed.), *The Fear of Conspiracy: Images of Un-American Subversion from the Revolution to the Present* (Ithaca, NY: Cornell University Press, 1972); Richard O. Curry and Thomas M. Brown (eds.), 'Introduction', *Conspiracy: The Fear of Subversion in American History* (New York: Holt, Rinehart and Winston, 1972); George Johnson, *Architects of Fear: Conspiracy Theories and Paranoia in American Politics* (Los Angeles: Tarcher/Houghton Mifflin, 1983); Frank P. Mintz, *The Liberty Lobby and the American Right: Race, Conspiracy, and Culture* (Westport, CT: Greenwood, 1985); David H. Bennett, *The Party of Fear: The American Far Right from Nativism to the Militia Movement*, rev. edn. (New York: Vintage Books, 1995 [1988]); Kovel (note 36); and Goldberg (note 49).
70. Frank J. Donner, *The Age of Surveillance: The Aims and Methods of America's Political Intelligence System* (New York: Vintage, 1981 [1980]), pp.47–8.
71. Hofstadter (note 69), p.17.
72. Ibid., p.14.
73. Thompson (note 41), pp.307–8.
74. Barkun (note 8), pp.47–9, 60–70, 106–7, 116–18, 205.
75. Minges (note 8), online.
76. 'What We Believe' (note 16).
77. Sometimes apocalyptic Christian movements that intervene in society are called post-millennialist because this tendency believes it must take over society before Christ returns; but theologically they must take over society and hold it for one thousand years before the Second Coming of Christ to be literally 'post' the 'millennium'; see also note 61. I think it is more accurate to catalogue Aryan Nations Christian Identity theology as a form of non-Rapture tribulationist, interventionist, coercive, dualistic, pre-millennial dispensationalism.
78. Minges (note 8), online.
79. Gordon W. Allport, *The Nature of Prejudice* (Cambridge, MA: Addison-Wesley, 1954), pp.29–67.
80. Hannah Arendt (note 3), pp.3–10. Arendt objected to the traditional use of the term whereby the scapegoats are portrayed as having no connection to an actual power struggle, but blameless unconnected innocents chosen at random.
81. See Allport (note 79), pp.243–60; David Norman Smith, 'The Social Construction of Enemies: Jews and the Representation of Evil', *Sociological Theory* 14/3 (1996), pp.203–40; and René Girard, *The Scapegoat* (Baltimore, MD: Johns Hopkins University Press, 1986).
82. Berlet and Lyons (note 24), p.8.
83. Landes, 'Scapegoating', in Peter N. Stearn (ed.), *Encyclopedia of Social History* (New York: Garland, 1994), p.659. Neumann has argued against using the term scapegoating when discussing conspiracist movements, but I support the Landes definition; Franz Neumann, 'Anxiety in Politics', in Richard O. Curry and Thomas M. Brown (eds.), *Conspiracy: The Fear of Subversion in American History* (New York: Holt, Rinehart and Winston, 1972), p.255.

84. Eli Sagan, *The Honey and the Hemlock: Democracy and Paranoia in Ancient Athens and Modern America* (New York: Basic Books, 1991), p.370.
85. Landes (note 83).
86. Girard (note 81), pp.43–4, 49–56, 66–73, 84–7, 100–1, 177–8.
87. James A. Aho, *This Thing of Darkness: A Sociology of the Enemy, 'A Phenomenology of the Enemy'* (Seattle, WA: University of Washington Press, 1994), pp.115–16.
88. Girard (note 81), p.44.
89. Lise Noël, *Intolerance, A General Survey*, trans. Arnold Bennett (Montreal: McGill-Queen's University Press, 1994), p.129–44.
90. Allport (note 79), pp.363–4.
91. Fuller (note 41), p.168.
92. O'Leary (note 41), pp.20–60.
93. Zeskind, 'Some Ideas on Conspiracy Theories for a New Historical Period', in Ward (note 42), pp.11–35, quotes from pp.13–14, 16.
94. S.L. Gardner, 'Social Movements, Conspiracy Theories and Economic Determinism: A Response to Chip Berlet', in Ward (note 42), pp.77–89, quoted p.83.
95. O'Leary (note 41), p.6.
96. Patrick Minges (note 8), online.
97. Kathleen M. Blee, 'Engendering Conspiracy: Women in Rightist Theories and Movements', in Ward (note 42), pp.91–112, quote from p.98. See also Kathleen M. Blee, 'Racist Activism and Apocalyptic/Millennial Thinking', *Journal of Millennial Studies* 2/1 (Summer 1999), Special Issue on Engendering the Millennium, online version http://www.mille.org/publications/summer99/blee.PDF, accessed 4 July 2004.
98. Portions of this section are adapted from material that originally appeared in other publications, see note 42.
99. Just insert the phrase 'Coca Cola culture' into any Internet search engine, (while noting that Coca Cola is a trademarked name).
100. Martin E. Marty and R. Scott Appleby (eds.), *Fundamentalisms Observed*, Fundamentalism Project 1 (Chicago: University of Chicago Press, 1994 [1991]).
101. George M. Marsden, *Fundamentalism and American Culture: The Shaping of Twentieth Century Evangelicalism, 1870–1925* (Oxford: Oxford University Press, 1982 [1980]); idem, *Understanding Fundamentalism and Evangelicalism* (Grand Rapids, MI: William B. Eerdmans, 1991); and Nancy T. Ammerman, 'North American Protestant Fundamentalism', in Marty and Appleby (note 100), pp.1–65.
102. Anthony F.C. Wallace, 'Revitalization Movements', *American Anthropologist* 58/2 (1956), pp.264–81.
103. Here we are using the broader definition of the term fundamentalist as suggested by the University of Chicago studies in their Fundamentalism Project; see Marty and Appleby (note 100).
104. Catherine Wessinger, 'Bin Laden and Revolutionary Millennialism', *New Orleans Times-Picayune*, 10 October 2001, http://www.mille.org/cmshome/wessladen.html, accessed 8 August 2004.
105. This was discussed at the conference on 'Millennial Texts and Apocalyptic Contexts: Implications for Congregational Life', at the Andover Newton Theological Seminary, co-sponsored by the Boston Theological Institute and the Center for Millennial Studies at Boston University, Newton, MA, November 2003. The distinction is often based on a theological notion of hating the sin, but loving the sinner. In demonising visions of fundamentalism and apocalypticism, the proponents hate both sin and sinner, and develop scapegoating narratives to justify aggression against the sinner based on some perceived group identity.
106. Karen Armstrong, *The Battle for God* (New York: Ballantine Books, 2001 [2000]), p.363; see also p.244.
107. David C. Rapoport, 'Comparing Militant Fundamentalist Movements and Groups', in Martin E. Marty and R. Scott Appleby (eds.), *Fundamentalisms and the State: Remak-*

ing Polities, Economies, and Militance, Fundamentalism Project 3 (Chicago: University of Chicago Press, 1993), pp.429–61, see esp. p.446.

108. Wessinger (note 104).

109. Mark Juergensmeyer, *Terror in the Mind of God: The Global Rise of Religious Violence* (Berkeley, CA: University of California, 2000), p.242.

110. Armstrong (note 106) pp.xii–xiv; citing in part Martin E. Marty and R. Scott Appleby, 'Conclusion: An Interim Report on a Hypothetical Family', in Marty and Appleby (note 100), pp.814–42.

111. Armstrong (note 106), p.xiii.

112. Ibid., pp.233–371.

113. Paul Boyer, 'John Darby Meets Saddam Hussein: Foreign Policy and Bible Prophecy', *Chronicle of Higher Education*, supplement, 14 February 2003, pp.B10–B11; Daniel Levitas, 'A Marriage Made for Heaven', *Reform Judaism* 31/4 (2003), online version http://www.uahc.org/rjmag/03summer/focus.shtml, accessed 22 November 2003; Chip Berlet and Nikhil Aziz, 'Culture, Religion, Apocalypse, and Middle East Foreign Policy', IRC Right Web (Silver City, NM: Interhemispheric Resource Center), online version http://rightweb.irc-online.org/analysis/2003/0312apocalypse.php, accessed 4 July 2004.

114. Gorenberg (note 61).

115. Juergensmeyer (note 109); and Jessica Stern, *Terror in the Name of God: Why Religious Militants Kill* (New York: Ecco/Harper Collins, 2003).

116. Among the more accessible sources are Stanley G. Payne, *A History of Fascism, 1914–45* (Madison, WI: University of Wisconsin Press, 1995), pp.245–89; and Roger Griffin (ed.), *Fascism*, Oxford Readers (Oxford: Oxford University Press, 1995), pp.169–226. Since these clerical fascist movements were virulently antisemitic, useful coverage can be gleaned from Israel Gutman (ed.), *Encyclopedia of the Holocaust* (New York: Macmillan, 1990); Lucy S. Dawidowicz, *The War Against the Jews 1933–1945* (New York: Bantam Books, 1975), pp.374–401; and Nora Levin, *The Holocaust: The Destruction of European Jewry 1933–1945* (New York: Schocken Books, 1973), pp.507–618.

117. Zeev Sternhell with Mario Sznajder and Maia Asheri, *The Birth of Fascist Ideology*, trans. David Maisel (Princeton, NJ: Princeton University Press, 1995 [1989]).

118. Payne (note 116), chart, p.15. Payne does not use the term 'clerical fascism'.

119. J. Wodka, 'Englebert Dollfuss', *New Catholic Encyclopedia* (San Francisco: McGraw Hill, 1967), pp.958–9.

120. For specifics, see Randolph L. Braham and Scott Miller, *The Nazis' Last Victims: The Holocaust in Hungary* (Detroit: Wayne State University Press, 2002 [1998]); Leon Volovici, *Nationalist Ideology and Anti-Semitism: The Case of Romanian Intellectuals in the 1930s* (Oxford: Pergamon Press, 1991); and Nicholas M. Nagy-Talavera, *The Green Shirts and the Others: A History of Fascism in Hungary and Romania* (Iasi and Oxford: Center for Romanian Studies, 2001); on the Catholic role in Hungary and Croatia, see Anthony Rhodes, *The Vatican in the Age of Dictators 1922–1945* (London: Hodder and Stoughton, 1973), pp.302–36; on Croatia, see Michael Phayer, *The Catholic Church and the Holocaust, 1930–1965* (Bloomington, IN: Indiana University Press, 2000), pp.31–40; and Livia Rothkirchen, 'Vatican Policy and the "Jewish Problem" in Independent Slovakia (1939–1945)', in Michael R. Marrus (ed.), *The Nazi Holocaust*, vol.3, section 8, 'Bystanders to the Holocaust' (Westport, CT: Meckler, 1989), pp.1306–32.

121. For example, the 'Political Soldier', a Third Position group, promotes Codreanu, adopting his oath for the Romanian Iron Guard Legionary Movement, and offering a painted oil portrait of Codreanu as a prize in a raffle, http://www.politicalsoldier.net, accessed 13 October 2002.

122. Volovici (note 120), pp.104–5, 110–11, 120–6, 134.

123. Ibid., p.98, citing N. Cainic, *Ortodxie si Etnocratie*, pp.162–4.

124. Phayer (note 120), p.8.
125. Roger Griffin used the term 'fascistised clericalism' in a series of email exchanges start-
     ing in October 2001 where we were trying to tease apart some of the taxonomic
     distinctions which are discussed at the end of this article. This was part of a larger elec-
     tronic conversation involving Douglas Kellner, Robert Antonio and Matthew N.
     Lyons.
126. Berlet and Lyons (note 24), pp.248–50. For more on Reconstructionism, see Bruce
     Barron, *Heaven on Earth? The Social and Political Agendas of Dominion Theology*
     (Grand Rapids, MI: Zondervon, 1992); and Clarkson (note 67).
127. Charles Bloomberg and Saul Dubow, (eds.), *Christian-Nationalism and the Rise of the
     Afrikaner Broederbond in South Africa, 1918–48* (Bloomington, IN: Indiana University
     Press, 1989); Walid Phares, *Lebanese Christian Nationalism: The Rise and Fall of an
     Ethnic Resistance* (Boulder, CO: Lynne Rienner, 1995); Ainslie T. Embree, 'The Func-
     tion of the Rashtriya Swayamsevak Sangh: To Define the Hindu Nation', in Marty and
     Appleby (note 45), pp.617–52; Partha Banerjee, *In the Belly of the Beast: The Hindu
     Supremacist RSS and BJP of India* (Delhi: Ajanta, 1998); and Walter K. Andersen,
     'Bharatiya Janata Party: Searching for the Hindu Nationalist Face', in Hans-Georg
     Betz and Stefan Immerfall (eds.), *The New Politics of the Right: Neo-Populist Parties
     and Movements in Established Democracies* (New York: St Martin's Press, 1998),
     pp.219–32.
128. Quinby (note 41), p.162. See also Lee Quinby, 'Coercive Purity: The Dangerous
     Promise of Apocalyptic Masculinity', in Strozier and Flynn (note 65), pp.154–65.
129. Catherine Wessinger, 'Introduction', in Wessinger (note 54), p.15, text and note 15.
130. Barkun (note 54); Robbins and Palmer (note 43); Katz and Popkin (note 54);
     Wessinger (note 54); and Carol Mason, *Killing for Life: The Apocalyptic Narrative of
     Pro-Life Politics* (Ithaca, NY: Cornell University Press, 2002).
131. Ellwood (note 32), p.253.
132. Fenn (note 32).
133. Richard Steigmann-Gall, *The Holy Reich: Nazi Conceptions of Christianity, 1919–1945*
     (Cambridge: Cambridge University Press, 2003), pp.19, 189, 261; quoted p.261.
134. Apocalypticism, dualism, conspiracism and populism are 'styles' used by organisers;
     however, Brenda Brasher has suggested in conversations that apocalypticism is usefully
     seen as a sociological 'master frame'.
135. Dick Anthony and Thomas Robbins, 'Religious Totalism, Exemplary Dualism, and the
     Waco Tragedy', in Robbins and Palmer (note 43), pp.264, 269.
136. Ibid., p.267. See also Dick Anthony and Thomas Robbins, 'Religious Totalism,
     Violence and Exemplary Dualism: Beyond the Extrinsic Model', in Barkun (note 54).
137. David Neiwert, *Rush, Newspeak and Fascism: An Exegesis*, online essay, http://dneiw-
     ert.blogspot.com, accessed 3 November 2003.
138. Matthew Rothschild, 'Bush's Messiah Complex', *Progressive*, February 2003, online
     archive http://www.progressive.org/feb03/comm0203.html, accessed 8 August 2004.
139. Sagan (note 84), p.363.
140. O'Leary (note 41), pp.6–7, 20, 42, 75–84, 218–20.
141. Wessinger (note 43); Catherine Wessinger, 'Introduction' (note 129).
142. Richard Landes, 'Patterns of Engagement', paper presented at the conference on
     Millennial Texts and Apocalyptic Contexts (note 105).
143. Emilio Gentile, *The Sacralization of Politics in Fascist Italy*, trans. Keith Botsford
     (Cambridge, MA: Harvard University Press, 1996).
144. For criticism of 'centrist–extremist' theory (including an extensive list of citations for
     other authors), see Chip Berlet and Matthew N. Lyons, 'One Key to Litigating Against
     Government Prosecution of Dissidents: Understanding the Underlying Assumptions',
     Police Misconduct and Civil Rights Law Report (West Group), in two parts, 5/13 (Janu-
     ary–February 1998), and 5/14 (March–April 1998), online version http://www.public-
     eye.org/liberty/Repression-and-ideology.html, accessed 4 July 2004.

145. Bale considers Ba'athism to be a genuinely fascist doctrine due to its telling combination of romantic integral nationalism (in this case in a pan-Arab form) and non-Marxist 'socialism'; see Jeffrey M. Bale, 'Ba'athism', in Cyprian Blamires (ed.), *Historical Encyclopedia of World Fascism* (Santa Monica, CA: ABC–Clio, forthcoming 2005), draft supplied to the author by Bale.
146. Steigmann-Gall (note 133), p.265; see also his essay in this issue.
147. Roger Griffin, email to author, 10 November 2003. Here and in the following paragraphs I am relying on extensive email dialogues between Griffin and myself concerning taxonomy and terminology starting in 2001 and continuing through to 2003.
148. For a fuller account of his argument, see Roger Griffin, 'Fascism', in Brenda Brasher (note 42), pp.171–8.
149. Ibid.; and Chip Berlet, 'Terminology: Use with Caution', *Public Eye* 15/3 (Autumn 2001), pp.14–17, revised online version http://www.publiceye.org/frontpage/911/clerical-911.html.
150. Griffin (note 148), p.175.
151. Avihu Zakai, *Exile and Kingdom: History and Apocalypse in the Puritan Migration to America* (Cambridge: Cambridge University Press, 1992), p.7.
152. Griffin (note 148), pp.171–2, 175.
153. Ibid., p.174.
154. Armstrong (note 106); and Marty and Appleby (note 110).
155. Griffin (note 148), p.175; see also the discussion on p.172.
156. The evidence for this can be found in numerous Christian Identity texts circulated by Aryan Nations. See, for example, Richard Butler, 'Sovereign Will', editorial, *Calling Our Nation*, newsletter of Aryan Nations, No.43, c.1984, p.1, in which Butler writes: 'The Adamic Aryan-born into flesh as images of an all-sovereign creator, given His delegated authority over earth and all contained therein to subdue, rule, and have everlasting dominion in LAW'; Robert Pash, letter from Australia, same issue, which begins 'Greetings in the name of YAHWEH the Mighty One of Israel', p.15; Bertrand L. Comparet, 'The Great Jubilee', excerpts form sermon (Special Alert No.69, Destiny Editorial Letter Service), *Calling Our Nation*, newsletter of Aryan Nations, No.50, c.1985, pp.18–20, in which Comparet writes: 'All Christians know that we have reached the point in time when this age is about finished ... the one hope of civilization remaining is the Second Coming of our Lord and Savior Jesus Christ'; Mark Thomas, 'Are There Any Connections?', *Calling Our Nation*, newsletter of Aryan Nations, No.83, c.1994, pp.2–11, an amazing biblical exegesis that pits Aryan Christian Identity, National Socialism and Odinism against the forces of the Antichrist: Jews and the Christian churches they 'control' on behalf of Satan.
157. Gentile (note 1), p.33, citing Raffaele Pettazzoni, *Italia Religiosa* (Bari: Laterza, 1952), p.7.
158. Griffin (note 148), p.174; with a tip of the hat to Umberto Eco, 'Ur-Fascism' [Eternal Fascism], *New York Review of Books*, 22 June 1995, pp.12–15.
159. For examples of attempts to sort out this particular issue, see Roger Eatwell, 'Introduction', in Roger Eatwell and Cas Mudde (eds.), *Western Democracies and the New Extreme Right Challenge* (London and New York: Routledge, 2004); Cas Mudde, *The Ideology of the Extreme Right* (Manchester: Manchester University Press, 2000); Martin Durham, *The Christian Right, the Far Right and the Boundaries of American Conservatism* (Manchester: Manchester University Press, 2000); Hans-Georg Betz, *Radical Right-wing Populism in Western Europe* (New York: St Martin's Press, 1994); Berlet and Lyons (note 24); and Eatwell (note 33).

INDEX